Developing Managers

* * * * * * * * * * * * *

*A Guide to Motivating
and Preparing People
for Successful
Managerial Careers*

* * * * * * * * * * * * *

Manuel London

Developing Managers

✳ ✳ ✳ ✳ ✳ ✳ ✳ ✳ ✳ ✳ ✳ ✳ ✳ ✳ ✳

Jossey-Bass Publishers
San Francisco • Washington • London • 1985

DEVELOPING MANAGERS
A Guide to Motivating and Preparing People
for Successful Managerial Careers
          by Manuel London

Copyright © 1985 by: Jossey-Bass Inc., Publishers
                    433 California Street
                    San Francisco, California 94104
                              &
                    Jossey-Bass Limited
                    28 Banner Street
                    London EC1Y 8QE

Library of Congress Cataloging in Publication Data

London, Manuel.
        Developing managers.

        (The Jossey-Bass management series) (The Jossey-Bass
social and behavioral science series)
        Bibliography: p. 241
        Includes index.
        1. Executives—Training of. I. Title. II. Series.
III. Series: Jossey-Bass social and behavioral science
series.
HD30.4.L66   1985   658.4'07124   84-43030
ISBN 0-87589-646-4 (alk. paper)

Manufactured in the United States of America

JACKET DESIGN BY WILLI BAUM

FIRST EDITION

Code 8516

A joint publication in
The Jossey-Bass
Management Series
and
The Jossey-Bass
Social and Behavioral Science Series

✳ ✳ ✳ ✳ ✳ ✳ ✳ ✳ ✳ ✳ ✳ ✳ ✳

For my parents
Meyer and Ruth London

Preface

Efforts to develop managers are often haphazard. Supervisors are not usually rewarded for developing subordinates and many do not know how to do it in the first place. Many individuals do not know what they can do to advance their own careers, and organizations are finding that career planning may raise expectations that cannot be met. Young managers face increased competition for a declining number of promotion opportunities, and pressures within organizations to improve productivity and reduce costs—in general to do more with less—have meant fewer opportunities for middle managers.

This book is about managers and how organizational practices affect their development. It is designed to help managers gain greater awareness of their career motivation, consider ways to enhance that motivation, and understand how to affect the work environment to expand their chances for a satisfying career. It is also designed to help supervisors and personnel professionals understand how their behavior and the organization's practices and procedures affect managers' career motivation.

Self-assessment techniques and action strategies are offered throughout this book to help readers analyze individuals' careers as well as organizational programs, and then to formulate practical steps to achieve necessary or desired changes.

Managers at all organizational levels and career stages will find that *Developing Managers* applies to their own careers as well as to their efforts to support their subordinates' career development. It gives special attention to beginning managers because the early career years are formative and early career experiences affect later career success. Middle managers—particularly those in midcareer who are not likely to advance further in the organizational hierarchy and who may think development is not for them—will also find this book a valuable resource.

Personnel professionals and top managers responsible for setting policies and developing programs for manager development will benefit from the detailed information about the impact of different approaches to manager development, guidelines for development, and numerous examples of programs offered in this book. Academics will find many ideas for further research on the development of career motivation and organizational conditions that affect it.

Beginning managers reading this book will find insights into the value of being proactive—of knowing their needs and interests, setting goals in relation to career opportunities, taking actions to achieve those goals, and being flexible in response to career barriers. The guidelines for manager development indicate the type of environment beginning managers should seek and, to the extent possible, create for themselves. *Developing Managers* will be especially valuable to career women who, perhaps more than men, have to analyze the work environment and seek support for career development as they juggle multiple roles, make role transitions, and face career barriers. Highly motivated (fast-track) managers may glean an increased understanding of the elements of career motivation and what they can do to avoid career barriers and create facilitating work conditions. Middle managers will benefit from the discussion of the meaning of midcareer development when further advancement is unlikely.

My approach to manager development is integrative and holistic. The elements of career motivation integrate personality characteristics, needs, and interests. The guidelines for manager development apply principles of good management. All these ideas are discussed in relation to career planning, socialization processes, the supervisor's style of management, training programs, the company's philosophy of manager development, and midcareer issues faced by managers.

A major theme of this book is that an understanding of managers' career motivation should guide manager development. To me, career motivation is not one thing, but a set of concepts connected with managers' resilience in the face of career barriers—their insight into their own strengths and weaknesses and how the work environment operates; their identification with the job, organization, and profession; and their need to advance in the organizational hierarchy. Because development and motivation occur together and result from the same actions and programs, the guidelines, programs, and action strategies for manager development offered throughout the book provide means of affecting the different elements of career motivation.

Overview of the Contents

Chapter One examines career planning from the individual's and the organization's perspective. My approach to career planning in both these spheres includes the need to keep goals flexible in order to accommodate the possibility of change.

Chapter Two explains how people are socialized into organizations. The main message here is that indoctrination is a crucial part of developing managers.

In Chapter Three, I analyze career motivation in terms of three domains: career resilience, career insight, and career identity. An assessment process to measure these elements of career motivation is described along with results from a sample of young managers. How the career motivation domains develop is the subject of Chapter Four. Self-assessment questions to help managers understand their own career motivation and a format for developing action strategies to enhance career motivation are presented.

In Chapter Five, I describe manager development in two companies that represent opposite approaches to the process. At one extreme is an organization that treats managers as corporate resources; at the other is an organization that treats managers as means of meeting current business needs, with little consideration for development to maximize their future contributions.

Chapter Six offers guidelines for manager development that suggest what the boss should do and what organizational policies and programs should be like to increase career resilience, insight, and identity. This chapter also outlines comprehensive programs for orienting new managers, developing high-potential managers, and maintaining the motivation of managers on a standard career track.

Chapter Seven addresses issues organizations should consider in formulating manager-development policies, such as the extent to which the organization should develop generalists or specialists. Development techniques and their potential effects on the elements of career motivation are described in Chapter Eight. The information in this chapter is designed to help organizations devise comprehensive development programs. Included is a plan for a workshop that will acquaint bosses with the concepts offered in this book.

Chapter Nine examines the boss's role in developing subordinates, using examples of bosses who have very different approaches to this issue. Self-assessment questions are presented that will help managers understand how they influence their subordinates' career motivation.

Chapter Ten is an analysis of training courses for developing managers. It clarifies the distinction between managing and leading and describes leadership development programs for promoting career resilience (proactive training), career insight (training for self-understanding), and career identity (ways to encourage visioning the future). Chapter Eleven covers development issues faced by midcareer, middle-level managers, with a description of strategies for coping with midcareer crises. The

Personal Career Graph, developed by Marshall G. Bryant, appears in the appendix to this chapter. This self-analysis instrument is designed to help midcareer managers evaluate their past careers, thereby gaining perspective for setting a direction for the future.

Chapter Twelve summarizes the major points in the book and indicates how they may be used by managers and personnel professionals.

Acknowledgments

I am indebted to Douglas Bray, who conceived the idea of studying career motivation and supported the research and initial development of the guidelines. I am grateful to Bent Jensen for the opportunity and encouragement to apply the results of the research. Many people contributed to this work. Eileen Hagen Fitzgerald, David Siegman, Joseph Fischer, Louise DuBois, and Walter Katkovsky were encouraging co-researchers. Thomas Vasko, Marjorie Leopold, Edward Mone, Thomas Thayer, Barbara Herr, and Marilyn McIlhone supported the development of the personal awareness workshops that were used in several manager-development programs. My own career resilience increased with these efforts as I learned to believe in myself, take risks, and act cooperatively. It could not have happened without the opportunities for achievement and innovation in an environment of concern and support. My wife, Marilyn, and children, David and Jared, are a never-ending source of reinforcement for my efforts. Finally, I appreciate Marlene Vigil's help in proofreading the many drafts of the manuscript.

Belle Mead   Manuel London
Montgomery Township, New Jersey
February 1985

Contents

Preface   ix

The Author   xvii

1. Strategic Planning for Manager Development   1

2. Early Career Experiences of Managers: Being
   Socialized into the Organization   19

3. Assessing Career Motivation of Managers   41

4. Developing and Strengthening Career Motivation   63

5. How Organizational Policies and Programs
   Affect Career Motivation   81

6. Designing Comprehensive Manager-Development
   Programs   103

7. Adapting Programs to the Organization's
    Philosophy and Needs   119

8. Selecting Human Resource Strategies and
    Techniques for Manager Development   137

9. The Boss's Role in Developing Managers   165

10. Training Programs for Developing Management
    Skills and Leadership   183

11. Motivating and Developing Midcareer and
    Plateaued Managers   207

12. Conclusion: Applying Manager-Development
    Strategies and Guidelines   231

    References   241

    Index   249

The Author

* * * * * * * * * * * * *

Manuel London is a district manager in charge of personnel research for AT&T Communications. He received his B.A. degree (1971) from Case Western Reserve University in philosophy and psychology and his M.A. (1972) and Ph.D. (1974) degrees from Ohio State University in industrial and organizational psychology.

London's main research activities have been in manager development and career decisions from the viewpoint of the individual and the organization. He has also conducted research on the relationship between work and nonwork behavior and has written on ethical issues in personnel decisions. He is a member of the editorial boards of the *Academy of Management Journal, Personnel Psychology,* and the *Journal of Management Development.* He has written over thirty papers and is the co-author of the book *Managing Careers* (1982, with S. A. Stumpf). London has been involved in organizational research and program development for AT&T since 1977. From 1974 to 1977 he taught in the business school at the University of Illinois in Urbana.

Developing Managers

✳ ✳ ✳ ✳ ✳ ✳ ✳ ✳ ✳ ✳ ✳ ✳ ✳

*A Guide to Motivating
and Preparing People
for Successful
Managerial Careers*

1

✻ ✻ ✻ ✻ ✻

Strategic Planning for Manager Development

One theme of this book is that we should create our own futures by recognizing reality. Creating the future involves exerting self-direction and initiative while being flexible in the face of career barriers and organizational changes. Another theme of this book is that organizations and bosses differ in their support for manager development.

These themes appear in this chapter's discussion of the interactive approach to career planning—that is, creating a vision for ourselves and then adjusting that vision, as required by organizational conditions. This chapter also considers how an organization's support of manager development is determined by the organization's own objectives and environment.

Chapter Two continues these themes in two ways: by examining the adjustments required of us when we start our careers and enter organizations and by discussing what organizations do to socialize us to their own values and accepted ways of behaving. These two processes affect not only how we view our careers but also our motivations for pursuing them within organizations. The discussion in Chapter Two sets the stage for understanding career motivation (Chapters Three and Four), how a company's manager-development policies and programs and bosses' management styles affect careers (Chapters Five through Ten), and the meaning of development for midcareer managers (Chapter Eleven).

Strategic Planning

The concept of manager development implies change and growth. It is the process of establishing goals and taking action to achieve them. From the individual manager's perspective, development refers to increasing managerial skills and abilities through job experiences and training, a task that requires learning and motivation. From the company's perspective, manager development refers to building the management team needed to run the business successfully. This task involves appropriate policies and procedures for recruitment, selection, training, supervision, promotion, transfer, and related issues. The actions that individuals take and the systems that organizations develop depend on the goals they want to achieve. These goals require strategic planning.

Strategic planning means determining a desired future and what it takes to get there. Strategic planning is usually applied to corporations, but it is also applicable to manager development. This chapter uses Ackoff's (1981) ideas about strategic business planning to discuss individual career planning. Ackoff argues that corporations should use control, responsiveness, and employee participation to create the futures they want.

Ackoff believes planning is a continuous process because of unanticipated events and because of changes in the values and assumptions that underlie goals and actions. Ackoff's observation applies to individuals planning for and taking action to accomplish their own development, and it also applies to organizations contributing to the development of managers. Thus, planning for development is a continuous process, because development itself is a continuous process. Ackoff distinguishes among four types of planning: reactive, inactive, preactive, and interactive. Here these four planning types are applied to manager development, first from the viewpoint of the individual manager and then from the viewpoint of the organization.

Career Planning: The Manager's Perspective

Reactive Planning. Most people take career opportunities as they come. They reach decision points in their lives (such as the need to find a job after graduation), they identify and evaluate their alternatives, and they make choices. A choice is likely to be based on what the individual wants now or will be comfortable doing. One graduate may want to live close to home or work with friends; another graduate may choose a company because her father or her aunt works there, or she may have a vague idea about what opportunities will be available in the company. Such decisions are based on reactive planning.

Being reactive also entails being dependent. Young managers depend on recruiters for their first assignments. They depend on their bosses for their projects. They depend on higher-level managers to recognize their abilities and offer them promotions. In short, they react as each opportunity arises. Reactive planning involves identifying deficiencies, so that an opportunity will not be lost because of a weakness. Planning, in this sense, is directed at what one does not want to be: If you know that in today's corporate world most young managers get an MBA, then you do the same.

I recently asked a group of managers to outline their career goals and then to describe which factors would facilitate achievement and which factors would be barriers. Generally, their goals were to advance several levels in the corporate hierarchy, usually to responsible middle-management positions. They thought they would achieve these goals because they would not be lacking in any requirements, and they believed they would overcome any weaknesses through training. They rarely saw themselves as barriers; they thought barriers were factors beyond their control, such as an economic downturn or a boss who would block a career move.

One manager kept a list of his weaknesses. Whenever he

felt he had overcome one, he began working on the next. For instance, he believed he needed to be better at giving presentations before groups, and so he joined the local Toastmasters Club. His next goal was to learn how to organize his work better, and he planned to attend a workshop in time management. The fellow in this example compartmentalized himself. He had an idea of the parts, but not the whole. The danger is he will never realize how his abilities work together, and he will never really see what he can accomplish.

Inactive Planning. Inactive planning is ignoring the need to plan. It is a conservative approach. The status quo is the ideal. The main goal is to not rock the boat. People adopting this approach fit nicely into bureaucratic corporations. They feel they have gotten along fine so far, and "if it isn't broken, don't fix it."

There is nothing wrong with being content with our lot in life, but the problem is that if we do nothing for as long as we can, we eventually have to act. This is often a reason for midlife crisis—which, by the way, can occur at almost any point in one's career. It is also a reason why the role of middle managers is being questioned in many organizations today (see Chapter Eleven). We eventually reach a stage where things have changed so much that we cannot remain the same. Change is so rapid in our world that there is often no time to react before the next change occurs. As Stein (1984) puts it, "the meantime between surprises" is decreasing every day. Inaction eventually leads to crisis.

A good example of such crisis is the way some telephone company managers were ready, even anxious, to leave their jobs after the Bell System breakup. Preparing for a competitive environment, AT&T saw the need to become "lean and mean." Company rhetoric emphasized the importance of taking risks, assuming more responsibility, and supervising more people. After working in a regulated environment, which required following standard practices to the letter, some managers were not ready for the transition, and they accepted the company's financial incentive to terminate. This was a difficult step to take for managers who had been loyal members of the corporate "family" for years. Nevertheless, there were many managers, young and old, who embraced the change and looked forward to working in a more dynamic environment. Those who left or who stayed halfheartedly were inactive planners. They found themselves adrift in a rapidly changing environment.

Preactive Planning. Some managers live in the future. They do all they can to accelerate the rate of change and to exploit change. Experience is irrelevant to them, while the ability to learn and adapt is crucial. They are not necessarily young. Many have known failure, yet they are willing to act. They are likely to have clear career goals, and they decide what is needed to achieve them. They plan their own careers, whether or not the company offers them a career planning program. They try to predict the future and prepare for it.

Sometimes a manager has little time to adjust to a major change. For instance, consider the situation faced by the first- and second-line managers at Westinghouse's steam generator and turbine plants in Philadelphia and Pittsburgh when the company closed these plants and built a modern facility in Orlando, Florida. Many of these managers had to decide whether to leave the company to which they had devoted their careers or leave the city in which they had lived all their lives. All the career planning in the world would not have helped them deal with this unforeseen event.

Another problem with goal setting is that we tend to focus only on accomplishing the established goals, and we often ignore other aspects of work or fail to perceive changes until it is too late. Murphy's Law applies to manager development: Whenever we think things will go our way or continue as they are, something changes or goes wrong.

Interactive Planning. Ackoff (1981) offers the following recommendations for creating a desired future: Appreciate your current situation; determine what you want, not what you do not want; identify ways to get what you want; develop needed resources; and implement your plan and control the process of creating your future.

One key to following these recommendations is not to assume that something cannot be accomplished. A goal may be seen as impossible only because the means to accomplish it do not exist now. For instance, you may want to go back to school part-time for an MBA at age forty, but you have family obligations, while tuition costs and the time requirements of your present job are also barriers. You may not be aware of the support available to help you achieve your goal (family encouragement and a company-sponsored tuition-aid plan) until you explore what is needed to bring it about. This is not to say that you should ignore reality; rather, you should take control of it. The key to our development as managers is planning for ourselves and realizing how our motivations and abilities affect our career decisions and behaviors.

Ackoff believes that the most effective means of control is responsiveness, which suggests the value of contingency plans. Instead of predicting what will happen, contingency planning (another term for interactive planning) identifies likely occurrences and outcomes of behavior. Contingency planning helps us respond to events rapidly and effectively, in contrast to reactive planning, which entails waiting for something to happen before responding. Contingency planning means designing and controlling the future by minimizing the effects of events beyond our control, but still being willing to change course when necessary.

Designing and creating the future and planning for contingencies require us to analyze underlying assumptions. For example, in establishing a career goal we may assume that there will be a job for us, the pay will be what we expect, the job will be challenging, and we will be respected. We may be wrong. One way to assess the validity of our assumptions is to compare them with the assumptions of others who have similar goals or who share ours. If we check our assumptions in this way, we may identify the needs that underlie our goals and discover other ways to meet our needs.

Planning is a continuous process, and a plan is not static. We do not necessarily come up with a plan one day and then let it guide the rest of our lives. We do the guiding. On any day of our lives we may be aware of the decisions we are making, the reasons for them, and how they fit into a plan, but the next day we may be making different decisions for different reasons, and so the plan takes on a different character. A career plan is not like a still photograph—constant, yet slowly fading with the passage of time. It is more like a motion picture or a piece of music—dynamic, changing, yet with a consistent theme or pattern pervading the whole.

To different degrees, each of us probably uses all the modes of planning. When it comes to our careers, we are more likely to be reactive planners than contingency planners. Many of us have only a vague idea about where we want our careers to go. How specifically can you answer the following questions?

1. Where am I in my career now?
2. If everything else were constant, what would I like to be doing now? Why is this what I want? What are my assumptions? What do I have to do to get what I want?
3. Where do I want to be in ten years? Why?
4. How can I get there? Can I create this situation?
5. How difficult will it be for me to change my goals along the way? How likely is it that I will have to change?

The case of Lydia Brown, below, demonstrates the guidelines of interactive planning. The reactive and preactive modes are evident in her case, but Lydia is also trying to create a future for herself. Lydia shows us the value of believing in ourselves and trying to get what we want. Her career prospects, which her boss agrees are good, nevertheless show the need for some flexibility. Her goals provide her with a guide for taking advantage of career opportunities. In reading about Lydia's case, consider the assumptions she is making about her future. How flexible will she be in changing her career plans, if necessary? What role does self-confidence play in her career?

Creating Your Future: The Case of Lydia Brown. Lydia Brown was an attractive and articulate woman of twenty-four. She had been with the company, a large industrial firm, for about a year when I first interviewed her. During her undergraduate days at a large state university, Lydia considered a variety of majors. She settled on business administration, not just because it was a practical way to earn a living but also because she thought it would lead to challenging job opportunities. After graduating with a B average, she had several jobs, first as an assistant buyer for a retail chain and later as a staff assistant in the sales office of a large manufacturer.

These jobs did not seem to be leading anywhere, and so Lydia decided to attend graduate school. By taking a night job managing a fast-food restaurant, she saved enough money to pay for her tuition. Two years after receiving her bachelor's degree, she enrolled in the MBA program at the state university and majored in finance.

Lydia had several job offers when she graduated. All were for positions in large companies that had manager-development programs. They all offered comparable salaries. Unlike the other companies, however, the one where she accepted a position offered a long-term development program. Rather than simply having a year-long program, the company claimed to prepare recruits to reach middle management through experience, in five to eight years.

Her first position in this company was as an assistant analyst in the cost accounting department. Her work involved establishing the costs for new products and services so that prices could be set appropriately. She loved the work and especially loved the contact with middle and top managers. She hoped to be promoted to cost analyst next. This position would require making presentations to top management in her department, as well as having contact with top people in the marketing and finance departments. Lydia looked forward hopefully to a series of increasingly responsible positions in cost accounting, finance, and marketing, and she let her boss know about her career goals. She hoped to reach middle management (third level in an organizational hierarchy of seven management levels) in five years. While such advancement was not impossible, it would be rapid for a time when the company was cutting down on promotions, since it already had too many managers. Lydia would have to maintain consistently outstanding performance and high ratings in advancement potential. Her ultimate goal was to be a company vice-president.

Lydia planned to have a family as well as a successful career. She did not have a steady boyfriend, but she hoped to be married in about two years. She wanted to have her first child five years after that, and a second child two years later. She stated that she would have a full-time nanny for her children and a part-time housekeeper, so that having a family would not hinder her career. She was confident she could balance work and family responsibilities and be successful at both.

When Lydia was interviewed again seven months later, she was working at the job she wanted: cost analyst, a second-level position. She was involved in organizing cost studies and presenting the results. She was also getting considerable exposure to higher-level managers. Twice, as part of an evaluation of a major new product offering, she had given presentations before the board of vice-presidents.

Lydia's boss found her to be an outstanding employee and thought that she had tremendous career opportunities with the company. He hoped she would move into another department to broaden her experience. In particular, he believed she could benefit from a management job in a department such as engineering or installation and repair; one or more such jobs would give her supervisory experience and acquaint her with the operations side of the business. When I asked Lydia about the possibility of such an assignment, however, she viewed it as a setback to her career. She said she would want a guarantee that she could return to the cost accounting, finance, or marketing department. Nevertheless, she was not the type to stand idly by waiting for the company to make its move. Lydia said that even if her boss convinced her that her next few jobs should be in operations departments and she secured such positions, she still would maintain contact with her old boss and others to ensure a future position for herself.

Lydia evidently gave a lot of thought to her career prospects. She knew where she wanted to go and did what was necessary to get there. She was a preactive planner, in that she had an ambitious vision for herself. In the past, she had decided what she wanted and then secured the resources necessary to get it. Now, she probably needed to do more interactive or contingency planning to weigh the advantages and disadvantages of different career options. Since job offers within the company would not necessarily be Lydia's choices, she might have to re-evaluate her situation when specific opportunities arose.

Career Planning: The Company's Perspective

Schein (1984) argues that an organization's manager-development activities reflect the way the organization does things. Margolis (1984) says that manager development should reflect the company's "essence." Essence is more than organizational culture, which refers to the company's climate and human systems; Margolis means the fundamental difference between the organization and its competitors, its beliefs and values, which color its activities and strategic direction. Essence is what must be transmitted to each new generation of managers.

The company's business strategy determines the skills and attributes necessary to take the company into the future. In designing a manager-development program, we can apply our knowledge in ways that are consistent with the values of top management and with how the company is structured and controlled. Our ideas about how we want the company to be and what we want managers to be should also guide the manager-development program. For example, Bristol-Myers is a decentralized organization (Margolis, 1984). It is a group of units that produce consumer products. Bristol-Myers often buys small consumer-products companies. These entities of the corporation operate semiautonomously. Each entity is responsible for the development of its own managers, with some coordination from headquarters. This procedure contrasts with those at a corporation such as GTE, which has a highly centralized training and development function. Some organizations, such as the new AT&T, are struggling with the question of how much to centralize personnel activities. In the old Bell System, each operating unit was responsible for the selection and development of its own managers, and these different companies had varying philosophies of manager development. These differences continue in the seven regional telephone companies divested from AT&T.

The new AT&T could centralize its training function and move managers among its entities for development purposes, or it could retain a decentralized training function, with manager development occurring primarily within each entity, particularly at lower and middle levels of management.

In most organizations, managers are probably more involved in planning the company's future than in planning their own careers. Organizations plan many facets of their operations—the financial picture, availability of raw materials, marketing approaches—because strategic decisions often have to be made many years before they are implemented. Human resource planning is also important for long-term viability and entails both estimating the numbers and types of people who will be needed at different levels of the organization and establishing policies and programs to be sure these needs are met. For instance, an estimate that the company will double in size in ten years may require hiring people now, to prepare them adequately for middle management and to identify and train future top managers. Thus, the organization's approach to human resource planning is likely to influence the type and degree of support it gives to manager development. Ackoff's four modes of planning can be applied to the human resource function, as the discussion below demonstrates.

Reactive Planning. Organizations that rely on reactive planning are often family-run, or else they view themselves as "one big family." Experience is believed to be the best teacher, and seniority is the most important criterion for promotion. Planning is designed to identify and remove deficiencies. The company wants and probably attracts loyal, long-term employees who are satisfied with the status quo and will follow standard operating procedures. This pattern is often true of government agencies. Reactive organizations are generally insensitive to the interaction of human resource systems, with typical results. Manager recruitment is likely to operate in isolation from manager training. Compensation is likely to be related more to tenure than to performance. Technical competence or experience in a specialty is probably valued more than supervisory and interpersonal skills. Managing is viewed more as organizing and planning than as leadership. Top managers deal more with "things" (numbers, records, programs) than they do with people. Employees are controlled and monitored. Decisions are made at higher levels and probably diffused over a number of managers, rather than proceeding from clear understanding of accountability and, as such, being made at the levels most affected by them.

Inactive Planning. This do-nothing policy results in crisis management: Problems are solved by turning off the heat, rather than removing the cause. A good example of a combination of inactive and reactive planning is the use of financial incentives to encourage managers to leave in an economic downturn. Several years ago, Polaroid offered such a plan and found that its best people left—the incentive was so good, they could not afford to stay. Another unintended by-product of such "golden parachutes" is that they reduce natural attrition: Managers eligible for early retirement delay retiring, hoping they will be offered a lucrative incentive to leave. One company offered such a program once and found that no one retired during the following year; even a formal announcement that the incentive program would not be offered again fell on deaf ears. Employees did not believe the announcement, and retirements took several years to reach normal levels again. Another company initiated termination incentives while simultaneously hiring sizable numbers of people who had different skills; the possibility of retraining was not even considered.

The rationale for termination-incentive programs is to rapidly and humanely decrease the number of managers as a way of controlling payroll costs, since these are often a large proportion of operating expenses. Another strategy is to stop hiring and lay off managers, without incentives. For example, a company in the Northeast implemented both strategies at once about fifteen years ago. Several years later, when the company desperately needed first- and second-level managers and engineers, its recruiters found a cool reception on the college campuses: Relations with college placement offices had deteriorated, and the company found it difficult to revitalize its recruiting effort and attract the best candidates. As a result, the company's selection standards were not as high as they should have been, and there was higher than normal turnover in subsequent years. Moreover, the legacy of this one-time layoff was a lasting distrust of top management and a fear for job security. Thus, solving short-term needs can lead to long-term messes; crisis management can result in solving the wrong problems and creating new ones. The need to reduce payroll costs could have been reinterpreted as a need to make current managers more productive and innovative, contributing to the growth of the organization rather than to its decline.

Preactive Planning. Here, the focus is on the future and on coping with an accelerated rate of change. Support is given to manager-development activities. Managers receive help in identifying their training needs and planning their careers. They are moved from department to department or even relocated across the country to prepare them for rapid advancement. The value of manager-training programs is accepted on faith. Emphasis is placed on the process, not on the content of development. Thus, there may be much activity but little substantive change. Momentum dissipates when the economic outlook suddenly grows bleak.

Interactive Planning. In part, organizations create their futures by the managers they hire and develop. For example, consider People Express. The concepts of employee ownership and participative management are guiding forces of this airline. Each employee handles several different jobs and shares in the operation and management of the business. It is a nonunion company that hires young people who are willing to take risks. This policy allows the airline to run with half as many employees per plane as most of its competitors do. Each employee is a capitalist with a stake in the business. Don Burr, president of People Express, designed the company on the basis of his vision of how the business should operate. He created the corporation's future by recognizing the interaction among its systems. This approach has not been trouble-free. Burr is the first to admit the communication problems and logistical difficulties in coordinating work schedules and in meeting the need for people to develop expertise in specialty areas. Turnover has been high, as the company shifts its priorities, and there is a need to adjust to changing market conditions. Overall, however, the approach is working.

Changes in a corporate environment require attention to interplay among the elements of the environment. Corporate change cannot be successful without consideration to manager development, and the recent shakeup at General Motors is a good example of this fact. GM is experiencing fundamental and strategic change in corporate philosophy and organizational structure, and this change reflects the type of company GM wants to be. The company has taken its five brand-name divisions and made them into two groups—one to produce small, economical cars and the other to produce large, luxury cars. The activities of the assembly and Fisher Body divisions have also been distributed between the two groups so that each group has total responsibility for its product lines, including design, engineering, and production of the automobiles. This redistribution should reduce decision times and increase the company's ability to respond quickly to car buyers' changing needs. It also should reduce duplication of functions. GM's action shows that old ways of organizing business, even in a mature industry, are inadequate and that sweeping change is necessary ("GM Shakeup . . . ," 1984). There should be implications for the expectations that GM has concerning its managers' actions and decisions. The redistribution also should affect the kinds of opportunities managers can expect from the company. There should be room for more innovative entrepreneurial behavior, improved communication and coordination between functions, and less competition between units within the company. Managers the company hires and develops during the next ten years will be less responsive to regimentation, less security-oriented, and more willing to take risks and recognize potential negative consequences of failure.

Another strategic corporate change that demonstrates interaction among organizational systems with impacts on manager development has taken place at Eastman Kodak. For a hundred years, this company had about an 80 percent world market share of the silver chloride–based photographic business.

The corporate culture was risk-averse. Decision making was centralized and overcautious. Middle managers were accustomed to pushing decisions to the top. As a result, the need for information and analysis consumed the time of top managers. The only power middle managers had was to say no. There was little tie between performance and financial compensation. The catch phrase was "Keep your head down, and don't make waves." Today, Kodak faces an eroding market share because of new technology and competition from Japan and elsewhere. Photographic technology has moved from a basis in chemical engineering to a basis in electrical engineering. Competition has meant erosion of the company's image of quality. Kodak now has a new CEO, who is implementing a new direction in corporate management philosophy. The organization's venture is becoming broader. Kodak is buying companies that have complementary technology. There is a shift from maintaining a geographic-functional management structure to developing lines of business. New ideas are considered seriously, even when they are outside the mainstream of the photographic business. The company has purchased small entrepreneurial enterprises and provided them with the financial backing for growth, allowing these new subsidiaries to manage themselves. These changes have major implications for Kodak managers:

1. Kodak's managers are being encouraged to think strategically, not functionally. Thus, managers must decide what they want their units to be like and how they can fit best into the new corporate strategy.

2. There is reduced tolerance of incompetence and low-quality performance in managers. For example, the company is experimenting with a new pay plan that emphasizes goal setting and puts a portion of each manager's pay at risk. Managers will be paid at 95 percent of the base rate for each level. They set goals, which they must achieve to earn the additional 5 percent. Unlike a bonus system, which pays a special merit award to the highest performers (perhaps only 30 percent of the management force), the Kodak system requires all managers to earn 100 percent of the base rate.

3. Kodak's managers are becoming generalists rather than

functional specialists. Training programs are offered to help managers operate in the new, decentralized environment. They have to learn not only how to participate in the corporate change but also how to lead it.

AT&T is yet another example of a company changing its corporate strategy, culture, and approach to manager development. As the organization faces an increasingly competitive environment, managers must change from a by-the-books strategy, aimed at providing the highest-quality service at any cost, to a more competitive mode. The AT&T manager must meet the needs of the customer by providing the most value at the lowest cost. This goal applies to managers in every department of the company. In this sense, all AT&T managers have clients, whether internal or external to the company. Top executives encourage middle- and lower-level managers to become risk takers and entrepreneurs; managers are encouraged to act when they see something that needs to be done.

Thus, General Motors, Kodak, and AT&T are becoming more flexible and decentralized. Johnson & Johnson, in contrast, needs more central control in adapting to a more competitive environment. J&J is a "family of companies" manufacturing pharmaceuticals, baby-care products, and medical supplies ("Changing a Corporate Culture . . . ," 1984). Each of its subsidiaries is fairly independent. J&J is now discovering the need to coordinate functions and offer package deals and central distribution facilities to such customers as large medical centers. This change requires J&J managers to coordinate their activities and recognize the implications of their decisions for other elements of the business.

The examples of interactive planning cited here show how companies react to changing environments by establishing visions of what they want to become. This process has implications both for organizational structure and for the roles managers play in corporations. Often, changes in the environment give managers more autonomy and cause them to be held accountable for their actions and decisions. Such changes may also call for more attention to managing contacts between units as well as more attention to interactions among people within units.

Manager/Organization Interaction

Both an organization and a manager can create the organization's future. Likewise, both can create the manager's future. Interactive planning entails recognizing the relationships between elements of a system. We have seen that environmental and organizational changes have an impact on managers' roles. As managers create visions of themselves, they must consider how well these visions fit with corporate directions. The idea of this fit will be clearer when the company communicates its directions, its progress in achieving goals, and changes in its goals. The managers of GM, Kodak, AT&T, and J&J are in the process of deciding whether they fit in with the new corporate objectives and what alternatives they have. At AT&T, some managers prefer early retirement to jobs in faster-paced, do-or-die environments. At J&J, some executives have chosen to quit rather than relinquish their autonomy to broader objectives.

One question is inevitable: "How can I be sure I am moving in the right direction?" This question deserves constant attention. Another term for interactive planning is contingency planning, the recognition that plans are likely to change. Thus, Anheuser-Busch does not write a corporate plan, but maintains files outlining major decisions. These files are updated as decisions change, and so it is possible to see where things stand at any moment. Another way to answer this inevitable question is to do some counterplanning. Applied in the pharmaceutical and medical products industry by Sheahan (1975), counterplanning is based on clearly defined assumptions that are largely unfavorable and unaccepted by management. Counterplans express fears and concerns that may not be voiced. Corporate counterplans are best developed by outsiders who have no jobs to protect, no reputations to enhance, and no psychological involvement with the growth or prosperity of a company. A counterplan alerts managers to eventualities that are unpleasant but realistic, so that managers can anticipate problems early enough to act on them. Counterplanning should precede most aspects of contingency planning for corporations.

Counterplanning is also valuable for individuals. It is difficult to face such questions as "What if my plans don't work out? What am I not considering?" An independent opinion from a career counselor or a trusted acquaintance can help us identify mistaken assumptions or factors we have not taken into account. Because most of us tend to be defensive when our ideas are evaluated, it is best to seek opinions from people whom we respect and who do not have vested interests in our success or failure. The goal of individual counterplanning is not only to accept criticism but also to anticipate unfavorable outcomes and consider constructive actions.

Conclusion

This chapter recommends that we plan our careers while realizing the possibility of unanticipated events and the likelihood that we will have to readjust our career directions periodically. Since an organization's policies, objectives, and programs also affect its manager-development strategies, organizations and individuals should create their futures interactively by establishing directions, counterplanning, and revising goals. These processes apply to us at all career stages, but (as the next chapter shows) it is particularly important to recognize these processes when we are starting our careers and are expected to adopt organizational values and accepted ways of behaving. Many of us learn the need for flexibility in our goals the hard way—by having our aspirations shot down. Interactive planning may help us avoid pain and increase our chances for career success.

2

* * * * *

Early Career Experiences of Managers: Being Socialized into the Organization

Chapter One urged us to design and create our futures. This chapter shows the importance of understanding the nature of the organization and the extent to which we fit in. The early career years start a mutual influencing process: We have to adapt to the company's ways of doing things, but we also influence the company by what we are willing to contribute and by the changes we make to improve our effectiveness and increase our sense of belonging. This chapter covers the meaning of socialization and how new employees are influenced by the corporate culture. It examines stages of influence susceptibility, methods of socialization, and socialization outcomes and, along the way, describes cases of companies and individuals. This chapter shows the interaction between individuals and organizations at a point when individuals are most susceptible to influence, and it sets the stage for later chapters, which offer a closer look at career motivation and how it is affected by organizations.

Socialization and Commitment

Companies expect their managers to sustain the wellbeing of the organization by having a sense of responsibility and dedication. According to Buchanan (1974), "the commitment of managers is essential for the survival and effectiveness of large work organizations." Buchanan points out that commitment has three components: identification, or adoption of the goals and values of the organization as one's own; involvement, or psychological immersion in the activities of one's work role; and loyalty, or a feeling of affection for and attachment to the organization. The process by which employees are transformed from outsiders to effective, committed corporate members is termed *socialization.* As Feldman (1976b) explains, "The success of the socialization process is critical for individuals, because the way their careers are managed by organizations influences both the quality of . . . work life and the quality of their outside lives. And as the success of organizations becomes increasingly dependent on the commitment of its members rather than on traditional control systems (such as pay), . . . organizational socialization becomes increasingly important to the organization as well" (pp. 64–65).

Organizational socialization is the process by which an employee learns the values, norms, and required behaviors that permit participation as a member of the organization. This process may also mean relinquishing attitudes, values, and behaviors that do not fit. Socialization establishes shared attitudes, habits, and values that encourage cooperation, integrity, and communication.

Corporate Values

To understand what is meant by an organization's values and norms, consider your own company (or school or any other organization with which you are affiliated) and write down what you think the organization stands for—not what the organization does, but how. Is there an explicit statement of corporate philosophy? For example, Hewlett-Packard, the computer firm, has a company credo given to all employees. One section states: "Objective: To help HP people share in the company's success, which they make possible; to provide job security based on their performance; to recognize their individual achievements; and to ensure the personal satisfaction that comes from a sense of accomplishment in their work." To take another example, Johnson & Johnson is committed to providing customers with the highest-quality products possible and putting the welfare of customers above all other goals, including profits or business volume. In 1982, when seven deaths were attributed to cyanide-laced capsules of Extra-Strength Tylenol, J&J acted quickly to recall 31 million bottles nationwide at a cost of $50 million. Later it was discovered that the few boxes of capsules in question had been tampered with in stores. To overcome the negative publicity surrounding this incident, J&J increased ad spending by more than 30 percent, to $56.8 million. In determining your company's values, ask yourself whether the company's espoused values differ from what it really does. The Tylenol case put J&J to the test, and the company's response was based on what the chairman, James Burke, believed the company stood for. At Hewlett-Packard, there is a no-layoff policy, which is adhered to even in hard economic times.

To understand the norms of your company, consider which behaviors are acceptable and unacceptable. For instance, do the men typically wear blue pinstriped three-piece suits, white shirts, and dark ties? (At IBM, this combination is sometimes referred to as the corporate uniform.) How common are beards and moustaches? Do most people come to work early and leave late? Is it necessary to follow lines of authority to communicate with someone in another department? For example, if I have a problem, must I take it to my boss, who takes it to his boss, who takes it to her counterpart in another department, who in turn sends it up the line? Or can I simply walk over to see a higher-level manager in another department? Speaking of norms, Pascale (1984) observes, "It is useful to distinguish between norms that are central to the business's success and social conventions that signal commitment and belonging.

The former are essential in that they ensure consistency in executing the company's strategy. The latter are the organizational equivalent of shaking hands. They are social conventions that make it easier for people to be comfortable with one another. One need not observe all of them, but one wants to reassure the organization that one is on the team."

Corporate culture is another important factor in many of the most successful firms. For instance, Peters and Waterman (1982) highlight attributes of corporate culture that they believe contribute to organizational success. These include such mottoes as "productivity through people" (meaning that concern and respect for employees is crucial) and "close to the customer" (meaning that employees are expected to understand and respond to customers' needs).

Thus, working in a company requires learning its values and norms. Employees who do not learn the values and norms, or who find that they cannot adhere to them, generally leave. There are cases of countersocialization, in which people who do not ascribe to existing values try to change organizations, but countersocialization is a long and arduous process, and there are few success stories. Consider Arch McGill, a former IBM marketing executive, who was hired by the Bell System to make it more competitive. During his ten years with the company, he instituted many changes in how products are introduced and sold. A certification process was developed for the sales force, and new pay incentive systems were introduced. McGill believed that the needs of the marketplace should determine which products are developed and manufactured, but this concept was hard to understand for a company used to developing and manufacturing what it believed customers should want. McGill left before the Bell System breakup, but his legacy lives on in the overarching goal of the new AT&T: customer satisfaction. The company has recognized the need to change, but the melding of research and development, production, and marketing is a slow process.

Management Culture

While there may be differences in corporate culture from one firm to the next, there may also exist one coherent management culture exhibited by managers across a wide range of contemporary organizations (Knudsen, 1982). This broad culture is based on belief in myths, including rationality, instrumentality, unilateral dependence on supervisors, unilateral control of subordinates, and the importance of the managerial role in an organizational hierarchy. The norms that dominate this management culture are typically masculine (Knudsen, 1982).

> Managers are expected to prioritize, divide tasks into separate components, delegate, keep to the point, and reach conclusions rapidly, all with a certain amount of aggression. . . . Emotions are seen as signs of weakness rather than strength. . . . Managers attempt to achieve their own objectives, maximizing winning, minimizing losing, minimizing negative feelings on the part of others, and maintaining a rational rather than an emotional posture. Pursuing these norms results in defensive behavior . . . , a lowering of commitment, and reluctance to take risks. This in turn affects organizational learning. Organizational effectiveness is decreased over time. . . . Managers are often unaware of their own involvement in a management culture. . . . It is probably only through considerable confrontation and reflection that managers . . . can understand the underlying assumptions on which a manager bases action, and the way in which others perceive the meaning of the action [Knudsen, 1982, pp. 13–14].

Socialization Never Ends

To some extent, socialization continues throughout an individual's career. Our needs change over time as we marry, have children, support them through college, and so on. We all undergo transitions, such as being promoted or changing jobs, and we are subject to feelings of anxiety. This anxiety is reduced if we conform to the norms and values we believe are expected. The sources of these expectations include colleagues, supervisors, subordinates, and clients (Knudsen, 1982, p. 15). If individuals change, companies change, too. For example, an organization's values change with economic fluctuations or shifts in the marketplace. Drug companies such as J&J experience declining market shares of some profitable products as patents run out and cheaper generic drugs enter the market. Competition from abroad in medical products also has eroded J&J's market share. J&J's response has been to take more central control of marketing strategy and product distribution. As a result, many managers in subsidiary companies owned by J&J have lost autonomy; some, particularly at executive levels, have left rather than change to suit the company's new management philosophy ("Changing a Corporate Culture . . . ," 1984). This organizational change eventually will affect the types of people hired at J&J and what they are led to expect in terms of control over products and processes.

Resocialization becomes necessary when an experienced manager changes jobs, is promoted, transfers to another department, or changes companies. The extent to which such changes require readjustment depends on how different the new position is from the former position. Except for radical midcareer changes, most job shifts are limited to similar areas and do not call for vastly different new attitudes or values.

Susceptibility to Influence

Socialization is a continuous process, but early career experiences are especially important for generating commitment to the corporation. This is the time when susceptibility to influence is greatest and attitudes toward the organization are shaped. In general, the earlier an experience, the stronger its effects, since it influences how later experiences will be interpreted. People in the early stages of organizational membership also have a special motivation to conform, and Buchanan called this *role readiness*. There are three stages of influence susceptibility: the first year, when people become acclimated to new roles; the second through the fourth years, when a role is incorporated into self-image; and the fifth year and beyond, when people's organizational attitudes have reached a mature stage of nongrowth, even though the intensity of these attitudes may change (at this point, the organization's socialization will be directed at maintaining and changing existing attitudes, rather than developing new ones) (Buchanan, 1974).

The First Year

This is a period of initiation, during which new managers learn what is expected of them. According to Berlew and Hall (1966), "The first year is a critical period for learning, a time when the trainee is uniquely ready to develop or change in the direction of the company's expectations. This year would be analogous to the critical period, probably between six and eighteen months, when human infants must either experience a close emotional relationship with another human being or suffer ill effects ranging from psychosis to an inability ever to establish such a relationship. . . . No organization can afford to treat this critical period lightly" (pp. 222–223).

The critical nature of early experiences in management is evident in the research finding that early job challenge and motivation predict job performance and motivation as many as sixteen years later (Bray and Howard, 1980). Newcomers learn what is expected of them and experience anxiety about their possible inability to live up to these expectations. One way of handling this anxiety is to develop bonds with others who can provide guidance and reassurance. Often, newcomers entering the organization at the same time give each other this support and provide each other a basis for comparing experiences. Nevertheless, the real subtleties of organizational culture stem from contact with veteran managers. The extent to which these veterans are good role models is crucial to newcomers' successful socialization. Assignment to a boss who is not a good performer or who may have a negative attitude about the company could lead a newcomer to adopt the boss's poor performance or negative attitudes; it would then be hard for the recruit to fit into the larger organization. The consequent delay in the newcomer's commitment to the organization during the crucial formative years could significantly decrease his or her career opportunities.

Another element of the first year is testing expectations.

The more expectations are met, the more satisfied newcomers are likely to be with a company. That is one reason why companies often try to give job candidates or very recent recruits realistic job previews, which generate expectations that can be met (Wanous, 1980).

Early job challenge is also important to being involved in one's work and to the development of intrinsic motivation. Intrinsic motivation is the desire to work because the task is stimulating. Jobs with motivating potential generally provide feedback on performance (from others or from observation), use a variety of skills, offer the freedom to work independently, require doing complete tasks rather than small parts of a task, and make a contribution to the organization. Jobs with these characteristics motivate those who want challenges on the job but may burden those who would rather devote their energies to other parts of their lives (Hackman and Oldham, 1980).

The natural reaction for first-year managers is to resist what may be perceived as the organization's attempt to control the individual. Organizational commitment is likely to be undermined to the extent that individuals feel threatened. Nevertheless, the more expectations are met, the more the newcomer learns to trust the organization. The outcome should be a sense of organizational loyalty.

There are four indicators that socialization is running smoothly (Feldman, 1976a, pp. 433-452):

- *Acceptance:* This is the feeling that newcomers trust and are trusted by others. The greater the sense of acceptance, the more likely it is that newcomers will receive, on an informal basis, information that will help them do their jobs.
- *Competence:* The more positive reinforcement is received, the more self-confidence increases. Early positive reinforcement is the start of a success cycle that leads to setting more difficult goals in achieving ever-greater success.
- *Role definition:* Newcomers are more satisfied the more they can set their own priorities and allocate their own time. The more employees have input to designing their jobs, the more they are committed to doing high-quality work.

- *Congruence of evaluation:* This occurs when employees agree with the feedback received from others about performance. Unfortunately, bosses often find it difficult to give feedback to subordinates, even when the feedback is positive. The less feedback they receive, the less newcomers are able to correct their perceptions of how well they are doing, adjust their behavior to do better, or know they are on the right track and continue to behave in the same way.

The Second through the Fourth Years

If the first year or so in an organization manages to satisfy the newcomer's security needs, then the next few years begin to provide a sense of achievement, a reinforcement of personal significance. Young managers develop competence and self-confidence and learn how to deal with apprehension about being evaluated. Unfortunately, fear of failure often has dysfunctional consequences, and new managers are prone to finding a style of management that is comfortable and has been successful in the past. If they stick to what they know best, there is no chance to learn from failure, to develop a deep ability to handle anything, or to vary behavior with changing conditions.

Fast-track manager-development programs may shield young managers from failure by moving them from job to job, to give them wide experience and train them as generalists. They are expected to make fast starts and visible contributions in each job, and then they are moved to new positions before they can develop expertise and understanding of the consequences of their decisions. Their tendency is to avoid taking risks in anticipation of coming promotions.

The Fifth Year and Beyond

After five years, managers enjoy continuity of reinforcements, signals of personal importance, and good working relationships with other managers. Established attitudes must now be maintained.

In past years, changes in organizational conditions were

generally slow enough so that major alterations in what companies expected of employees were not required. Futurists now recognize that change is occurring more rapidly; in some cases, the manager does not have time to react to one change before the next change appears. For example, the Bell System adhered to the same values for most of a century. The dominant value during that time was commitment to universal service. When divestiture was announced, the company had only two years to prepare for its new orientation to a competitive mode. The need for cost control, the search for a new identity, the ability to take risks without following standard regulated practices— these were all formidable new issues. Divestiture occurred early in 1984, and loyalties as well as management styles are still changing.

Methods of Socialization

Organizations have many options for inducting new managers (Van Maanen, 1976). Here are a few examples, along with their intended outcomes.

- *Selection:* Candidates are subjected to a rigorous selection process, or at least it is made to seem rigorous. Candidates who receive job offers are made to feel part of an elite group; thus their sense of self-confidence and belonging increases.
- *Realistic job previews:* Information about organizational conditions and what it is like to be a manager is given to individuals either prior to job offers or immediately after acceptance. These previews include information about job duties, promotion, and transfer opportunities. Their purpose is to reduce reality shock.
- *Management orientation:* An introduction to organizational policies and procedures contributes to organizational loyalty and group cohesiveness.
- *Assignment to a new group:* The process of organizational socialization is similar to the process of group development (Wanous, Reichers, and Malik, 1984). Newcomers to an or-

ganization may be assigned to a new work group or they may be made to feel part of a class of new employees entering the company together and meeting as a class every few months to share experiences. As newcomers work together, group norms and identification with the group and organization develop simultaneously.

- *Technical training:* Information about, and training in, skills required for specific job functions contribute to role clarity. Training could include, for example, teaching a new manager in data services about the use of computer systems and the flow of information.
- *Apprenticeship:* Learning the ropes with an experienced manager generates group cohesiveness, realization of expectations, and reduced reality shock.
- *Bottom-up experience:* Management recruits are assigned to menial line positions that require them to learn the business at the most basic levels. These assignments provide shared experiences and increase recruits' knowledge of the business.
- *Mentorship programs:* Newcomers meet periodically with higher-level managers during the first years to discuss experiences and organizational conditions. This practice encourages role clarity and prevents reality shock.
- *Performance feedback:* Frequent reviews of performance during the first year or so in management, perhaps quarterly, build newcomers' confidence in themselves.
- *Competition:* Newcomers are measured by a succinct set of criteria, so that it is easy to compare them to each other in the same area of a business. For instance, product managers are compared on market share or market share growth. These measurements let the recruits know where they stand in relation to all the others who will be competing for limited promotion opportunities. Such comparison also highlights the importance of achieving visible results, although it has the potential disadvantage of generating intraorganizational conflict.
- *Departmental meetings:* In many organizations departments have meetings away from the office, often in remote loca-

tions, to discuss departmental goals, progress, and other issues. Departmental meetings generate a sense of belonging and a basis for shared experiences.

- *Assignment to special projects:* New managers may be assigned to special projects of fairly short duration (say, from one to three months). This practice establishes feelings of personal importance, intrinsic motivation, and achievement.
- *Assignment to undesirable tasks:* The norm in some companies is to assign the newest manager in a group to collect for the United Way or organize a departmental meeting. This custom is not unlike other initiation experiences, such as fraternity or sorority hazing. This "hazing" works because people rationalize their experience as a reflection of their commitment to the organization. It also provides a shared experience, which other managers already have gone through, and this bond tends to generate organizational loyalty.
- *Exposure to company folklore:* Newcomers are bombarded with stories of heroic sacrifices or strokes of genius that saved millions of dollars, kept the company in business during hard times, or demonstrated the firm's commitment to its employees or its customers. Sharing company folklore enhances newcomers' commitment and provides a model for individual work goals.
- *Statements of values:* Banners, newsletters, token gifts, and so on, can highlight such organizational values as safety, customer satisfaction, and secure employment. Values statements generate common goals, a sense of purpose, and an overlap with personal values.
- *Up-or-out decisions:* After a probationary period (say, six months or one year), new managers' performance can be evaluated and a decision made to retain or terminate them. This process weeds out the uncommitted and forces those who are not succeeding to find a better organizational match elsewhere. It also encourages employees early in their careers to evaluate for themselves whether they belong in the company and, if not, to quit before being fired.

Socialization is an incremental process: Each experience

contributes to making the person feel more a part of the organization and less a newcomer. Socialization experiences provide newcomers with reasons and reinforcements for accepting new role behaviors. They also provide others in the organization with a basis for incorporating newcomers into activities. Special training programs for bosses may be necessary to support new-manager orientation. Such training deals with how to give frequent performance feedback, design job assignments, structure work-group activities, and do whatever else is necessary to increase newcomers' involvement. Bosses also should understand their new subordinates' needs and interests, especially because young people today differ considerably from older employees in their values, interests, and ambitions (Howard and Wilson, 1982).

Company Fears about Socialization

Companies tend to avoid the word *socialization* in describing the strategies outlined above, because the word smacks of "control, incest, and myopia," while a phrase like *learning the ropes* is thought to give companies more latitude to implement change and execute business strategy; "strong-culture firms empower employees . . . by supplying continuity and clarity" (Pascale, 1984). While there is some danger in overemphasizing the norms of superficial behavior, it is important for individuals to understand and contribute to corporate goals and to do so in a way that is consistent with corporate values. To avoid becoming too narrow and inward-oriented, strong-culture companies like IBM and Procter and Gamble focus outward—on customer satisfaction, concern for quality, market share, and so on. Companies whose dominant focus is inward (the Delta Air Lines focus on "family feelings," for example) may be riding for a fall.

Electronic Data Systems: A Strong-Culture Firm

Socialization reinforces and maintains a company's culture. Consider the policies of Electronic Data Systems Corporation, a Dallas-based computer services company recently acquired by General Motors. Unlike its new parent, which manages by committees and has a bureaucracy similar to that found in large government agencies, EDS manages by small teams and delegates responsibility to low levels. Ross Perot, founder and CEO, institutionalized competitiveness and determination in the company's culture. Here is how _The Wall Street Journal_ reported it (Lehner, 1984):

> In some ways, EDS is run like a corporate version of the Marine Corps. Its Dallas headquarters resembles a fortified encampment; it's encircled by barbed wire and patrolled by armed guards. Discipline inside is strict. Years ago, one of the duties of a female treasurer was to measure, with a tape measure, the length of some employees' skirts to ensure proper length.
>
> To this day, male employees can't have beards. They must wear light shirts, ties, and short hair, a startling contrast to many other computer-related companies, whose employees often look like refugees from 1960s communes. EDS's written conduct code cites different kinds of offenses—including discussing salary—for which employees will be fired. One former EDS employee says she was told two years ago by her supervisor that she would be fired if the company found out that she was living with a man to whom she wasn't married.
>
> Such policies would be unacceptable at most companies, but at EDS they are part of a socialization process designed to weed out the uncommitted. That process starts with hiring. EDS hired mostly veterans until the early 1970s and still prefers to hire "lean and hungry" graduates of less prestigious schools rather than possibly self-satisfied Ivy Leaguers. But the most important part of the inculcation is a grueling training and trial period, which lasts as long as two years for systems engineers who maintain and design customer programs. Employees estimate that 25 percent of the trainees don't survive EDS's boot camp.
>
> But the result is that most of EDS's 13,500 employees display an unusual esprit de corps and devotion to hard work. "They do things when they

say they will, whatever it takes," says Marlin Johnston, commissioner of the Texas Department of
Human Resources [pp. 21, 24].

The Wall Street Journal article went on to liken the merger of
EDS and GM to a Green Beret outfit's joining up with the Social Security Administration.

Individual Differences Affecting Socialization

While managers are most susceptible to influence and indoctrination early in their careers, some individual characteristics are likely to influence the degree of susceptibility and enhance both the extent to which socialization is successful and
how quickly it occurs. These factors affect how newcomers
define established expectations, as well as how they internalize
role and cultural knowledge necessary for successful adaptation
(Jones, 1983).

For example, personal background and past experience
affect how people make sense of uncertain and ambiguous situations. Prior learning experiences are likely to be used in dealing
with new situations. Thus, individuals who moved frequently as
children and learned to be aggressive in making friends probably
act the same way at work. Again, one goal of socialization is to
make newcomers feel important and to reinforce positive self-
image, but many people enter work organizations with a fairly
well established sense of their general competence and a feeling
that they control what happens to them. Those who are competent may find it easier than those who are less competent to
assimilate role and cultural knowledge and see learning experiences as opportunities to demonstrate skills. Similarly, those
with high growth needs (for example, the desire to have a challenging job) may be more likely than those with low growth
needs to value new, uncertain environments. Still another factor
is how newcomers interpret role-related information. Newcomers and established organizational members neither know each
other well nor have the same knowledge and experiences, and
so they are liable to misinterpret each other's behavior and pay

attention to different aspects of the same situation. Consequently, there is always the potential for misunderstanding during the
socialization process. Feedback may quickly resolve newcomers'
misconceptions, but many times newcomers and established organizational members are not even aware of disparities in interpretations. For instance, established members simply take for
granted the reasons behind particular organizational procedures
and norms, such as why members behave or dress in certain
ways. It is therefore difficult for newcomers to make sense of
organizational behavior and of why they are expected to dress
or behave in the same ways. It is likewise difficult for established members to make sense of newcomers' behavior. Such
unrecognized misunderstandings impede socialization.

Thus, socialization can be seen as an interaction between
individual characteristics of newcomers, on the one hand, and
the socialization processes and programs offered by organizations, on the other. Van Maanan (1976) offers four possible
socialization outcomes, which he characterizes as individual
modes of adjustment and labels as personality types. *Team players* are people who conform both to group and to organizational expectations. *Isolates* fulfill expectations of the organization, but not of the immediate work group. For example,
ratebusters put in far more than the expected energy to out-
produce others. Persons protected by good connections also run
the risk of isolation from their peers. *Warriors* are accepted by
their peers, but fight the organizational system. Organizations
with strong institutional norms and regulations are ripe for
warriors. Finally, *outsiders* fail to meet either group or organizational expectations. They are usually quick to leave the organization, although it is possible for them to be tolerated and
become isolates or warriors.

Socialization is a two-way street. On one side, the organization tries to indoctrinate newcomers to its way of thinking
and to have newcomers meet its expectations. On the other
side, newcomers evaluate the extent to which the organization
meets their expectations. To some degree, newcomers and the
organization influence each other's expectations; for instance,
the organization may try to impart realistic expectations before

the applicant even accepts a job offer, while, for the newcomer, being a team player may require no adjustment at all or may require new skills, social behaviors, and frames of reference. Warriors, in contrast, try to change the organization but remain unaffected themselves. Still another possibility is for personal and organizational development to occur simultaneously.

Some socialization experiences increase the newcomer's commitment to the job. For example, special assignments, feedback on performance, and assignment to a boss who is a good role model are likely to generate intrinsic motivation and a sense of personal achievement. Experiences such as orientation and training result in feelings of camaraderie and identification with the organization. The first few jobs and bosses are probably the most important factors in socialization because they have immediate and direct impact on daily life. The following two cases demonstrate how early career experiences can interact with perceptions of self and with goals, affecting important early career decisions (for example, whether to stay in or leave a first job). Each case is an example of a mismatch between a newcomer's expectations and those of the organization.

Talent and a Poor Job Match. Marilyn Bentley, the daughter of a surgeon, grew up on "the right side of the tracks" in Roanoke, Virginia. She attended a well-known private university in the South and majored in philosophy. Her grades were outstanding, and she was involved in many extracurricular activities.

She had traveled extensively, both as a child and during college, and she knew several foreign languages. She had always had a wide circle of friends and many interests. She said that she liked to feel continuously challenged and would never want to be involved in anything that was routine. Realizing that the demand for philosophers was not high and believing that she had had enough schooling, she decided to find a job after graduation. She accepted a job as a first-level manager in a large company's high-potential manager-development program. The recruiter painted a picture of tremendous opportunity for career growth, and Marilyn liked what appeared to be a friendly atmosphere.

Marilyn's first job was in the business research department. She skip-level reported to a very supportive third-level manager, who gave her many interesting assignments. These helped her shift from academic life to a business career. During this time, she was also temporarily assigned to a second-level manager to work on a special project. Marilyn had never before dealt with anyone so irrational and illogical. Nevertheless, she persisted, working from 7:30 A.M. to 8:00 P.M. for several weeks to complete the project. In the end, her second-level boss scrapped everything she had done. This angered her; it was the first time in her life that she had ever felt incompetent.

After five months with the company, Marilyn was transferred to the installation and repair department. Her new job was to supervise ten women who processed service orders. Marilyn was disappointed, because she had had no input to the decision to place her in this job. After she had been on the job for several months, however, it became fairly enjoyable. She described it as an incredible learning experience, both in terms of being a supervisor and in terms of dealing with nonmanagement people who were much older (all her subordinates were forty to sixty years old, and Marilyn was only twenty-three years old at the time). The biggest adjustment for her on this job was that everything needed immediate attention, whereas on her previous job she had had several weeks to think about any one issue.

Marilyn had been with the company for ten months when I first interviewed her. Her job was beginning to bore and frustrate her. She disliked having to explain everything to her subordinates again and again before they understood, and she was afraid she seemed like a snob. She also felt that she was too young to commit herself to a lifelong career with this company. She was considering returning to school for an MBA, but she did not like the idea of a part-time degree program, and she hoped the company would give her a leave of absence to complete a full-time program. Marilyn felt an MBA would be valuable, because she was encountering credibility problems: Supervisors in several departments had told her that as a philosophy major she did not have the background to work in their areas.

Marilyn resolved to stay with the company for one more year, after which she would decide whether to return to school or to extend her stay with the company. Meanwhile, she was enjoying her life as a single young woman. She believed the proverb that a healthy body goes hand-in-hand with a healthy mind, and so she swam every day and also biked. In addition, she was taking a graduate course at night at a local university; she liked the idea of keeping one foot in the academic world, without being totally immersed.

When I talked with her seven months later, Marilyn's career outlook was pessimistic. For several months she had been responsible for two positions at once, and she found this arrangement challenging and exciting. When one of the jobs was taken over by a new employee, it was a letdown for Marilyn. She had already demonstrated her value to the department; she believed that her supervisor saw her as irreplaceable and so was stalling about moving her to a new position. Because she had approached her boss about a promotion, her relationship with him had worsened. He thought that she should not be thinking about promotion so early in her career with this company. In general, Marilyn thought her boss was ineffective, and she did not respect him as a supervisor. Her view was that she had proved herself in all her positions, especially when her workload had been doubled, and that her potential for advancement therefore should have increased. Despite her perception of slow career progress, Marilyn claimed to maintain her energy level and said she was just as much a self-starter and compulsive worker as ever.

When I tried to contact her a year later, I found that Marilyn had left the company for a full-time MBA program at a school on the West Coast. Contacted by telephone, she stated that she had no desire to return to the company. She was extremely involved in her studies and in several extracurricular activities. While she had forfeited a salary considered high for someone her age, she felt that the trade-off would repay her. After completing the two-year MBA program, she hoped to find a position that would make better use of her skills. Her two years of business experience already had fulfilled an entry requirement for the MBA program, and Marilyn also saw that period as a solid background in supervision at a low level of management. She thought this experience would help her find another position after graduation.

Marilyn's job experiences had not been sufficient to capture her involvement in her work or in the company. Her good experiences were outweighed by such disappointments as lack of support from her bosses, not having input to decisions affecting her career, and slower advancement than she had expected. While Marilyn did seem to have the intellectual ability required for early career success, she lacked the interpersonal skills necessary in her positions. Perhaps if she had been in a staff job, she might have done much better and stayed with the company. As it turned out, Marilyn was not committed to the company, and she chose to use her experience as a springboard toward obtaining an MBA degree and then looking for a more important position.

The manager-development program that initially attracted Marilyn represents one way to socialize young, high-potential managers. For example, the managers in the program are made to feel part of a special, very select group (in most companies, high-potential managers are about 5 percent of all managers); the participants are given special assignments, especially during the first year; orientation programs help participants understand the business and share experiences; they receive frequent feedback on performance; they are given more responsibility than many other people their age; they are moved from job to job every twelve to eighteen months to train them as general managers; and they are promised rapid advancement. Of course, such programs do not always work as intended, as we saw in the case of Marilyn Bentley, but this is not necessarily a disadvantage: One of the functions of such programs is to separate team players from others, who either leave the company, stick with it but continue to be frustrated, or try to change the organization to suit their own needs.

The second case is about a man who was disillusioned by his co-workers' lack of involvement in their work and so found it difficult to identify with the company.

"Give Me a Reason to Care!" Jim Boyd, thirty-five, was a first-level manager who had been with the company, a large service provider, for three years when I interviewed him. He had worked for a government agency for eight years before joining this company, but had left the agency because the pay was not high enough to support his family. His new job in the company's real estate management department gave him a higher salary, but his responsibilities were much less than they had been when he was working in government. His work standards were very high and he was thinking about advancement, but his ambitions reached no higher than second-level management.

Jim took his family responsibilities seriously and gave them a much higher priority than work. He was very cynical about the company and admitted he stayed primarily for the money, although he noted that he was developing many new skills. He felt that advancement beyond the second level would be pointless, and he saw little opportunity for advancement anyway. He complained that his co-workers were indifferent, that they had no sense of what they were contributing to the company and did not seem to take pride in their work. He also felt that he was not being challenged. Jim complained that he did not receive the positive feedback that he deserved from his boss. He worked as hard as he could when he was at the office, but he did not see how his hard work could pay off for him.

Jim's boss's reaction was quite different. He considered Jim's performance excellent and thought he had considerable opportunity for movement in the company. In his boss's eyes, Jim's low self-concept was unjustified. It seemed that Jim's frustration could have been alleviated by better feedback, some encouragement, and more meaningful job assignments, but Jim was used to thinking of himself as a person who plugged away without sufficient reward.

Jim's work environment did little to encourage his sense of contribution. He received insufficient information about himself and the organization, and there did not seem to be enough opportunities and rewards to encourage either his motivation for advancement or his commitment to his work and to the company.

In Jim's case, lack of support from his boss inhibited his feelings of job involvement. Jim was also frustrated by his perception that his co-workers did not care about the quality of their work. At this point in his career, Jim intended to stay with the organization because of the money, but it seemed that the company still could have done much more to increase both his enthusiasm for his work and his commitment to the organization.

Conclusion

To some extent, socialization occurs every time we change jobs, shift assignments, get a new boss, or experience any significant role change, but we are most susceptible to influence early in our careers, when we want to become established and feel a part of the organization. Some of us want this feeling more than others do. Certain people try hard to change the organization. Still others never feel comfortable, and so they leave. Companies such as EDS have such strong expectations and indoctrination processes that people can only adapt or leave; other companies allow more choices of behavior.

The next two chapters consider the individual characteristics that determine career motivation, and how these characteristics develop and change over time.

3

❋ ❋ ❋ ❋ ❋

Assessing
Career Motivation
of Managers

The term *motivation* refers to what we want, how much we want it, and how hard and long we try to get it. For example, work motivation is our desire to do our current jobs; managerial motivation is the desire to carry out the role of a manager—to exert leadership, conduct administrative activities, and so on. The term *career motivation* includes work and managerial motivation but also goes farther, to cover motivation associated with a wide range of career decisions and behaviors. These include searching for and accepting a new job, revising career plans, deciding to stay with a company, seeking training and new job experiences, and setting and trying to accomplish goals.

Career motivation is not just one thing or one concept; it has multiple facets. It can be understood in terms of needs, values, interests, and personality characteristics. It can also be understood in terms of career decisions and behaviors, which can be grouped into three domains of career motivation, each with several components:

1. *Career resilience* shows the extent to which we keep our spirits up when the going gets tough, how resistant we are to career barriers or disruptions affecting our work. People who are high in career resilience see themselves as competent individuals able to control what happens to them. They get a sense of accomplishment from what they do. They are able to take risks. They also know when and how to cooperate with others and act independently.

2. *Career insight* demonstrates the extent of our realism about ourselves and our careers and how accurately we relate these perceptions to our career goals. People who are high in career insight try to understand themselves and their environments. They look for feedback about how well they are doing, and they set specific career goals and formulate plans to achieve them.

3. *Career identity* is the extent to which we define ourselves by our work. People who are high in career identity are involved in their jobs, their careers, and their professions, and they are likely to feel loyalty to their employers. Career identity reflects the direction of career goals—whether we want to advance in the company, be in positions of leadership and higher status, and make more money, and whether we want to accomplish these goals as soon as possible.

What Managers Say

To find out how these concepts apply to managers, we conducted some interviews. We wanted to find out how managers view their own careers, how they like their jobs, and how work gives meaning to their lives. We started by asking when and how people gained a sense of accomplishment. Here are some of the answers we received.

I got a sense of achievement when I was an operations manager. That job, in many respects, was similar to running my own small business. I had a lot of autonomy—my boss was not even in the same building. I ran the operation the way that I thought was most appropriate or that worked the best.

I get a sense of personal accomplishment from my job because for the first time I have a little bit of freedom in what I do, which is more than I had when I was in a clerical position.

We really didn't know we were going to make it until absolutely the last day. We could not pretest. We accomplished all of our front-end objectives prior to throwing the switch. On June 31, we threw the switch, and it worked! It was a great accomplishment, an achievement for all of us who participated in it.

When we were setting up the new organization, seven of us who had no background in designing an organization sat down. Within a few months, we had a whole organization of another 135 people in place and operating with a design that was strictly ours.

We also wanted to know what it is like to feel vulnerable in the face of assignment to unfamiliar tasks. A certain amount of anxiety is expected in taking stands or making decisions in controversial situations. We asked managers how they felt when they embarked on new assignments or took actions with uncertain outcomes.

My feelings about a new job are mixed. When I am experienced in a job, it's a nice feeling of security. There is nothing that anyone can ask me about my job that I don't know. Coming into a new area shakes that feeling. I am like the new kid on the block. I have to ask so many questions, and I have to look at so many manuals. Before, it was all second nature. It's almost as if I want to jump up and say, "I do know a lot about something, but it's just not what I am doing right now. Ask me about my background—I'm good at that, and I will be good at this, but not yet."

There was no question that we had to turn
that office around. I was given all the options and
support required to do it or at least make an attempt. I thought then that if I failed, it would be
the end of my career.

The need or desire for emotional support and approval
from bosses and colleagues varies from manager to manager. We
asked managers how, when, and to what extent they depended
on others.

I think most of us become aware early in the
job what the job structure is. We don't really try to
seek specific approval. We know what's expected,
what's correct, what's incorrect, and try to do it on
our own.

Most of the work I do requires a lot of initiative—a lot of decision making as to how to handle
my job and my responsibilities.

Being new, the first two or three weeks I
didn't look to my supervisor for concurrence, but I
needed direction as to where to go, how to go
about it, and what the procedures were. The other
side of the fence is that once I know what has to
be done and how it has to get done, I need almost
no supervision.

I learn from others. People come into their
jobs with various experiences, and if I can draw on
others' experiences I can learn quite a bit.

It has been said often that the only certainty is change.
We asked managers to look into the future and tell us if they
had specific career goals and also to tell us how they find out
about career opportunities.

My career goals are vague to me right now.
What I need to do first is learn my department and
my new job.

There are so many different jobs I would
like to have. I would like to have a job in marketing and in engineering.

I get information about career opportunities from my boss; from peers and contacts within the corporation; mainly from exploring the contacts that I run into doing my day-to-day job functions.

Well, there is a job-ad package that I see regularly. Also, being with the company a few years, I have a network of people that I have dealt with in previous assignments.

There is no specific way to get career information, and it's not an easy thing to do. A lot of it is just dumb luck. You run into a job opening that appeals to you, but you didn't even know the job existed before.

We asked managers whether they knew their own strengths and weaknesses—in a word, if they thought they could look at themselves objectively and whether they had sufficient feedback to be realistic.

I think the information I get about myself with respect to my career is largely from myself, my own feelings about how I performed a particular job. I also get input from my boss and others every day.

A lot has to do with the job. There isn't always an opportunity to discuss my job performance openly with others.

Right now I am happy with the amount of feedback I get. On my last job, I was "feedbacked" to death.

My boss never tells me how well I'm doing.

On certain assignments you can fool everyone else, but you can't fool yourself. I think you need to be objective to realize what you cannot do, as well as be perceptive enough to realize what you can do and can do well.

You can go down the wrong path in picking an area that you think you want to go into, without realizing that it's not your strength. To a certain extent, that's not going to hurt you. As long as you do it early, you don't get too far off the track, and you still have a common thread through all of your career moves.

I target myself to jobs where I will be able to capitalize on my greatest strengths.

Just being able to look at a task and say, "I can't do that without help" shows that you know yourself. It's very important—I think it's a sign of strength to point out your weaknesses.

Work involvement is another issue we explored. Managers varied in how much time they spent on the job versus the time they spent with their families, friends, or in self-development.

Basically, my job is scheduled seven and a half hours a day, five days a week. It's a sort of unwritten code that we take the necessary time to do the job. If we can't do everything we should while we are on the job, then we just stay as long as we have to.

It's hard to have one good part of your life and one not-so-good part, so it's very important to balance them out, because if they are balanced, they're both good. If your work takes over 80 percent of your time, the other section of your life, the enjoyment section of your life, begins to suffer.

I don't mind spending the time it requires to do a job well and, as a consequence, spending less time now with my family and in other leisure activities. You know, I am a runner, and I haven't run as many miles as I used to.

Perhaps the most obvious element of career motivation is the question of advancement. Advancement seemed important to the managers we interviewed but had different meanings to each of them.

I think advancement is a reward for doing my job in a more than satisfactory manner—in such a way that my boss will say, "He's doing this job really well; I think he's ready to take on more responsibility and do something bigger for the company."

I am interested in advancement, don't misunderstand, but right now I'm trying to work things out in my home life and my personal life.

I want the opportunity to make decisions and be responsible for projects. I realize that you probably can get more of that responsibility as you move up the hierarchy.

More than the money and the change in status and the nicer office, advancement is being able to continue to learn, to develop as a manager, to have new experiences. Advancement is important to me.

I would like the opportunity to prove to myself and to others that I can achieve at a higher level. With that comes the fact that I may have to relocate, and I may have to sacrifice some of my relationship with my wife and kids. I'll have to address those issues when I come to them.

Knowing Yourself

To understand your own career motivation, ask yourself the following questions, and think about how your responses compare with those of the managers in our sample.

1. *When and how do you gain a sense of achievement from your work?* Our managers talked about having autonomy and discretion, implementing projects or programs and seeing them work, and doing tasks for which they had little background.

2. *How do you feel when you embark on new assignments or take actions with uncertain outcomes?* One manager talked about having mixed feelings about a new job, knowing that it would take time to become an expert but that one day expertise would come. Another manager talked about the perceived risk of failing.

3. *How, when, and to what extent do you depend on*

others? The managers mentioned determining what is expected and then doing it. Managerial work often requires taking initiative, but it also entails learning from others who have more experience and taking direction when it is needed, especially during a learning period on the job.

4. *Do you have specific career goals, and how do you find out about career opportunities?* Several managers indicated vague career goals and many things they wanted to do in their lives. They also talked about formal and informal ways of getting information about career opportunities. One manager thought that a lot of what happens in a career is "just dumb luck."

5. *Are you getting enough feedback? Where does the feedback come from? How important is it for you to know your strengths and weaknesses? Why?* Our managers indicated that feedback came from themselves and others during daily interactions, depending on the job. They implied that some jobs (and some bosses) give more feedback than others. But it is also possible to have too much feedback. Knowing yourself can help you move in a direction that uses your strengths and avoids your weaknesses. One manager stated, "It's a sign of strength to point out your weaknesses."

6. *How much time do you spend on the job, versus time on nonwork activities?* One viewpoint is that managers must work as long as it takes to get the job done; another viewpoint is that life is a balance of work and nonwork activities. Spending too much time at one means that the other suffers.

7. *How do you define advancement, and how important is it to you?* Advancement was seen as a challenge, a learning opportunity, and a way to realize full potential. It is something to strive for, but it may require some sacrifices.

Coming to know your own ideas and feelings in answering these questions will help you recognize your career interests and needs. Managers differed in their responses to each question. Your interests and needs today affect what you will be doing ten years from now, and how you see yourself will help you guide your future.

Career Motivation Research

My understanding of career motivation and its components grew out of an intensive study of the needs, interests,
abilities, and personalities of young managers (London and
Bray, 1983, 1985). The idea for the study stemmed from earlier
research, which showed that there had been a cultural shift in
values toward well-balanced life-styles (Howard and Bray, 1981;
Howard and Wilson, 1982). For some people, this balance meant
less emphasis on work, less motivation to advance, and generally
less commitment to a management career. This finding led to
several basic questions: What is career motivation? What are its
antecedents and consequences? How stable is career motivation,
in the light of organizational constraints, unmet expectations,
and other factors limiting advancement? What are the implications of career motivation for career planning and development
in a changing environment? (The chronology for the study is
outlined in Table 1.) After identifying the issues and determining

Table 1. Career Motivation Research Study Chronology.

Problem Identification
  Earlier research findings indicated that young managers are equal in
ability to those of twenty-five years ago, but they are not so motivated to
lead or advance in the company (Howard and Bray, 1981). This finding is
a problem, since need advancement and other indices of motivation predict success (level attained) twenty years later. It led to this research question: *What conception do today's young managers have of their careers?*
This question was differentiated to include these questions: *What is career
motivation? What factors contribute to it? What are its antecedents and
consequences?* The result of the problem-identification phase was a study
of managers' early career experiences in two companies.

Development of Dimensions
  The research method was the assessment center. This method uses
a variety of measures (behavioral exercises, paper-and-pencil tests, interviews, and so on). It provides an in-depth study of a fairly small number
of people. The development of dimensions to be assessed defined career
motivation. After numerous revisions, we arrived at three domains—career
insight, career identity, and career resilience—with dimensions falling under each domain.

(continued on next page)

Table 1. Career Motivation Research Study Chronology, Cont'd.

Assessment Center Development
    As the dimensions were developed, we designed the assessment center. We drew from other research assessment centers and also designed new tests and exercises.

Administration
    The assessment center was administered first to a trial group of six people and then to forty-eight young managers from two companies (twenty-four from each company). The companies are called here by the fictitious names ECHO, Inc., and DYNAMO Corp. The participants were selected by the companies on the basis of our selection criteria: employed in a general management position, with one to three years of experience; approximately half the participants male and half female. The companies were selected because of their availability, willingness, and proximity.

Data Analysis and Integration
    Tests were scored, reports typed, and so on, in preparation for the integration sessions, during which the staff rated the dimensions. Statistical analyses of the quantitative measures were conducted.

Individual Feedback and Follow-Up
    To give the young managers something in return for their participation and to determine how they viewed our conclusions about them, we met with each participant to give feedback on selected test scores seven months after the assessment, and we used this occasion to discuss what had happened to the participants in the interim.

Primary Reports
    The companies were given group results. Many differences were found between the two companies. In general, motivation was significantly higher on many dimensions in DYNAMO than in ECHO. The company differences were attributed to several factors: different selection policies; different development programs attracting different types of people; different company philosophies of management development (ECHO viewed young managers as filling current business needs, while DYNAMO treated young managers as corporate resources for the future). The vice-presidents of personnel from the two companies suggested that we do additional research to investigate the impact of situational conditions on the career motivation variables and then to recommend programs and policies for early career development.

Participant and Boss Interviews
    About one year after the feedback, we interviewed the participants again and conducted separate interviews with their bosses. The interviews focused on organizational conditions (for example, department policies, supervisory style) that contribute to career motivation. In addition, group sessions were held with other young managers and separate group sessions were held with bosses of young managers to discuss the same issues.

Table 1. Career Motivation Research Study Chronology, Cont'd.

Development of Situational Dimensions

As we conducted the interviews, we generated and revised dimensions of the situations that influence each individual characteristic associated with career motivation.

Impact of Results

ECHO, Inc.: The personnel vice-president ordered the development of a program for all new employees, not to prepare them for promotion but to give them challenging and interesting work assignments. The program, which is now operating, assigns new managers to mentors and features meetings with fellow new managers and company officers. The program lasts one to two years. DYNAMO Corp.: The company used the results to defend its own development program and to argue for its continuation in the company and its extension to the other companies in the region.

In addition, we reviewed the literature, with particular attention to research on early career experiences of managers. This review, together with the results of the career motivation study, was used to develop a set of guidelines for manager development, based on the situational dimensions associated with young managers' career motivations. Existing programs and program components were evaluated for their costs, benefits, and likelihood of affecting the different career motivation domains. The best components were combined to form an orientation program for new managers and two career tracks: *New-Manager Development Program*, for all new managers, to orient them to the company and to managerial responsibilities; *High-Potential Development Track*, for a select group of young managers; *Standard Career Track*, for all other managers. (These programs are described in Chapter Six.)

what we wanted to measure, we devised and administered assessment methods. The results led to the need for more research on the same sample, and the project concluded with the design of guidelines and programs for early career development.

The method chosen for the research was a specialized assessment center focused on individual characteristics relevant to career motivation. In assessment center work, such characteristics are called dimensions. Dimensions lead to the selection or development of exercises (tests, interview guides, behavioral simulations, and so on) designed to produce evidence for evaluating assessees on those dimensions. The dimensions in our career motivation assessment center were split into the three domains of career resilience, career insight, and career identity. (For an explanation of career motivation domains and an extensive description of their components, see London, 1983.)

The Assessment Center

Fundamental to the assessment center method is that ratings on the dimensions are not derived in any mechanical way from test scores, but are, in effect, assessor judgments. The bases for such judgments come from a variety of assessment devices, including interviews, biographical data, self-description inventories, projective tests, and behavioral simulations. Our career motivation assessment center was similarly designed. (The methods used in the assessment center are outlined in Table 2.)

Table 2. Two-Day Career Motivation Assessment Center.

Preassessment Mailing
   Personal history form and background questions

Day 1: Projectives
   Thematic Apperception Test (60 mins.): The participant is asked to write a story about each of six picture cards, describing what is happening in the picture, what led up to the events, and what the outcome will be.
   Rotter Incomplete Sentences Test (30 mins.)
   Bell Incomplete Sentences Test (30 mins.)

   Intellectual Abilities
      School and College Ability Tests (80 mins.): A timed test of quantitative and verbal ability.

   Personality Measures
      Edwards (60 mins.): Total of 225 forced-choice items measuring fifteen personality variables originating from a list of manifest needs (developed by H. A. Murray and others). The needs measured are achievement, deference, order, exhibition, autonomy, affiliation, intraception, succorance, dominance, abasement, nurturance, change, endurance, heterosexuality, and aggression.
      Sarnoff (10 min.): Eighteen items measuring need for upward mobility, need to advance and get ahead, and value of money and position.
      Expectations Inventory (25 mins.): Fifty-six statements describing the situation in which a manager might find himself or herself five years later.

   Background
      Interview (120 mins.): A semistructured interview covering

Table 2. Two-Day Career Motivation Assessment Center, Cont'd.

four major areas. (1) A brief account of the person's life up until graduation from high school. (2) The person's college years. (3) The person's current life, including work and nonwork pursuits. (4) The person's perceptions of the company and his or her career so far.

Day 2

Personality Measures

Guilford Zimmerman Temperament Survey (50 mins.): Measures ten personality constructs: general activity, restraint, ascendance, sociability, emotional stability, objectivity, friendliness, thoughtfulness, personal relations, and masculinity.

Reid-Ware Three-Factor Internal-External Scale (10 mins.): A forty-five-item forced-choice questionnaire measuring three factors—self-control, social systems control, and fatalism.

Bass (20 mins.): A fifty-eight-item measure of authoritarianism (belief in power, punishment, toughness, conventionality, cynicism and judgmental attitude).

Rokeach Value Survey (20 mins.): Subjects are presented with two lists of eighteen values. Subject arranges each list in order of importance.

Q-Sort (30 mins.): Subject sorts seventy statements in order of how well each one describes him or her.

Interests

Strong-Campbell Vocational Interest Blank (30 mins.): Asks the person 325 questions that elicit preferences (likes, dislikes, or indifferences) concerning various occupations, school subjects, activities, amusements, and types of people. Generates three types of scores: (1) General Occupational Themes (Holland's six types); (2) Basic Interest Scales; and (3) Occupational Scales.

Fact-Finding Exercise, Career Projectives, and Cases

The Fact-Finding Exercise (30 mins.): Subject is given three hypothetical job choices: assistant branch manager of a bank; staff member in the new-services development department of the bank; or assistant product manager in a consumer products company. The subject then has an opportunity to question a resource person (an assessor) about the alternatives.

Career Projectives (Management Apperception Test) (30

(continued on next page)

Table 2. Two-Day Career Motivation Assessment Center, Cont'd.

mins.): Six pictures focusing on career-related topics; originally developed by H. T. Ballard, K. S. Calhoun, and J. L. Moses. Each picture used as a basis for discussion between the participant and an assessor.

Six Cases (40 mins.): Each case asks the subject to advise a character in the case about a life–career decision. Issues deal with different problems faced by men and women in balancing work and family; career stagnation; advantages and disadvantages of advancement; women supervising men; and equal employment opportunity. An assessor questions each participant on his or her reaction to each case.

Career and Life Expectations Measures

Future Time Line (25 mins.): The person lists positive and negative events he or she expects will happen at different times in future. Separate lists are made for career, family, and self-development.

Ideal Business Day (10 mins.): The subject is given a blank page from one day on a calendar and asked to indicate what he or she would be doing each hour of the day on an ideal job.

What You Want In Life (15 mins.): Asks the subject to list what he or she wants most from life and a career.

Growth Need Strength Measure from the Job Diagnostic Survey by Hackman and Oldham (1980) (10 mins.): A measure of the extent to which the individual wants a challenging job.

Expectations Discussion (55 mins.): A semistructured interview covering career and life goals for the next five years, in such areas as family, spare-time activities, personality, financial matters, health, career, relations with supervisors and peers, training, and job performance; actual expectations in each of these areas; and long-term aspirations and expectations.

A number of the assessment exercises we used were also used in other research based on the assessment center method (Bray, Campbell, and Grant, 1974). Among these were the projectives and most of the personality inventories, as well as the mental ability test. In addition, several new exercises were devised for our study. One of these was an individual behavior simulation, a career fact-finding exercise focusing on career decision making. Administration of the assessment took place in fourteen hours, spread over two days.

The goal of the assessment was a better understanding of career motivation in young people. Our intention was not to answer all our research questions definitively, but the study did provide descriptive data on the level of career motivation for comparison with other existing data. In-depth information on subjects' backgrounds and early career experiences yielded information on development and changes in the career motivation domains. Comparison of the data from the companies involved also suggested the importance of situational characteristics. This discovery led to additional development of the theory, to include environmental variables and the processes by which they interact with individual characteristics that reflect career motivation (Howard and Bray, 1981). It also led to an exploration of organizational strategies for increasing career motivation, including a comprehensive early-career manager-development program (described in Chapter Six).

Conducting the Assessment Center

The assessment staff consisted of two psychologists and one graduate student, who was the test administrator. Four subjects participated in each session of two consecutive days. Two groups completed the assessment center each week. Forty-eight first-level managers were assessed, twenty-four from each of two companies. The companies were similar in operations and were located in similar geographical regions. The sample size was deliberately small because the purpose of the research was to study in depth the early career experiences of relatively few people. The participants were general managers, often with supervisory responsibilities, in a variety of departments. (Managers in specialist positions, such as computer programming, were excluded from the study.) The sample included twenty-five females and twenty-three males, forty-one whites and seven nonwhites. All participants were college graduates who had been with their companies for one to three years; therefore people who left their companies during the first year or so were not included in the study. The sample was limited in this way because our goal was to study managers' first few years in organizations. We also wanted to study people who were knowledgeable about organizational opportunities, policies, and programs, and we knew from other research that managers with only a few months of service know very little about their organizations.

To avoid biased responses (that is, participants giving us what they thought we wanted), we did not tell the subjects that this was a study of career motivation. Rather, the research was described in general terms and called the Early Career Experiences Study. Confidentiality was guaranteed; the participants were assured that no identifying results would ever be given to their companies. The participants were promised personal feedback, however.

Integration sessions, designed to rate each participant on the dimensions and domains, were held several months after the assessment center. The raters consisted of the three assessment staff members, the clinical psychologist who wrote the projective test reports, and an advanced graduate student in clinical psychology. It took two to two and a half hours to review the reports and test scores and to rate each participant. Ratings were made on five point scales. After making all the ratings for a given subject, the raters stated what rating they had given for each dimension and domain. If the raters disagreed by more than one scale point, they discussed the rating until they reached that level of agreement.

Summary of Results

We obtained the following results for the total sample with respect to each domain of career motivation:

1. *Career resilience:* The participants were slightly more vulnerable than resistant to career barriers, as was evident from some notable differences among the subdomains making up the domain of career resilience. They seemed to think well of themselves, but they were not risk takers and they relied on others, especially for career opportunities.

2. *Career insight:* The participants were rated as having

fairly clear career goals and working toward future goals, but they were also seen as slightly higher than average on goal flexibility and need for change. This finding suggested that to some extent they had multiple, possibly conflicting goals and were interested in new and different career experiences.

3. *Career identity:* The participants were highly committed to managerial work, but they were attracted to change. At the same time, they were concerned with job security and making money. These are, of course, conflicting tendencies. The participants' advancement motivation appeared to rest on this interest in financial return and on the need for recognition, rather than on the motivation to lead.

These results were consistent with other research on larger samples (Howard and Bray, 1981). As we shall see later, however, further analyses of the data showed differences in results between companies, leading us to consider situational impacts on career motivation variables.

Feedback to Participants

Seven to eight months after the assessment center, the participants were presented with face-to-face feedback on selected personality test scores. Since this study was not intended to go on for many years, we felt that the feedback would not contaminate future data and could benefit the research, in addition to giving the managers something in return for their participation. The research purposes of the feedback were to explore the extent of corroboration with self-perceptions; resolve or affirm inconsistencies; identify defense mechanisms (for example, rationalizations); and, as a by-product, gather reactions to changes taking place in the companies. The potential value of the feedback for the participants was to help them recognize internal conflicts and inconsistencies, identify patterns suggesting possible dysfunctional behaviors, and consider advancement and achievement needs in the light of organizational opportunities. We examined dependency needs, discussed adjustment scores (for example, emotional stability and objectivity), and considered the participants' ability to deal with change and uncertainty. Our feedback strategy was to explore the participant's reactions tactfully, taking care to protect his or her self-concept. In a few cases, personal change strategies were discussed, but only if this question was raised by the participant.

Reactions to feedback seemed very positive. There was generally high agreement with the results, although disagreements were noted occasionally. Career and personal problems were evident in a few cases. We limited our advice to suggesting that professional help be sought, and this advice was given only when the investigator's opinion was requested.

Follow-Up Interviews

One year after the feedback, the participants were interviewed again. Their current bosses were also interviewed separately. The purpose of these interviews was to learn what had happened in the interim. The vice-presidents of personnel from the companies involved also wanted to know more about how organizational context and style of supervision influence early career development, and they felt we should go back to our original participants to investigate these issues, since we knew so much about the participants already and could try to analyze the effects of the work environment, taking individual differences into account.

Case Studies

The assessments, feedback, and follow-up interviews provided rich data on people, many of whom were experiencing organizational change and making important decisions about their careers. These data were the source of the case studies in this book. To protect confidentiality, the cases presented here have been disguised by changes in names, departments, and identifying events. For the same reason, the cases are limited primarily to work experiences; detailed information collected on each person's childhood, family, and other nonwork life experiences is not included, although this information, along with the test scores and other assessment center reports, was used by

the staff to rate each participant on the career motivation domains and dimensions. The average ratings on the domains are
incorporated into the cases, along with occasional excerpts
from the clinical psychologist's reports. To understand how our
ratings of each person's career resilience, insight, and identity
supplemented the background material, let us review the cases
of Lydia Brown (Chapter One) and Marilyn Bentley and Jim
Boyd (Chapter Two).

Lydia Brown. Recall that Lydia was an average student
who, after a succession of jobs, decided to work her way through
an MBA degree, majoring in finance. Looking for a job after
graduation, she was attracted to a manager-development program that offered long-term development and advancement. She
had a positive self-image. Her style of planning was to create
the future she wanted, although she was beginning to realize the
impact of unanticipated events and opportunities.

The assessment staff evaluated Lydia as high in career
resilience, moderate in career insight, and high in career identity. Her high career identity stemmed from high need for advancement, high need for recognition, high need for dominance,
and high financial motivation. She was involved in her work and
committed to a career with the company. She was not concerned about job security, feeling that she could do well wherever she was and that she had many opportunities. Lydia's only
moderate career insight stemmed, on the one hand, from high
goal clarity and high concentration on the future and, on the
other hand, from low self-understanding, fairly accurate perception of the social environment in the company, and low realism
of expectations. Her high career resilience stemmed from high
self-esteem, high need for achievement, high initiative, willingness to take risks and tolerate uncertainty, and high competitiveness. She was high in some dependency needs, in that she relied on her boss for obtaining her next assignment and on both
her boss and higher-level managers for positive feedback. Lydia
did not sit back and wait for opportunities to come her way,
however. She made contacts with managers at higher levels, and
she let everyone know about her career ambitions.

The clinical psychologist's report found Lydia to be active, motivated, and determined to structure her life in ways that would bring her the rewards and satisfaction she wanted. Nevertheless, the psychologist felt that her goals reached out in many directions, with lofty dreams of great success and accomplishment as well as a realistic focus on what she called the basics ("love, happiness, and health"). The psychologist wrote, "Most of all, she is seeking self-fulfillment, and at present this takes the form of establishing her independence and seeking new experiences. She reports having a happy state of mind and, for the most part, is pleased with the developments in her life. But she continues to look forward to changes and improvements. She is optimistic about the future and feels confident that she will be able to achieve what she wants."

The assessment staff was unsure of whether Lydia's career goals were problematic for her career identity. One assessor did not believe she clearly knew what she wanted. Others felt she knew exactly what she wanted, although her goals were ambitious. There was disagreement among the assessment staff in predicting whether or not she would stay with the company. On the one hand, she seemed to have a very high need for change. Since many opportunities would be open to her in the future and because she tended to be somewhat impatient, she was likely to leave. On the other hand, one assessor felt that as Lydia matures, and if she experiences reasonable success in the company (which he thought was likely), she would not look outside the company for career opportunities.

Marilyn Bentley. Marilyn expected challenging assignments befitting her self-perceived high abilities. She also wanted respect from her colleagues, which was difficult to attain in her line positions supervising and working for older, more experienced people. She was often seen as a snob, and she felt she was not recognized and rewarded for having proved herself. She realized that an MBA would give her added credibility in business, and she left the company to enter an MBA program at a prestigious university.

The assessment staff found Marilyn to be a bright young woman who learned fast and thrived on change. She liked being active and was definitely a doer. Although her career goals were not very clear, she knew that she wanted to stay in business and that she wanted to guide her own career. The staff rated her as high in career resilience, moderate in career insight, and moderate to low in career identity.

Marilyn's career identity seemed to stem from a need for recognition. Her needs for advancement, leadership, and money were fairly low, however. She was not committed to the company or to the nature of her work, and she did not exhibit a need for job security. She seemed to be very high in need for change. Her moderate career insight score stemmed from a combination of low goal clarity and high goal flexibility. She received high ratings on social perceptiveness, self-understanding, and realism of expectations. Her high career resilience stemmed from strong self-esteem, need for autonomy, and need for achievement. She exhibited high inner-work standards and a strong development orientation. Her fear of failure was evaluated as very low, her risk-taking tendency as moderate, and her tolerance of uncertainty as quite high. Her dependency needs were about average, except that she seemed to have an above average need for peer approval. The clinical psychologist's report, based on the projective tests, found Marilyn to be responsive and open. The report stated, "She is a spontaneous, cheerful person whose reactions are natural, unpretentious, and relaxed. The feature that stands out most clearly is her enthusiasm. She is excited about the pleasures and new experiences she anticipates having and is eager to live her life fully, enjoying each minute."

Jim Boyd. Jim was disappointed with the lack of commitment his co-workers showed to their own work and to the company. He also felt his skills were underutilized, since he had had more responsibility in his previous job with the government. Not surprisingly, the assessment staff saw Jim as low in career identity. His career insight was high, however, because he had a clear conception of his career goals, which were not very ambitious. He was also perceptive about his co-workers' lax attitude toward quality of work. Jim needed a sense of achievement, but his self-concept was low. He was not a risk taker. He exhibited little initiative regarding his career development; overall, his career resilience was low.

Conclusion

Career motivation is defined here in terms of three domains and eight components, as follows:

A. *Career Resilience*
    1. Believing in oneself
    2. Needing achievement
    3. Being willing to take risks (being innovative without fear of failure)
    4. Being independent, yet cooperative
B. *Career Insight*
    5. Establishing goals
    6. Having career perceptiveness (self-knowledge of strengths and weaknesses; understanding of the work environment)
C. *Career Identity*
    7. Having career involvement (identifying with job, organization, and profession)
    8. Desiring advancement (and the attainment of what usually goes along with advancement—recognition, leadership, money, and so on)

The assessment center is certainly the most thorough and probably the most accurate way to measure a set of personality characteristics, needs, and interests that are closely tied to past and current behavior. Integrating the information in the form of assessor judgments is important for understanding a person's career motivation, because the elements of career motivation are conceptually interrelated and may also build on each other. The next chapter considers how the domains of career motivation develop and offers some techniques to guide thinking about individual career resilience, insight, and identity.

4

*   *   *   *   *

Developing
and Strengthening
Career Motivation

How do the domains of career motivation develop and change? This chapter offers speculation on answers to this question and is based on my own opinions, my understanding of relevant theory and research in psychology, and my interpretations of the cases taken from the career motivation assessment described in the last chapter. It is hoped that this chapter and the exercises at the end will help readers understand their own career motivation.

Career resilience is probably fairly well established when people start their careers, although it can be altered. Career insight and identity, in contrast, are less stable and depend on information people receive about themselves and the environment. It is also probable that career insight and career identity are affected by information about career opportunities, support received for career development, seeing what others do, and available rewards and opportunities, while career resilience is composed of more ingrained personality characteristics and is affected by early successes and failures.

Developmental Processes

Past experiences and the current situation determine one's psychological state at any given time, and the reinforcements one receives make an important contribution. One tends to repeat behaviors that have positive outcomes or that eliminate or prevent negative outcomes. There is also a tendency to avoid behaviors that have negative outcomes or that do not have positive consequences. Understanding career motivation requires a careful review of past personal history, an attempt to document what has controlled behavior, and the use of this information to interpret career resilience, career insight, and career identity. This line of reasoning follows the conceptualization of work motivation by Campbell and Pritchard (1976). Reinforcement is most effective when experienced personally, but personal experience is not necessary for relationships between behavior and rewards to have a personal impact. One's interpretation of observed events will also have an effect on processing information about oneself and others. This effect is termed *social learning*.

Thus, we learn indirectly by observing the actions of others and the consequences of those actions and by copying the behaviors of others. Moreover, we develop standards for evaluating behavior, and this process affects how we react to others (Bandura, 1977; see also Salancik and Pfeffer, 1978).

The domains of career motivation (career resilience, insight, and identity), since they stem partly from thoughts that make sense of our past actions and the social environment, depend on the consequences of our behaviors, the salience and relevance of information, and the general need to develop socially acceptable and legitimate rationalizations for our actions. Each of these processes may contribute to the formation of the individual characteristics that constitute career motivation, but the strength of their effect is likely to vary. Reinforcements experienced directly are likely to have the strongest and most permanent effects on us, whereas individual characteristics that arise from social learning and information processing are likely to be less stable and more easily changed.

Career resilience is likely to arise from reinforcements experienced during childhood and adolescence. For instance, need for achievement, a dimension contributing to career resilience, may develop because of rewarding achievement experiences in the past. Career resilience arises fairly early in life, but this is not to say that it is static; recent reinforcement experiences in new contexts may alter certain individual characteristics.

Career identity and insight tend both to be more directly associated with current circumstances and to be less stable than career resilience. Career identity and insight are also likely to be more work-related than career resilience (a dimension whose characteristics are also evident in other areas of our lives). While career resilience reflects what one has become, career insight reflects what one is and what one wants to be. Career insight depends on what others say about us, how others react to us, and how they treat us. It also depends on our own thoughts as we evaluate the extent to which information applies to us and as we set goals for ourselves. We may seem to have insight one day and the next day be in a state of confusion or naiveté. Career identity is based on our interpretation of the past and of the current situation. It may be affected by what we learn from watching others and by the value we attribute to what we think will happen when we behave in a certain way. Thus, this discussion suggests that career resilience arises prior to the start of one's career, while career identity and career insight arise concurrently with the beginning of one's career, and that career resilience, while not unchangeable, is more stable than either career identity or career insight.

The Relationship Between Career Resilience and Career Insight. As mentioned above, career resilience is likely to precede the development of career insight. Career resilience helps one establish one's role in the organization. People high in career resilience are likely to believe in their own ability to understand and affect the environment, whereas those low in career resilience doubt this ability in themselves. Consequently, people high in career resilience may gain career insight earlier than those low in career resilience. In general, low career resilience discourages the development of career insight, whereas high career resilience facilitates the development of career insight.

This argument suggests that career resilience affects career insight. To a lesser extent, however, the relationship may be reciprocal. Once established, career insight may reinforce the level of career resilience. As we gain a fairly concrete sense of ourselves and the environment, we will probably try to manifest a consistent picture of ourselves in our self-confidence, need for achievement, willingness to take risks, and desire to be independent. Realizing our weaknesses may be the first step toward trying to increase our resilience.

The Relationship Between Career Identity and Career Insight. Analyzing our expectations and setting clear and realistic goals—two components of career insight—set the stage for career identity. The extent to which our careers are important to us depends on the opportunities we have and the likelihood that these opportunities will meet our needs. Commitment to the organization, the job, and the profession may increase as we realize the expected value from these work elements.

Career insight, in turn, may be affected by career identity. For instance, the desire to advance in the corporation—an element of career identity—is likely to prompt individuals to set clearer goals and establish ways to achieve them; and these, of course, are elements of career insight.

The Relationship Between Career Resilience and Career Identity. Low career resilience combined with high career identity produces an incongruous state, which is likely to be frustrating. For instance, a person may dream of being the company president but doesn't have the ability or backbone to even come close to this goal. Individuals in this state who also have high career insight realize that their goals will probably not be achieved; they are their own worst enemies, and they know it. If their insight is low, however, they are in for continued disappointment as they confront barriers to their career goals but fail to understand why they cannot overcome these barriers.

Individuals high in resilience and low in identity are also

in an incongruous state. Moreover, theirs is a pattern in flux: If their career insight is high, they will realize that they have not yet found themselves and may anticipate that their career identity will emerge as they have more experiences and glean more information about themselves and the organization; if their insight is low, they may feel dissatisfied with their lack of career direction.

The extent to which congruence emerges between career resilience and career identity, and how long congruence takes to emerge, will depend on the situation and on what happens to the individual. Some people may never resolve an inconsistency between low career resilience and high career identity because they never gain the insight necessary to perceive and alter the incongruence. Others may receive accurate, constructive feedback that contributes to self-insight and may be encouraged to set goals and establish career paths on the basis of either this feedback or self-assessment. Thus, the relationship between career resilience and career identity may be stronger when career insight is high than when it is low.

This argument views career resilience as a cause of career identity, but career identity may reinforce a particular level of career resilience. For instance, being thrust into an advancement-oriented environment (for example, being sent to a summer course for managers at the Harvard Business School) may initiate the development of a need for advancement, which is an element of career identity. If the individual's sense of self-confidence is initially moderate, this experience is likely to enhance self-confidence. If, however, self-confidence is initially low, it would be inconsistent with the need for advancement and would probably block the development of such a need.

Patterns of Development

The previous section described proposed relationships between career resilience, career insight, and career identity and suggested that changes may occur over time, as a modification in one variable affects another variable. Several possible patterns of domains are outlined in this section.

Pattern 1: Healthy Development. Individuals who have had fairly positive experiences throughout childhood and adolescence should enter the work world with a generally high level of resilience. This is not to say that the individual will have had no negative experiences or that all the individual's relevant personality characteristics will indicate high resilience. In this pattern, career insight and identity will probably be fairly low at the outset of the career, although it is likely that some career direction will have emerged before this time. College students, for instance, are usually expected to declare a major before the junior year. This decision may be changed, but for many it is the first formal statement of career direction. Nevertheless, college graduates with similar educational backgrounds may seek jobs in many different organizations, sometimes even in very different industries. Ultimate career identity is likely to depend on which organization is joined. The next stage in this pattern is the emergence of career insight and career identity; when a person starts a career with high career resilience, career insight and identity are likely to follow.

This pattern applies to Lydia Brown. Recall from Chapter One that self-confidence was her hallmark. Raised in a large family, Lydia learned early in life that she would have to fend for herself to get what she wanted, and she also learned early that she could be successful at meeting her needs. Trying out several jobs and then supporting herself through business school, she demonstrated her sense of independence and her willingness to take risks. Her career insight emerged as she set her own standards and goals and did what was necessary to achieve them.

When I met Lydia, her career identity was blossoming. She wanted to advance in the company, and she had a sense of the role she wanted work to play in her life. In the future, she may find that some of her goals are beyond her reach and that she cannot control which opportunities will be open to her, but she has the resilience and insight to readjust her goals in a direction meaningful to her.

Pattern 2: Redirection. Individuals who have established their career identity and appear to have career insight will not necessarily maintain these dimensions. Changes in circumstances may not be perceived because career identity is so strong. As a result, career insight may diminish. Another possibility is that insight may remain strong, but identity may diminish or be redirected as the individual puts new information to use. For example, information about a particular career direction may be negative and may make the goal seem less attractive or more difficult to pursue; additional information may make another career identity seem more desirable. Alternatively, the individual may lose career identity and not establish another immediately; learning from past experience, the individual may take more time than before to seek and process career information and establish career direction. If career resilience remains fairly stable, the individual may not hesitate to make a commitment to a new career direction. If risks do not pay off, or if supervisors encourage dependency, resilience may decrease, and it may become difficult to re-establish career identity or insight.

Jim Boyd, who was introduced in Chapter Two, is an example of someone searching for career identity. Having worked his way up in a government agency, he changed jobs primarily for more money. Now earning a higher salary, he has less responsibility and finds that his co-workers do not meet his standards for work quality. His boss has a higher evaluation of Jim's career prospects than Jim himself does. Jim is a family man and likes living in a small town. He is not ambitious. At this point, he is not committed to the company, except that he sees his job as the only way to make a decent living and maintain his present life-style. Whatever encouragement he gets from his boss and from job opportunities in the company will determine his future work involvement. If he does not receive this support, he will be likely to direct his energies to nonwork pursuits.

Pattern 3: Intervening Self-Doubt. Career insight and career identity may not develop during the first years of work if the individual is isolated from others, given unimportant assignments, or has substantial nonwork responsibilities that do not permit sufficient attention to work. Career identity may be absent and insight may remain low. Initially, self-doubt will arise. If the individual has had sufficient evidence of his or her own competence in the past, he or she is likely to take some risks, experience some successes, and develop a greater sense of independence. The eventual outcome will be, optimistically, higher career resilience, insight, and identity.

This was the case for Marilyn Bentley (Chapter Two), who found that her early work experiences did not give her the recognition she thought she deserved. She had several challenging assignments that lasted only a short time, and she soon became bored and felt that her efforts were not appreciated. Disillusioned with the company, she experienced some self-doubt, and she needed to rethink her career directions. For Marilyn, any drop in self-confidence was not lasting, and her two years with the company provided her with the experience she needed to apply to a prestigious MBA program. The following case is another example of intervening self-doubt.

Reversing Early Career Failure: The Case of Wayne Converse. Being considered a poor performer early in one's career can be the kiss of death. If performance is sufficiently low, the company will probably dismiss the individual. Early dismissal may be the best thing for employees who are able to seek more promising careers elsewhere, but in some cases dismissal is either not justified or is an unpleasant step the boss wants to avoid. Consequently, poorly performing individuals may be transferred to other departments or placed in other, less demanding jobs. The reputation of having failed is likely to persist and become a barrier that must be overcome if there is any desire for advancement. Occasionally, such negative experiences are due not to the inability of the individual but rather to poor supervision or to a mismatch between the job requirements and the employee's abilities. Wayne Converse's story indicates that early failure, due in part to poor supervision, can be overcome when the job and the boss change.

Wayne was an economics graduate of an Ivy League school who chose to work for the company because of what promised to be a challenging manager-development program and because of the high starting salary. His first boss had never, in his thirty years with the company, supervised a newly hired college graduate. Wayne's job was in the engineering planning department, and it involved evaluating the cost effectiveness of possible equipment changes. Wayne enjoyed the work but was frustrated by his lack of rapport with the boss; the boss gave Wayne little help and direction, but Wayne never asked for any help. His boss never gave him feedback on his job performance. Wayne had the feeling that his contributions were not being used by the department, and so he started to exert less effort. He never received a negative comment until he had been on the job for ten months, when his boss surprised him by telling Wayne that he was a borderline case; he was considering firing Wayne.

Wayne felt that the boss's evaluation was completely unprovoked. Wayne's reaction was to work harder, and his efforts paid off: After several months, the boss made the decision to retain him. One reason Wayne had disliked his job was that there was very little interaction with other people in the department. It was a small department, and everybody worked in the same area, but Wayne was not even sure what some of the other managers' names were. They all had separate projects, and they were not encouraged by the boss to use each other as resources.

Fortunately for Wayne, one of his co-workers was transferred, and Wayne was assigned to work directly with a fourth-level manager on a special project. During the next four months, Wayne developed a close relationship with this manager. He worked with several other upper-level managers, and they listened to him.

After eighteen months in his first job, Wayne was transferred to a planning position in the marketing department. This job involved doing pricing studies for various products. His new boss was a young woman, and there was an excellent working atmosphere in the department. This department was much more relaxed than his first department. Everyone worked on group projects and often socialized off the job.

When I first interviewed Wayne, he was doing well. The negative feedback from his first boss had disconcerted him, but he kept working and eventually occupied several important positions that allowed him to demonstrate his abilities. He was beginning to develop an excellent reputation; his latest boss had evaluated him as having officer-level potential. During the inter-

view, Wayne showed me two letters of commendation he had
received.

Wayne was evaluated by the assessment staff as high in
career identity, moderate in career insight, and high in career
resilience. His ratings showed high advancement needs and high
job involvement. His self-concept was positive, and he had a
high need for achievement. He was seen as moderately high in
fear of failure and somewhat low in risk taking. To some extent,
this finding may have resulted from the initial negative performance appraisal, since this was the first time he had had reason
to question his positive self-concept. In his first position, Wayne
had felt inexperienced, yet did not think he should ask for assistance. His personality test scores suggested that he often pro-
jected a mask of emotional control and resisted close personal
relationships. While his current boss evaluated him highly, she
felt that Wayne tended to shy away from work that was new to
him.

Wayne had a strong self-concept, which was shaken for
only a short time. His bosses' styles of management were important to his ultimately having successful work experiences.
Rather than give up after his first failure, Wayne worked even
harder. Fortunately, he was placed in positions where his abilities could shine. (Recall that this was not the case for Marilyn
Bentley, who felt she was assigned to positions that were be-
neath her, but which probably required interpersonal skills she
did not have.)

Pattern 4: Breaking Away from an Ineffective Pattern.
This pattern starts with low career resilience. A pattern of low
career resilience, low career insight, and low career identity may
be temporary. There are several ways to reverse this pattern, but
low resilience is likely to be difficult to change. Resilience may
increase only after insight and identity have developed to some
degree. One possibility is that insight may emerge as the organization requires setting goals or as organizational policies and
procedures are made clearer. As the individual uses this new insight (and, it is hoped, experiences some success), the feeling of
self-confidence and the willingness to take risks may grow and
dependency needs may decrease. Another possibility is that vul-

nerability (low resilience) may be an immediate but temporary result of a setback (for example, losing one's job). The individual may demonstrate resilience fairly soon if no additional adverse experiences occur, and especially if positive experiences are forthcoming (for example, the individual finds a new job that is more rewarding than the first). Unfortunately, in some cases low resilience may be too difficult to overcome, and a chronic state of low self-confidence and high dependency may result.

Making It on Your Own: The Case of Carol Baylor. Carol had taught high school for a year before taking a job in business. Her staff position in the company's construction department required taking extensive in-house courses, and she was very busy during her first few months on the job. Taking the position required moving to a new city, away from her family and friends. Her new co-workers were older, married men, and she had trouble making friends on the job because she thought that rumors would start if she spent too much time talking to any one of her co-workers. After a year with the company, she still had no close friends at work.

Carol found her job exciting at first, but the excitement wore off quickly. The problem was that her workload was very low. Her boss was aware of the situation, but there was not much he could do about it. The department would not let its people transfer because the workload was anticipated to increase. The department did not want to lose people, especially people as able as Carol, when replacing them could not be justified.

Carol toyed with the idea of quitting and enrolling in a full-time MBA program. Her own boss and his boss were supportive of this idea and wrote letters of recommendation for her. She was accepted at two local universities, but the financial aid package was insufficient, and so she dropped the idea. She made plans to enroll in a part-time MBA program but did not pursue them because she believed that the degree would not help her much in the company and that if her boss were ever transferred, she might not have the same support from a new boss.

At the time of the initial assessment, Carol felt inadequate in doing her work because she did not have sufficient on-the-job experience; the workload had not been enough to give her that. She felt stuck in her job, and she could not get out without jeopardizing her career within the company. She reasoned that, since it would not be politically feasible to complain about her job and ask for a transfer to another unit, she could bide her time and find something to amuse herself, like taking a course and studying on the job. Another alternative was to leave the company, but she did not believe she had enough experience to find a job with comparable pay. She lamented that she did not trust her supervisor: He had a reputation for making things very unpleasant for people he did not like. Her hope was that being a female in the construction department would pay off in the long run.

The assessment staff evaluated Carol as low in career resilience, insight, and identity. Her self-esteem was weak, and she was dependent on others for her career progress. While emotionally dependent on others, she resisted going to others for help. She did not have a strong identification with the company, but leaving did not seem to be a viable solution at the time. She had been with the company for three years, and she was not yet worrying about promotion opportunities. The lack of both job challenge and social interaction were emotionally debilitating.

When Carol was interviewed seven months after the assessment, she felt more positive about herself and the company. She said that as a result of the assessment process she had decided to seek some help. The company's employee assistance department referred her to a private counselor, who helped her deal with her feelings. This process led her to request a transfer, since she felt she had nothing to lose. She carefully composed a letter and sent it up the line through her boss and his boss to the fourth-level manager. The letter was well received, and it led to a meeting with the fourth-level manager. While he did not promise anything, he said he would consider her request carefully. Two weeks later, the third-level boss announced that no one would be allowed to leave the department, and this news depressed Carol. Several weeks after that, however, the fourth-level manager asked Carol if she would be interested in a transfer to the company's corporate headquarters in another state.

Carol was intrigued with the possibility. She was interviewed for the position and was offered the job. It meant an immediate promotion to second level and required relocating. The company paid for her move, and she purchased a condominium. A year later, her career was still on an uphill swing. She loved her job and was looking forward to new and challenging assignments. She was also planning a long-term career with the corporate headquarters. Her timid initiation of a career change had been successful. Her work environment was much improved, and her involvement in the company and her hopes for advancement had increased.

Carol was low in career resilience, insight, and identity at the time of the initial assessment—a pattern of career motivation that does not contribute to career success or personal happiness. The lack of support for career development, low job challenge, and perceived lack of control over her career depressed her but also probably reinforced her pattern of low career motivation. She was apparently very bright, and her boss rated her job performance as excellent. With the support of a counselor, she was able to break away from an ineffective pattern of career motivation. While her bosses were slow to respond, her efforts paid off. After she was promoted into a challenging job in a supportive environment, Carol's career motivation began to blossom. She had successfully avoided a career barrier and made major changes in her life. In doing so, she probably paved the way for stronger career resilience.

Conclusion

This chapter has considered how the domains of career motivation may develop. Career resilience is composed of ingrained personality characteristics and is affected largely by successes and failures prior to the start of a career. Career insight and identity stem from information about career opportunities, support received for career development, seeing what others do, and available rewards and opportunities. It was suggested that career resilience sets the stage for the development of meaningful career insight and career identity. The possibilities for different patterns of career motivation domains and how they might change over time were explored. Next, the reader is offered some guides for increasing career motivation.

Taking Action to Increase Career Motivation

This section helps you identify actions to increase your career resilience, career insight, and career identity. Try one or more of the following self-assessment exercises.

1. Describe your life and career to date. Be explicit; write your description down. Start by describing yourself, your family, educational experiences, jobs, career interests, and career concerns.

2. List your career decisions to date. What have you done to manage your career?

3. Answer the seven questions ("Knowing Yourself") posed in Chapter Three (pp. 47–48). First, answer each of the questions in terms of where you are today. Then, for each question, consider how and why you have changed and where you hope to go in the future. Remember that the first three questions pertain to career resilience, questions 4 and 5 pertain to career insight, and the final two questions focus on career identity.

4. The two exercises shown in Exhibits 1 and 2 will help you identify and implement general, long-term objectives and activities. First, for Exhibit 1 ("Key Action Steps"), review each step and then select one or two under each category that you feel are most relevant and realistic for you at this time. Put an X next to your selections. While all of the action steps are desirable, try to find the ones especially important to you.

Next, continue with the action plan shown in Exhibit 2.

Exhibit 1. Key Action Steps.

---

1. *Need for Achievement* (these items refer to doing a job in a more than satisfactory manner and to having the desire to excel in the job).

    _____ Set a difficult but not impossible goal.
    _____ Design a better way of doing something.
    _____ Take the time to do the best job possible.
    _____ Try to do the best job possible on a task, even though few people will notice it.
    _____ Take one or more work-related courses outside the company.
    _____ Take one or more work-related courses offered within the company.

    OTHERS:

2. *Approach to Unfamiliar Tasks* (these items refer to believing in yourself to the extent that you are willing to take actions with uncertain outcomes—in other words, to take risks).

    _____ Make suggestions, even though others may disagree.
    _____ Look for opportunities to interact with higher-level managers.
    _____ Accept a job assignment for which you have little or no experience.
    _____ Clarify a job assignment on your own.
    _____ Establish a schedule for completing an assignment with a firm due-date commitment.
    _____ Ask your boss for feedback when you complete a special project or assignment.

    OTHERS:

3. *Balance Between Dependency and Autonomy* (these items deal with how, when, and to what extent you depend on others).

    _____ Evaluate your job performance against personal standards, rather than comparing it to what others do.
    _____ Learn from others' experiences.
    _____ Help a co-worker do his or her job.

(continued on next page)

Note: Exhibits 1 and 2 owe much of their development to assistance provided by Marjorie Leopold and Barbara Herr.

Exhibit 1. Key Action Steps, Cont'd.

_____ Make and maintain friendships with people in different departments.
_____ Seek out other sources of information (for example, manuals, co-workers) before asking your boss for information to help do the job.
_____ Outline ways of accomplishing jobs without waiting for your boss to do it.

OTHERS:

4. *Establishing Goals* (these items refer to thinking about career opportunities, thinking about career objectives, and figuring out how they can be achieved).

_____ Ask for information about future job opportunities.
_____ Obtain information about organizational changes that may affect your career.
_____ Ask others (friends, other managers, a supervisor) for career advice.
_____ Identify specific career goals.
_____ Discuss your career with your boss.
_____ Map out in writing what steps you should take to achieve your career goals.
_____ Change or revise your career goals in light of new information about yourself or your situation (for example, organizational changes that may affect your career).
_____ Seek a change in job assignment to allow you to achieve your career goals.

OTHERS:

5. *Objectivity About Strengths and Weaknesses* (these items refer to assessing strengths and weaknesses with respect to career objectives).

_____ Informally ask others what they think about a finished project that you worked on.
_____ Keep a record of your job performance.
_____ Keep track of how a project is progressing, in terms of meeting the designated objectives.
_____ Make a list of your strengths and weaknesses.
_____ Ask significant others (subordinates, peers) for feedback on your managerial performance.
_____ Be sure that when you receive a performance appraisal, you discuss it with your boss.

OTHERS:

Exhibit 1. Key Action Steps, Cont'd.

---

6. *Work Involvement* (these items refer to the focus and quantity of time spent on work versus time on other interests and responsibilities).

    _____ Improve your managerial skills.

    _____ Keep abreast of developments in your field.

    _____ Spend more free time on an activity that will help on the job (for example, take courses toward a job-related degree; be active in a professional organization).

    _____ Put the necessary time into the job, even if it requires working overtime and on weekends.

    _____ Keep current on company affairs (legislation, labor-management issues).

    _____ Participate in company-sponsored volunteer programs (safety fairs, community action programs, charities).

    OTHERS:

7. *Importance of Advancement* (these items refer to working toward more responsibility and achieving recognition).

    _____ Make a good impression on a higher-level manager.

    _____ Look for another job with better advancement opportunities.

    _____ Request to be considered for a promotion.

    _____ Volunteer for an important job assignment.

    _____ Let others know what you accomplish.

    _____ Volunteer for or assume a leadership role.

    _____ Learn about company policies and procedures that deal with advancement.

    OTHERS:

Exhibit 2. Action Plan.

Now be brutally honest with yourself. You know better than anyone else what the demands are on your time; you know better than anyone else how well you fare on New Year's resolutions and similar commitments to a more virtuous life.

Go back over your list of selected key action steps and select one or two (absolutely no more than two) action steps that you will honestly and seriously attempt to do. Your selection may fall under a dimension

(continued on next page)

Exhibit 2. Action Plan, Cont'd.

you think is particularly weak, or it may be an action step from a dimension where you feel you are already strong, but which you want to enhance. The critical factor here is that you really try to follow through. No one else can do this for you; it is up to you.

Once you have selected your action step, use the following action plan form. Be as specific as possible. List names and dates wherever appropriate. This is your action plan; make it meaningful for yourself.

Dimension (Need for Achievement, Approach to Unfamiliar Tasks, etc.):

Action Step: _____

What, specifically, are you going to do? (names, dates, other specific points)

Potential Obstacles? Possible Solutions?

5

* * * * *

How Organizational
Policies and Programs
Affect Career Motivation

Companies differ in what they expect of their managers, in how
their managers are treated financially and interpersonally, and
in the career opportunities available to managers. Companies
also differ in recruitment techniques, selection standards, procedures for transfers and promotions, how policies are commu-
nicated, the availability of challenging job assignments, and
supervisor-subordinate relationships. These and other factors are
likely to affect the types of people hired and the extent to
which people develop and enhance career resilience, insight, and
identity.

This chapter, by looking at how managers in two companies differ in dimensions of career motivation, explores the
impact of organizational policies and procedures on managers'
career motivation. In considering the reasons for these differences, we shall examine the importance of situational conditions to career motivation. This examination will set the stage

81

for generating the guidelines and programs for manager development that are offered in the next chapter.

So far, we have reviewed several individual cases to examine career motivation. Company policies were not discussed in these cases except to mention that some individuals entered a company-sponsored manager-development program for high-potential people. Recall that the cases came from a career motivation assessment of managers from two companies, twenty-four from each company. While the sample was small and unrepresentative, there were enough significant differences between the two companies to warrant a consideration of those elements in a situation that can affect career motivation.

The companies, given the fictional names ECHO, Inc., and DYNAMO Corp., were in the same industry and in the same geographical region, and they faced similar economic conditions, but they differed in their philosophies of manager development. College graduates hired by DYNAMO entered a manager-development program; DYNAMO treated these young managers as corporate resources for the future. ECHO hired college graduates to meet current business needs; the possibility of future job assignments and developmental opportunities was secondary and often not relevant to the company at all. Before exploring these situational differences in more depth, let us look at the study results.

The differences between the companies are summarized in Table 3. The table presents only the statistically significant differences. The participants from DYNAMO were higher on many of the personality characteristics that reflect advancement motivation, including need for advancement, need for recognition, need for exhibition, expectations for a favorable career, ascendance, enterprising, and extraversion. The DYNAMO managers aspired to higher levels in the organization and rated the importance of advancement more highly than those from ECHO did. The growth-need strength score (an index of challenge motivation) was also higher at DYNAMO. Variables that reflect interpersonal orientation (need for nurturance and friendliness) were higher at ECHO. The participants from ECHO were higher on authoritarianism and need abasement, a finding that

Table 3. Statistically Significant Differences Between Companies
($p. < 05$).

	Company	
	ECHO	DYNAMO
Variables Reflecting Advancement Motivation		
Need for Advancement Dimension	2.64	3.37
Need for Recognition Dimension	3.63	4.22
Need Exhibition[a] (Desire to be Recognized)	53.92	70.58
Expectations Inventory[a]	9.67	39.04
Ascendance[a]	55.21	79.63
Enterprising	54.38	58.92
Extraversion (Inverse Scale)	45.71	37.25
Ultimate Goal for Level in the Company	3.33	4.46
Importance of Advancing to the Next Level (Self-Rating)	4.21	4.88
Importance of Advancing Two Levels (Self-Rating)	3.70	4.54
Growth-Need Strength	5.19	5.71
Variables Reflecting Interpersonal Orientation		
Need for Nurturance[a] (Need to be Nurturant to Others)	71.00	51.13
Friendliness[a]	53.50	38.92
Authoritarianism[a]	54.42	37.08
Variables Reflecting Career Stability		
Goal Flexibility Dimension	2.84	3.36
Need for Change Dimension	2.88	3.53
Need Abasement[a]	56.58	35.75
Commitment to Managerial Work Dimension	2.56	3.32

[a]Mean percentiles based on company norms.

means they were more likely to adhere to conventional values and accept guilt than those from DYNAMO. The young managers from ECHO were lower on goal flexibility and need for change, while those from DYNAMO were higher on commitment to managerial work. Participants from DYNAMO were paid a bit more and had slightly higher undergraduate grade-point averages than those from ECHO. There were no differences between the two companies on the intellectual ability measures.

Clearly, the DYNAMO managers were more advancement-oriented, less interpersonally-oriented, more flexible in their goals, and more committed to managerial work than the ECHO managers were. Some of these psychological differences may have been due to background factors, differences in selection criteria between the companies, or an unknown bias in how the subjects were selected for the study. The differences also may reflect basic characteristics of the two companies.

The personnel vice-president from ECHO was very concerned, because the results reflected poorly on his company. He wondered whether the ECHO managers in the study were selected as carefully as those from DYNAMO and whether such a discrepancy could have accounted for the findings. He asked that we interview bosses to determine the quality of the people who participated in the study. These interviews revealed no substantial differences in the managers' abilities, as judged by the bosses. Moreover, the data available on the background of the managers indicated no substantial differences except for the slightly higher grade-point averages among DYNAMO managers. The quality of the colleges attended also seemed to be about the same for both companies. Two questions arose: How similar were the results from ECHO to those for other, comparable companies? Would the participants from ECHO have exhibited the same career motivation if they had been hired by DYNAMO?

Some data were available to answer the first question. The average scores from the twenty-four ECHO people were compared to data taken from similar tests administered during another assessment-center study of a larger, more representative sample of companies in the same industry and in the same geographical region as ECHO. This study—as opposed to the career motivation assessment center, which was geared to assessing needs, interests, and personality variables associated with career motivation—had the primary aim of measuring managerial abilities. Comparisons were made where the variables were the same. There was considerable similarity between ECHO and the data from the larger-sample study. In fact, several results were in favor of ECHO. For instance, the ECHO managers tended to be higher on desire for advancement and need to be a leader than participants from the larger sample. The ECHO managers were less dependent on emotional support from others. A negative finding, however, was that they expected much less favorable careers than managers from other companies in that geographical region.

Overall, it could be concluded that ECHO was very similar to the other companies, and that the results from DYNAMO were something of an aberration. The managers from DYNAMO were higher than those from ECHO on desire for advancement and need to be a leader. They were higher than ECHO as well as the other companies in that geographical region on need for achievement, and they were lower on need to nurture others. An important finding was that managers from DYNAMO were much higher than both groups on expectations for a favorable career.

Unfortunately, quantitative data were not available to answer the question of whether the career motivation of ECHO managers would have been different if they had been at DYNAMO. Nevertheless, a closer examination of both ECHO and DYNAMO took into account personnel practices and programs, organizational climates, and the extent to which each may have influenced the career motivation and attitudes of younger managers. The influences of factors like these would indicate the extent to which the study findings were generalizable to each company as a whole.

Information gleaned from the managers during the career motivation assessment center, and subsequent interviews with company personnel, revealed many organizational differences. At ECHO, the managers in the sample had been brought in during a hiring surge. While there was no indication that standards were sacrificed, there was evidence that some expectations were generated that could not be met. Some new college graduates were led to believe that they would be treated as general managers, with opportunities for movement into other departments of the company, but it turned out that increasing segmentation between departments (because departments acted independently) made such movement very difficult. Some managers felt that their talents were underutilized. Most were viewed by the company as filling positions that met present business needs, rather than undergoing preparation for middle management in the future.

At DYNAMO, the managers were participants in the manager-development program. They were transferred between departments once every twelve to eighteen months. Such movement was intended to increase their knowledge of the business and to give them more responsibility. DYNAMO managers were also given special assignments, which enhanced their self-image and their feeling that they were valued by their company. Financial conditions limited advancement opportunities in both organizations, but the young DYNAMO managers seemed to understand why, and although they hoped for promotions, they sought opportunities for challenge in other ways. Since they were given challenging assignments, in many cases their work was visible to top executives. Elements of the DYNAMO manager-development program are summarized in Table 4.

Table 4. DYNAMO Manager-Development Program.

1. The program is intended for college graduates hired into the first level of management. It is not intended for specialists (attorneys, accountants, computer programmers) who are hired for their expertise in a specific area and intend to remain in that area while employed with the company. All other college hires are assumed to be in general management positions. While they will learn specific skills associated with their departments (engineering, construction, installation and repair, real estate), emphasis is placed on developing such managerial skills as decision making, leadership, organizing, planning, and so on.

2. The program begins by recruiting high-quality college graduates. The successful job candidate must have a strong academic background and demonstrated leadership skills. The recruitment process emphasizes the risk entailed in the program (the possibility of termination after the first year). It also highlights the possibility of high reward (rapid advancement to middle management—third level).

3. A program coordinator monitors the progress of the trainees for their first five years in the company but maintains close contact with the trainees only during their first year.

4. A course acquaints the trainee with the development program and emphasizes that trainees should take responsibility for their own growth and development in managerial abilities.

5. The trainee becomes a sponsor of the department he or she is assigned to first. While the trainee may move to other departments and subsequent assignments, the intention is for the trainee to return to the sponsoring department unless another department is willing to assume sponsorship responsibilities, whereupon the two departments negotiate a transfer.

6. The trainee's first assignment is reporting to a third-level boss. The bosses are selected for the program because they are good role models who have demonstrated leadership skills and have shown ability

Table 4. DYNAMO Manager-Development Program, Cont'd.

to develop subordinates effectively. The boss is supposed to provide the trainee with challenging job assignments, which increase in scope and responsibility during the year. The boss acts as a coach, periodically giving feedback and guidance. At the conclusion of the year, the boss evaluates the performance and advancement potential of the trainee.

7. During the first year, the program coordinator holds group sessions with the college hires in the program that year. These sessions give the trainees the chance to compare their experiences. In addition, the coordinator holds several individual sessions with each trainee to discuss his or her current and future assignments.

8. At the end of the first year, if the boss feels a trainee does not have potential to reach third level within five years, it is in the trainee's and the company's best interests that the trainee seek employment elsewhere. Trainees who demonstrate potential for advancement to third level are given new assignments. Thus begins a sequence of assignments within the sponsoring department and within other departments. These assignments often alternate between line and staff jobs. The trainee now reports to a second-level boss until being promoted to second level. The length of time until promotion to second level (and, subsequently, to third level) depends on the individual's continued performance and demonstration of advancement potential and on the availability of promotion opportunities.

9. The trainee is expected to develop a career plan, which is revised annually. This plan lists the types of jobs the trainee would like to have in the next several years.

10. Financial compensation is slightly above average, as compared to other companies in the labor market. Salary increases periodically on a regular schedule for thirty-two months, unless the trainee is promoted to second level. Merit increases are possible for trainees rated outstanding.

Presidents' Letters

Additional evidence of differences in organizational climate between the two companies was found in the presidents' letters to stockholders, included in the annual reports, over the last five years. (Management scientists have used annual reports to learn about companies' attitudes toward people and events; see, for example, Salancik and Meindl, 1984.) There was no change in president at either company during that time. There was a clear difference between the presidents in their orientation to employees and in the company policies and programs they described to stockholders. In general, company presidents contribute to organizational climate and also reflect that climate in their actions and statements; the differences in these two presidents' letters corresponded to the findings, reported above, of the differences between the two companies in their young managers' career motivation.

ECHO's orientation toward its employees was typically encapsulated in brief concluding remarks in most of the ECHO president's letters. There was usually a single sentence thanking the employees for their work and loyalty to the company, and the president then usually asserted his confidence that the employees would meet the challenges of the coming year. In each annual report—a lengthy message—these concluding remarks were the only reference the president made to the company's employees.

In contrast, the DYNAMO president's letters to stockholders during the same period had much to say about the company's employees. One year, the president emphasized the importance of the employees in maintaining high-quality customer service. He observed that as new technologies arose, there would be changes in the number, mix, and content of jobs. He vowed that the company would make adjustments in the work force, taking employees' personal objectives, aspirations, and concerns into consideration. He also stated that the employees had every right to expect the company to provide a good place to work, a meaningful job, the opportunity for advancement, and adequate financial reward. He noted that the company had recently surveyed employees' attitudes and welcomed their opinions about areas for improvement. He mentioned that training at all levels had assumed new importance in a time of quickening technological change. He then described various seminars and training programs run for middle and top managers to discuss crucial policy issues facing the corporation. Subsequent sections of the annual report dealt with safety, equal employment opportunity gains, and a description of several employees who performed heroic acts during the year, risking their lives to save others. The report concluded with a statement of confidence in the employees and in the company. All this discussion of employees was part of a more lengthy annual report, which covered other topics important to stockholders.

The DYNAMO president's letter in another annual report began with a statement of the employees' contributions. Once again, the challenge of technological advancements changing the nature of jobs was mentioned. Later in the report, the president stated that the company was making every effort to treat employees fairly, to make their jobs meaningful, and to provide wages and benefits comparable to their skills, since this was crucial to keep and attract skilled, talented people. The president noted that the company had expanded its employee communications effort, making it more comprehensive; the goal was to give all employees the opportunity to learn about the business while seeking their solutions to operations problems. This participative management approach, the president stated, informed employees of actions taken as a result of their suggestions, and he reported that many ideas for service improvements had been discovered through this communications process. At the conclusion of the report, the president mentioned that he was engaged in discussing the company's goals at face-to-face meetings with managers across the company, and he expressed his confidence that these goals would be achieved.

The following year, the president again complimented the DYNAMO employees on their excellent performance and stated that the company sought to provide in return commensurate financial rewards, a productive working environment, and varied developmental opportunities. He emphasized that the company was dedicated to creating and maintaining a work environment where employees could be recognized and treated as individuals and have varied career development opportunities and direct involvement in the career decision-making process. He mentioned a recent survey, which revealed that employees felt better about DYNAMO as a place to work, felt more secure in their jobs, and saw more opportunity for advancement than in previous years. He also recognized that employees wanted more participation in decision making and goal setting. He promised to maintain open communication, up as well as down the organizational hierarchy, as a way to build trust and understanding. He described a new program, initiated that year, which povided a communication channel for employees to ask questions (or voice concerns anonymously if they chose) and to receive answers from the company executives best qualified to respond. He also mentioned that during the year group sessions had been held with all the company's managers. The president then reiterated his commitment to seeing that all DYNAMO employees had the opportunity to speak their minds.

Another DYNAMO annual report described a year of record high interest rates and persistent inflation, which had had serious impact on the company's costs and slowed its real economic growth. The president wrote about efforts to improve efficiency in all areas and about how the company was examining management and staff departments to be sure they were in line with the needs of the field operations they guided and supported. The president said he was gratified to report improvements in most productivity measures. He assured stockholders that the company was uniquely equipped with the knowledge and skills to satisfy customers' needs.

The next annual report returned to the theme of making management jobs at DYNAMO more meaningful by increasing opportunities for initiative and decision making. In his letter, the president described a plan to broaden spans of control, not only as an economic measure but also as a way to increase managers' job challenges.

Attitude Survey Results

In 1981, both ECHO and DYNAMO administered the same attitude survey, asking employees how they felt about various aspects of their jobs and of the company. The company differences on the survey reflected the same differences in climate and concern about employees that were evident in the annual reports and in the career motivation study. The recent survey results from a representative sample of first-level managers showed that DYNAMO's managers were better informed about job openings than managers from ECHO (this finding was derived from the item "I'm well informed about job openings").

In both companies, however, most managers did not respond favorably to this item; 23 percent responded favorably from DYNAMO, compared to 7 percent from ECHO. Other items revealed that satisfaction with the opportunity to get a better job was also higher at DYNAMO (31 percent responded favorably) than at ECHO (20 percent responded favorably). DYNAMO's managers were more satisfied with advancement and transfer opportunities, the effectiveness of top management in the company, the pace of change in the company, the amount of pressure on the job, the amount of training provided for the job, and job security.

The survey results combined newly hired recent college graduates in first-level management with all others in first-level management. Additional analyses were conducted to examine responses for first-level managers who were under thirty-five years of age, had worked for the company from one to five years, and had graduated from a four-year college. This was the group from which the career motivation study sample was drawn. Young managers from DYNAMO were more satisfied with the company, more satisfied with their jobs, and felt better informed about job openings in the company than young managers from ECHO seemed to feel. There were no differences in satisfaction with advancement and transfer opportunities. Participants from ECHO felt more satisfied with information they received on company happenings and, compared to those from DYNAMO, were more likely to say that promotions were based on merit rather than on friendship. The young managers from DYNAMO were less satisfied with feedback on advancement potential given by immediate supervisors. Overall, the young managers from DYNAMO were more critical of the promotion process, how much information they received about it and about their own advancement potential, and the fairness of promotion decisions.

Group Sessions

When the results of the career motivation study were presented to the vice-presidents of personnel at the two companies, they suggested that group sessions be held both with recently hired managers and separately with their bosses, to help us understand the statistically significant company differences. These sessions did not include the managers who participated in the assessment-center study. Four sessions were held, one with bosses and one with recently hired managers in each company.

The discussions were a microcosm of many problems associated with early-career manager development and were rich in information about young managers' attitudes. One finding from the attitude survey—that the young managers at DYNAMO were dissatisfied with some elements of their career development prospects—also emerged in the group discussion with the young managers. This dissatisfaction may have been due in part to the high expectations created by the manager-development program, expectations that the company was finding difficult to meet in poor economic times and under conditions of organizational change. First-level managers in the program had been promised promotion to third level within five to seven years of entering the company, but they were finding that in fact it would take much longer to reach third level. Several seemed almost obsessed with reaching second level and were frustrated because it was taking so long. To some extent, they were distracted by their desire to be promoted, and they seemed to spend more time thinking about their career development than they did about their work. The company was committed to the manager-development program and had retained it for over twenty years, through good as well as bad times. Nevertheless, the first-level managers thought that if promotion opportunities became scarce, the college graduates coming into the program should not be misled; they felt that creating realistic expectations would not make the program less attractive. In general, they were happy with the first year in the program, during which they reported to third-level managers and were given special assignments. Several complained about the quality of their bosses, but on the whole they found the experience to be exciting and challenging.

After their first assignments, the first-level managers at DYNAMO were generally given line jobs and reported to second-level managers; suddenly they were in the real world. This change led to conflicts between the young managers and their experienced second-level bosses, who in some cases were not college graduates. The first-level managers thought that their bosses were threatened by having rising stars under their control. They also complained that the second-level managers did not give them meaningful assignments, possibly because the bosses thought their new subordinates would not be in their departments long enough to accomplish meaningful assignments. This was true, to some extent, because the participants in the manager-development program were moved every twelve to eighteen months. The young managers depended on their bosses for information about career opportunities and hoped their bosses would be influential in obtaining better jobs for them.

The bosses at DYNAMO did not empathize with the frustrations expressed by the young managers in the manager-development program, feeling that these newcomers to the company had to get used to the real world. The bosses could see advantages as well as disadvantages of the manager-development program. One problem was that the program set the college graduates aside from all those others who were not in the program. One advantage was that young managers who were dissatisfied could feel free to complain to higher-level managers and to the program coordinator. The bosses in the group sessions were second- and third-level managers, yet they seemed naive about manager-development policies within the company. For instance, they had trouble describing what factors constitute a good manager, they were not sure how promotion decisions were made in the company, and they felt they had very little control over these decisions. Like the first-level managers, the bosses felt that the company must convey accurate information to recruits about career prospects.

At ECHO, the first-level managers in the group did not express the same frustrations as the young managers from DYNAMO. The young managers from ECHO were resigned to bleak futures. They perceived that, overall, there were not many career opportunities, and they expressed this perception as a fact of life. Some were already in dead-end positions. They felt that expectations generated upon their entrance into the company

had not been met, in that they had expected to be able to
change departments if they did not like their first assignments
or if they wanted to learn about different parts of the business.
Movement between departments at ECHO was difficult, however, because of each department's desire to develop independent expertise.

Some of the ECHO bosses felt that young managers
should take more initiative in handling their own careers. They
noted that career opportunities were greater in some departments than in others; some departments frequently promoted
first-level managers to second level after two or three years. The
philosophy in these departments was to train first-level managers as professionals in the area and then give them second-
level status once the training was complete. Responsibility increased with promotion, but opportunity for movement to
other departments was nil.

The young managers from ECHO mentioned conflict between college graduates and up-from-the-ranks managers, a
problem also noted by the DYNAMO managers. ECHO managers
felt that a college degree was not necessary for some of the jobs
they were doing. Ironically, they saw that the possibilities for
transfer to another department increased for managers who
were viewed as replaceable—or, to put it another way, the more
valuable they were to the department, the less the department
was interested in transferring them to develop their skills and
make them more valuable to the company as a whole. The suggestion was made that more attention be given to matching new
managers to bosses who would take the time to train them. Like
their counterparts at DYNAMO, the ECHO first-level managers
wished they had more information about career opportunities.
We knew from the attitude survey, however, that as a whole the
young ECHO managers did not feel as strongly about this point
as their DYNAMO counterparts.

The bosses at ECHO felt that young managers needed
more information about career opportunities. They also felt
that more should be done to foster manager development. They
recognized that a college degree is often not necessary to do the
work and also felt that the young managers in the company

were overpaid, and that this overpayment had the effect of decreasing their motivation. Nevertheless, it also locked them into their jobs, since there were few opportunities for employment at the same rate of pay outside the company. They called this phenomenon "the golden handcuffs." The bosses at ECHO felt that their hands were tied when it came to motivating subordinates, since they could not promote outstanding performers. They felt that some cross-training between departments would be desirable to give young managers a better idea of how the business operated, but cross-training need not necessarily mean moving them from job to job in different departments; it could also be accomplished through training programs or by giving them temporary assignments in other departments. Recognizing the lack of promotion opportunities, the bosses felt the need for a development program that would not be a fast track to middle management but instead would enhance the quality of management at lower levels. This goal could be accomplished by attracting motivated people with high ability and giving them challenging assignments.

Generally, it seemed that the problems at ECHO were on a different plane than those at DYNAMO. The DYNAMO first-level managers had expectations for advancement and challenge, and they were disgruntled that these expectations were not being met fast enough. At ECHO, the first-level managers felt neglected. They were given no special treatment except to be placed in positions and given salaries that took up-from-the-ranks managers many years to attain. Young managers at both companies felt that their expectations had not been met, and this finding suggested the need to impart realistic information during recruitment. Both companies mentioned conflict between up-from-the-ranks managers and recently hired college graduates.

The career motivation study suggested that managers at DYNAMO were more highly motivated to advance than those at ECHO because of the manager-development program, yet this program generated problems stemming largely from expectations that could not be met. Nevertheless, it was generally believed that a strong manager-development program, coupled with a careful recruiting process to attract the most able and highly motivated managers, could have positive benefits. Evidence supporting this belief is reviewed below.

Comparing Young Managers
in Different Development Programs

Data from another study conducted in the same industry compared managers from several companies, all of which had development programs for their young managers. DYNAMO was also included in this sample. One other company, called HI-TECH here, recruited more able and highly motivated managers than the other companies in the study were able to attract. In addition, the development program at HI-TECH offered a more challenging experience than the programs at the other companies. For example, at HI-TECH, successful managers were promoted sooner, and unsuccessful managers were dismissed more readily. The HI-TECH managers were significantly higher in decision making, leadership skills, oral communication, behavior flexibility, personal impact, forcefulness, perception of social cues, energy, resistance to stress, and the importance of work in their lives than the young managers from the other companies. The HI-TECH managers also displayed higher need for advancement, financial motivation, and adjustment. They were rated as more likely to reach middle management and, in general, were predicted to attain a higher level in management. The young managers from the other companies were higher on need for security, need for peer approval, and willingness to wait for advancement. Therefore, it seemed that the more rigorous development program was better at attracting more able people, maintaining their motivation, and presumably developing their skills than were the development programs at the other companies.

Another analysis compared young managers from the companies with development programs (excluding HI-TECH) with young managers from companies, in the same industry, without development programs. This analysis revealed fewer differences on the career motivation variables. Young managers involved in development programs were significantly more forceful and were also higher in energy and importance of work in their lives. There were a number of differences between these two groups on personality test scores. There were no differences in ability measures between managers who were in development programs and those who were not, but a development program seemed to attract more-motivated individuals, or at least those who had personality characteristics and needs that suggested achievement orientation and a sense of independence.

When turnover data were examined, there was no significant difference between companies with young-manager development programs and those with none. While the existence of such programs may not affect whether a participant stays or leaves, it seems advantageous for a company to attract and select the most able and highly motivated people, so that those who remain are of high quality. If a program does not live up to the expectations of its participants, there will be a mismatch between the participants' needs and what the program offers. Of course, reasons for turnover go beyond programs offered by companies, but encouraging realistic expectations at the outset is one factor that generally decreases turnover (Wanous, 1980).

The Value of Productivity Through People

Peters and Waterman (1982) describe the management strategies of forty-three highly regarded American companies that met criteria of long-term economic success. The firms represent a broad spectrum of industry and include such companies as Boeing, Hewlett-Packard, IBM, Procter & Gamble, and 3M. One of the principles Peters and Waterman observed in these companies is that they obtain productivity through people; they treat their employees with dignity and respect. This principle includes a willingness to train people, set reasonable and clear expectations for them, and grant them practical autonomy to contribute to their jobs. The companies view themselves as extended families and celebrate their success with enthusiasm. The employee is made to feel important, and his or her successes are rewarded. By emphasizing quality, reliability, and service, the excellent companies generate excitement in the average employee down the line. Peters and Waterman claim that the excellent companies avoid lip service, gimmicks, and such disasters as having programs on the books that do not operate as intended, making promises which cannot be kept, abandoning programs in midstream, and changing policies without explanation or proper communication.

Now consider ECHO, Inc. The young managers at ECHO were attracted by the possibility of moving between departments. The fact that the company was large and performed many functions made it reasonable to assume that a variety of opportunities would be available, but this was not the case. A program for high-potential managers was designed, implemented for a very short time, and then dropped. Layoffs from almost ten years before had created a lingering fear for job security. DYNAMO, in contrast, had maintained a manager-development program for many years. The company did have trouble meeting the expectations generated by the program, and we have seen the negative effects in the frustrations expressed by young managers, but the company nevertheless seemed concerned about its employees. This attitude prevailed at the top of the company, as conveyed by the president's letters in the company's annual reports.

Peters and Waterman state that excellent companies "create environments in which people can blossom, develop self-esteem, and otherwise be excited participants in the business." While DYNAMO may not be the epitome of excellence in Peters and Waterman's terms, it is certainly closer to excellence than ECHO is. DYNAMO, like Peters and Waterman's excellent companies, had a deeply ingrained philosophy that said, in effect, "respect the individual, make people winners, let them stand out, and treat them as adults." As Peters and Waterman elaborate, "The excellent companies are measurement-happy and performance-oriented, but this toughness is born of mutually high expectations and peer review rather than emanating from table-pounding managers and complicated control systems. The tough side is, in fact, probably tougher than that found in the less excellent and typically more formal systems-driven companies, for nothing is more enticing than the feeling of being needed, which is the magic that produces high expectations. What's more, if it's your peers that have those high expectations of you, then there's all the more incentive to perform well" (p. 240).

How ECHO and DYNAMO Used Our Results

As noted above, after the career motivation assessment center, and after the feedback interviews that were conducted seven months later, the results were presented to the vice-presidents of personnel at the two companies. In preparation for the meeting, we sent the vice-presidents a list of questions to think about regarding their development policies for young managers. The vice-president from ECHO, who had only been in his position for about six months, had not thought much about the questions; in fact, he admitted that he did not know the answers to most of them. His major concern was how the participants from his company had been selected for the study and whether they had included the best people.

The vice-president from DYNAMO wrote an answer next to each of our questions and came to the meeting with a binder filled with material. Aware that the discussion would center on career motivation, he had held group sessions with participants in the manager-development program and their supervisors to discuss career motivation issues.

The vice-presidents agreed that additional work should be done to follow up on participants in the study, interview their bosses, and collect information from other first-level managers and their bosses about manager-development policies at both companies. This conclusion led to the final interviews, approximately a year and a half after the study had begun. It also led to group sessions with managers who had not been in the study and to examining data from the attitude survey. In addition, as reported above, we compared the ECHO and DYNAMO results to results found at other companies.

The two companies used the results of the career motivation study in different ways. At ECHO, the vice-president decided that a manager-development program should be initiated, and he assigned a third-level manager to the task. Part of the assignment was to work with the executives of the company and, later, with middle- and lower-level managers to change the organization's culture. The initial intention was to make the manager-development program applicable to any college graduates hired into the company in the future so as to prepare them for a fast track to middle management, as was done in the development program offered at DYNAMO. When an outline of this program was presented to a task force of middle-level managers, however, it was severely criticized. The central problem was that every department already had many young managers currently rated promotable, but there were very few promotion opportunities. Consequently, these managers could not see the need for a new program to prepare additional people for middle management. As a result, the company redesigned the program to make it applicable to all newly hired first-level managers in supervisory as well as nonsupervisory roles, not just to high-potential young managers. The purpose of the program is to enhance job challenge, provide relevant job training, and give periodic performance feedback during the manager's first year with the company. Training the boss is an important part of the program. The new managers meet every few months to share common experiences and discuss issues with officers of the company. A mentor program was also established, which assigns each young manager to an experienced middle-level manager.

ECHO hopes these programs will not only attract highly qualified college graduates into the business but also make the jobs more interesting and rewarding, even without the promise of rapid advancement. The company assumes that young managers interested in career development and advancement will take advantage of opportunities to learn the business and demonstrate outstanding performance and, in the process, put themselves in competitive positions for promotions. So far, the program is a success, and the company is beginning to think about a program for identifying high-potential second-level managers and giving them experiences to enable them to move rapidly up to third-level management.

DYNAMO used the study results to support its existing development program. Top managers recognized deficiencies and discussed them openly. They recognized the problem of unrealistic expectations, mentioned in the group reports. They held their own group sessions, which identified other problems. They made changes in the program to be sure that expectations would be met and that more realistic expectations would be established in the future. Finally, they used the information to argue for continuing the program. Aside from trying to lower expectations for advancement, however, DYNAMO did not anticipate major changes in the program; for example, no effort was made to increase the length of the program, as had been suggested by some of the participants.

Conclusion

The career motivation study was intended to be exploratory. The differences between ECHO and DYNAMO could have stemmed from many factors. From what was known about the two companies, however, it was clear that there were substantial differences in policies and procedures regarding career development. A manager-development program seems desirable for attracting highly motivated college graduates. It may also be desirable for enhancing elements of career motivation. Chapter Four argued that the components of career resilience are fairly well established by the time the college graduate enters the business world, but that individuals' career resilience may also be enhanced by programs and policies that encourage individual contributions and personal growth, provide opportunities for risk taking, and offer appropriate levels of interpersonal concern (enough to promote good working relationships without creating overdependence). Likewise, career insight and career identity may be enhanced by programs and policies that encourage involvement, provide opportunities and rewards, and offer support for career development. How this kind of enhancement can be accomplished is the topic of the next chapter.

While major differences were found between the two companies in the career motivation study, the experiences of the young managers varied within each company, partly because of differences in departmental policies and supervisory styles. One reason for conducting the boss interviews was to ask bosses about their philosophies of manager development. We wanted to understand how the bosses felt they influenced the career motivation of young managers as well as how the company's personnel policies and procedures influenced career development. (The role of the boss in subordinates' career development is discussed in Chapter Nine.)

6

* * * * *

Designing Comprehensive
Manager-Development
Programs

Career opportunities are important in attracting and motivating managers. The type of training the company offers, the rate of advancement, the level of pay, the extent of job challenge, and so on, are important to college graduates seeking management positions. To attract able and highly motivated managers and maintain that motivation over time, an aggressive recruiting effort and a challenging development program, such as the one offered by DYNAMO Corp. (discussed in the last chapter), are required.

Approaches to manager selection and development depend on current career opportunities within the company and on the personnel available to take advantage of those opportunities (that is, the number of vacancies and the number of employees rated promotable). Manager-development strategies also depend on anticipated future needs in middle management, since these needs determine the extent to which the com-

pany should hire and begin developing lower-level managers today.

Goals for Early Career Development

The discussion above suggests the need for the following
major goals for early career development:

1. Attract highly motivated and able managers, maintain their
    interest, and minimize their turnover.
2. Identify young managers with high potential, and prepare
    them for rapid advancement when advancement opportuni-
    ties exist or are anticipated.
3. Offer a standard career track for those not designated as
    having high potential. This track would provide opportuni-
    ties for challenge and advancement, but at a pace slower
    than that of the high-potential program. It would be sup-
    ported by career planning and development activities.
4. Maximize all managers' career motivation by positively af-
    fecting their career resilience, career insight, and career
    identity.

When companies accomplish these goals, managers will be challenged and will feel their skills are being fully utilized. Moreover, managers will develop realistic expectations that are based
on current and anticipated future needs of the company.

To help companies accomplish these goals, the following
section offers guidelines organized around the elements of career motivation, identifies situational conditions that affect the
components of career motivation, and describes specific programs for implementing the guidelines.

Manager-Development Guidelines

Research and review of the management literature suggest
that there is a set of situational variables that may influence the
individual characteristics of career motivation. These situational
conditions are based on psychological principles in the areas of

job design, leadership style, goal setting, performance appraisal, feedback, and reinforcement. These conditions can be summarized in eight general guidelines for enhancing the three domains of career motivation.

First, to support *career resilience*:

1. Encourage self-confidence through feedback and positive reinforcement.
2. Generate opportunities for achievement.
3. Create an environment for risk taking (reward innovation; reduce fear of failure).
4. Show interpersonal concern and encourage group cohesiveness and collaborative working relationships.

Second, to support *career insight*:

5. Encourage goal setting.
6. Give career information and performance feedback.

Third, to support *career identity*:

7. Encourage work involvement through job challenge and professional growth.
8. Provide opportunities (for example, for leadership and advancement) and rewards (for example, recognition and bonuses).

In Chapter Four it was hypothesized that while career resilience is already fairly well developed by the time a person graduates from college, it is also maintained and enhanced on the job by positive reinforcement, opportunities for achievement and risk taking, and a positive work climate. In addition, it was argued that career resilience is necessary for the development of career insight, and that career insight in turn enhances the development of career identity. Organizations that support goal setting and give career information and performance feedback to managers will contribute to managers' career insight. Career identity is likely to be stronger when the organization

encourages work involvement through job challenge and professional growth and when there are opportunities for leadership,
advancement, and higher salary. While research is still necessary
to show the relationships between these eight guidelines and the
career motivation domains, the guidelines, as organized above,
are a way of conceptualizing and integrating principles of good
management.

Motivation Strategies

These eight guidelines assume that career motivation is affected by the nature of supervision and by the company's policies, procedures, and programs. Motivation strategies can be
organized into two major groups: one type tries directly to affect managers' behavior and attitudes, and the other tries to
change situational conditions (such as the boss's behavior) and
organizational policies that may influence managers' motivation.

One example of the direct approach would be a selection
method developed to identify individuals who are high in career
resilience and have sufficient social perceptiveness and self-
understanding to develop career insight and career identity soon
after entering the organization. Interviews and assessment-center
methods already used to measure managerial skills and abilities
can be adapted to measure individual characteristics associated
with career motivation.

Another approach focusing directly on individual characteristics would be to make the individual aware of where he or
she stands on the career motivation variables, and the career
motivation assessment center described in Chapter Three may
be useful here. Recall that seven months after the assessment,
the participants were presented with individual face-to-face
feedback on selected personality test scores. The research purposes of the feedback were to update the background interview
and to discuss the meaning of the results with the participants,
with the goals of exploring the extent to which the study cor-
roborated self-perceptions, trying to resolve or affirm inconsistencies, identifying defense mechanisms (rationalizations),

and gathering reactions to company changes. The potential benefits of the feedback were for the participants to recognize internal conflicts and inconsistencies, identify patterns suggesting possible dysfunctional behaviors, and consider advancement and achievement needs in the light of organizational opportunities.

Career motivation assessment and feedback for individuals could be implemented on a voluntary, company-wide basis. Careful prescreening could ensure that only those who really need it are assessed. The assessment could be integrated into a career counseling program as one available tool.

A less expensive approach would be to offer self-assessment workbooks to individuals who have the desire and initiative to learn about themselves. These workbooks could be organized around the career motivation variables. Training on the dimensions of career motivation could also be beneficial in helping individuals consider their own needs and personality characteristics with respect to career ambitions.

In general, information about where one stands on the career motivation dimensions can be beneficial, particularly if the information also offers comparison with where others stand on the dimensions. For instance, learning that others are higher on need for advancement may cause an employee to consider the extent to which he or she really wants to advance, and why. Some people may think that they are high in need for advancement until they learn that others are much higher. This discrepancy may cause them to think both about what motivations lie behind the need and about the strength of that need.

As the eight manager-development guidelines indicate, bosses can contribute to the development of subordinates' career motivation. Bosses should realize how subordinates' career resilience, insight, and identity contribute to productivity. Subordinates who are high in the three career motivation domains are likely to need less direction and control, to welcome more responsibility, and to seek feedback on job performance. Subordinates who are low on the three domains are likely to be dependent, to require more interpersonal concern and support, to misperceive their strengths and weaknesses, to have poor

understanding of the organization's political and social environment, and to require more guidance; they are unlikely to be
highly involved in their careers, and so they will probably require more prodding and closer supervision.

Company policies and procedures may also contribute to
managers' career motivation—for example, when bosses have
freedom to implement the eight career motivation guidelines.
Formal career planning programs, performance appraisal methods, and training that fosters accurate and thorough performance evaluations and feedback can enhance subordinates'
career motivation. Flexibility of work methods and goals; information about career opportunities within the company; and opportunities for advancement, recognition, and financial gain are
other elements that contribute to career motivation. Manager-
development programs can also positively affect career motivation by assigning participants to good role models: bosses who
are concerned with their subordinates' career development, who
give young managers especially challenging assignments, who
hold group meetings for young managers to share experiences
and career ambitions, and who provide information and counseling on career opportunities. (These motivation strategies are
listed and described more extensively in Chapter Eight.)

The Need for Comprehensive Development Programs

Traditional motivational strategies entail changing one
element of the environment (for example, the compensation
system or the job design) to increase motivation and thereby enhance job performance. Another traditional approach is to hire
people who have not only the requisite skills and abilities but
also psychological profiles related to the jobs in question. The
untraditional idea that some individual characteristics may
change over time and be affected by situational conditions in-
troduces possibilities for new motivational strategies. Once
there is a better understanding of how a situation can activate
different individual characteristics, it will be possible for organizations to affect motivation by changing the salience of different situational variables: Attention may be focused on different

elements of the environment by changing them, or perhaps merely by discussing them or communicating information about them. For example, a company may offer its employees a voluntary, self-administered career management program consisting of several workbooks. Because such a program entails considerable work, with no immediate benefit to one's career, the program may not be completed by many employees. Just the knowledge that the program exists, however, may focus the attention of many more employees on career goals, factors affecting those goals, and employees' responsibility for their own careers. This kind of insight could ultimately affect career decisions and behaviors.

How people interpret the environment also has implications for motivational strategies. For instance, a given situational change may not affect motivation if it is not perceived as intended. Understanding which individual characteristics are relevant to the interpretation of different situations may suggest ways of controlling the interpretation process.

The multidimensional nature of career motivation suggests that motivational strategies will have to deal with broad sets of variables. For example, a new pay system may be designed and implemented—along with a career development program, a supervisor-subordinate joint goal-setting process, and new transfer and promotion policies—as an integrated system. Such a system could be designed with the aid of knowledge about relationships between groups of situational characteristics, individual characteristics, and career decisions and behaviors. To take another example that deals with multiple variables, an employee communications program, coupled with training to help subordinates set and carry out career goals, may affect career insight variables. Nevertheless, these sorts of programs may have no effect if prior circumstances have generated low career resilience. Consequently, programs intended to affect resilience dimensions (for example, ways of providing constructive feedback while reducing the negative consequences of failure) may also be necessary.

Thus, it would seem that human resource systems must be integrated to be effective. Appendixes A, B, and C to this chapter outline three comprehensive development programs, each of which has a number of different components, and Figure 1 shows how these three comprehensive programs fit together.

Figure 1. Development Program Linkages.

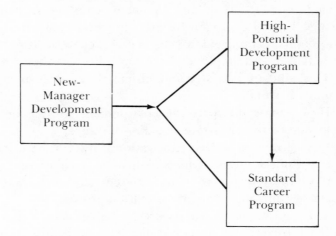

The new manager may be a recent college graduate newly hired by the company or may have been promoted from the nonmanagement ranks. The new-manager development program (Appendix A) encompasses the first year in management, during which newcomers are given an opportunity to learn their jobs and demonstrate potential for advancement to higher levels. Managers with advancement potential are placed in a high-potential development program (Appendix B). This program may include only 5 percent of the new managers. Managers of longer tenure may also be placed in the program if their bosses feel that they have recently demonstrated potential for advancement. The standard career program (Appendix C) provides opportunities for professional growth for managers not in the high-potential program (London, 1984).

There are several ways, including supervisory nomination and performance in an assessment center, for managers in the standard career program to enter the high-potential program. Some companies allow managers to nominate themselves, a policy that forces higher-level managers to consider subordinates' potential for such a program.

Being in a high-potential program is not a guarantee of promotion, however; rather, the program provides opportunities and experiences that prepare managers to handle higher-level responsibilities early in their careers. Managers in the standard career program also have such opportunities and may be promoted, although probably at a slower pace than those in the high-potential program.

Some companies put newly hired managers on a high-potential/fast-track program immediately, believing that this is how to attract the best people. These companies often worry about whether managerial talent will surface on the job. They also worry that it may be perceived as unfair to select someone for a high-potential program when others are not selected even though they are performing equally well. Since potential to work at a higher level of management is an amorphous quality, which is often difficult for peers to see, an assessment center can be very valuable in making such judgments.

Many new managers like having a year or so to get used to both the job and the company while having the chance to demonstrate performance and potential. While fast-track programs offer potentially higher rewards, they also entail higher risks, in that new managers who do not succeed on the fast track are let go. The other approach is to hire new managers for specific jobs, which they can always keep on a standard career track.

Ultimately, decisions on hiring people directly into high-potential programs depend on business needs. If there are many advancement opportunities for which it is necessary to prepare people quickly, then it may be desirable to hire people directly into high-potential programs. If there is a need for people at lower levels and there are few advancement opportunities, then there is no point in hiring many competitive, advancement-oriented people and making promises that cannot be kept. Giv-

ing the new manager a period of time to demonstrate performance and potential on the job will probably predict future
success better than college records and employment interviews
do. Nevertheless, a small number of "superstars" (highly ranked
MBA graduates from the top business schools) may be hired directly into fast-track programs as an aid to recruitment.

Conclusion

This chapter has offered guidelines for attracting highly
able and motivated young managers and maintaining their commitment to the organization. The guidelines, together with the
motivation strategies presented in this chapter, constitute a career motivation model.

The model assumes that career resilience, career insight,
and career identity are desirable. It also assumes that following
the guidelines improves the quality of work life and ultimately
increases productivity. Organizations are encouraged to follow
all the guidelines, not just a few. We know from the literature
on job redesign that trying to increase productivity by changing
specific job characteristics often leads to failure if other elements of the organizational context are not also considered
(Hackman and Oldham, 1980). The same principle is likely to
apply to the career motivation guidelines. For instance, a career
development program is likely to be ineffective in the absence
of performance feedback, positive reinforcement, and opportunities for achievement.

Another assumption of the career motivation model is
that managers can learn to apply the guidelines to their work
groups. This task will be easier for some managers than for others, but the guidelines do incorporate basic principles of good
management. Many of these guidelines involve bosses, but more
needs to be said about organizational contexts, since a company's philosophy of career development is crucial to the successful application of this model. The next chapter considers
how to adapt manager-development programs to organizational
philosophies and needs.

Appendix A. New-Manager Development Program.

Development Program

Purpose: To acclimate new employees to the policies of the organization, give them a chance to learn their jobs, and give their bosses a chance to evaluate their performance and potential. The employees also become familiar with available career opportunities and career paths. The program concludes with establishing realistic expectations and initial career plans.

Duration: First year in the company.

Description: The program consists of several components:

Orientation to the company, provided by the boss, and a standard training program (or sequence of programs). This phase covers the work done by different departments within the company and includes training on important management skills. (An orientation workshop is outlined at the end of this appendix.)

Quarterly appraisal feedbacks from the boss during the first year, to let employees know where they stand and what can be done to enhance their performance.

A *career planning module* to help individuals develop career goals and paths to achieve them on the basis of currently available career opportunities. Employees must understand that their goals should be revised periodically to reflect changing career interests and changing organizational conditions. This module is administered at the conclusion of the program.

Participants: Entry-level personnel. The content of the program differs for recent college graduates hired into the first level of management and for nonmanagement employees promoted to first management positions. The program is also different for technical people hired into specialized positions (computer programming, accounting, legal services) that have special career tracks.

Control: The content of the program may be developed centrally, although organizational units may wish to add material pertinent to their own areas. The program is administered locally, with the immediate supervisor of the new employee held responsible for the employee's completion of the program.

Advantages: The program provides a ready means for communicating standard policies and procedures, puts all new employees on an equal level with respect to information available on career opportunities, and prevents new employees from developing expectations which cannot be met.

Disadvantages: Discussing opportunities and establishing plans early in a person's career may be unnecessary and counterproductive if there are actually few opportunities or if the person was hired to do a specific job that meets a current business need and if the person is expected to continue in the job for some time.

Costs: Initial development costs for orientation training, for development and administration of a supervisory training program, and for updating information.

Recommendation: Vary the program for different groups of young managers, depending on why they were hired, the jobs they hold, their departments, and the likelihood of their movement to other jobs. In some cases, the program should be limited to initial orientation; in others, there should be heavy emphasis on early performance and potential appraisal and on career planning. What is done should depend on the opportunities likely to be available and on the company's and the department's philosophy of manager development. It is important to guard against raising expectations that cannot be met.

Orientation Workshop[a]

Number of participants per session: 15-20.

Unit I—Networks and Alliances: Increase awareness of jobs, departments, and functions in the company; build networks.
  Present overview of company.
  Share information about jobs.
  Show how two performance objectives affect other departments in the company.
  List people in the seminar who can be contacts for mutual help with jobs.

Unit II—Management Skills: Increase awareness of methods and principles of interpersonal communication; give feedback and recognition; show behavior-modeling tapes on feedback and recognition.
  Present learning principles.
  Observe role models on tape.
  Practice giving feedback to fellow participants on previous day's presentations.
  Discuss how these skills apply to jobs.

Unit III—Personal Motivation Awareness: Increase awareness of career motivation dimensions and viewpoints of other new managers and bosses; develop action plans.
  Watch videotape of interviews with new managers as they describe getting a sense of achievement from work, dealing with new assignments, taking actions with uncertain outcomes, depending on others, balancing work and nonwork activities, the importance they give to advancement, forming career goals, and receiving feedback.
  Discuss tape.

Watch videotape of interviews with bosses as they describe perceptions of new managers, bosses' management styles, subordinates' motivation levels, problems with and barriers to supervising, encouraging work involvement, opportunities and rewards, giving career information, giving feedback, encouraging risk taking, perceptions of rewards for supervising, and how bosses can improve.

Discuss bosses as barriers to and facilitators of career development and what can be done about it.

Establish priorities for development.

Set action steps for highest priorities.

Share priorities and action steps in group session and get feedback from group members.

---

[a]This workshop was developed by Barbara Herr, Marjorie Leopold, Manuel London, Marilyn McIlhone, Edward Mone, Thomas Thayer, and Thomas Vasko.

Appendix B. High-Potential Development Program.

Purpose: To provide job experiences and training that will prepare high-potential young managers for promotion to the next two levels.

Duration: The program begins with one year of concentrated attention to prepare the person for the next level. After the first promotion, the second phase of the program, lasting two to five years, prepares the person for the next promotion.

Description: During the first year, the employee is assigned to a supervisor two levels higher in the organizational hierarchy (a first-level manager reports to a third-level manager). Thus, the employee has an opportunity to model the behavior of the higher-level boss, and the boss has an opportunity to evaluate the employee's potential for advancement. The employee can be removed from the program upon evaluation, which occurs once every six months. Only high-performance bosses are used for the program. They are trained to evaluate the program participants, give them developmental assignments, and generally give them the attention required to prepare them for early promotion. This attention includes giving participants frequent feedback on performance, keeping them informed about departmental and organizational occurrences, having them sit in on higher-level meetings, having them give presentations to executives, and so on. Another valuable experience is attendance at periodic meetings with other program participants, to share experiences and discuss common issues. The second and third years of the program involve reassignment to a different boss, one level above the participant, preferably in another department or in a different area in the same department. This reassignment broadens participants' knowledge of the business and gives them experience interacting with different co-workers and dealing with different sets of programs and work methods.

Participants: The program applies to first-level managers who, during their first year with the company, have demonstrated good job performance and high potential for advancement. More experienced managers who have demonstrated performance and potential can also be placed in this program during an annual nomination period. (It is important to note that potential and performance are not identical; a person may have outstanding job performance, but may not show potential to be effective at a higher level. It is also possible, although not as likely, that low performance is due to factors beyond the employee's control; nevertheless, he or she may still demonstrate advancement potential in the way he or she handles the job.)

Control: Bosses are responsible for the development of the high-potential employees assigned to them. The boss's evaluation is the major determinant of whether or not the person stays in the program. Departments are responsible for identifying high-potential employees. A central office tracks each participant's progress.

Applicability: The company must be committed to the program from the top down; the program also operates company-wide, because if each department were left to design, implement, and operate its own high-potential program, the program would dissolve. Central control is necessary to ensure that participants receive meaningful experiences, are evaluated fairly, and are moved into new positions at appropriate times. If the program is to be credible, it must be continuous, with a new group starting each year. Promotion is not automatic: Successful graduates of the program must compete for promotion with employees who are not in the program and who have more experience, outstanding job performance, and a rating of "ready now for promotion." The size of the program is based on the human resources needs anticipated at higher levels one to three years in the future. When many job opportunities are forecast, more people are sought for the program, even if economic conditions are bad currently. The program assumes that middle-management positions are filled primarily from within the company, because experience at lower levels is desirable for managing the company at higher levels.

Advantages: The program treats high-potential employees as corporate resources. It provides these employees with challenging experiences to broaden their scope, enhance their motivation, and guarantee a supply of talented individuals for higher-level positions.

Disadvantages: The program can create a schism between those selected for the program and those not selected. The participants may have difficulty interacting with others, who may view them as "prima donnas." In addition, the participants may have a tendency to focus more attention on building networks and attaining the next position than on performing assignments. These problems can be handled by proper program administration.

Costs: Costs include administrating of the program (for example, having a company coordinator) and running special training sessions and meetings for participants. The highest cost is relocating participants when they are transferred to new jobs in different geographical areas. One way to control this cost is to use temporary assignments, which do not require selling one's home and moving one's family. Another way is to take advantage of the variability of job types in the geographical area. In some cases, it is possible to gain a broad background in the business by transferring to different jobs in different departments within the same area. Some businesses want their high-potential people to have a stint at headquarters, however, and this may require moving to and from headquarters in a few years.

Recommendation: Develop and institute the program only if there is commitment to maintain it for a long time and to follow through on the expectations it generates.

Appendix C. Standard Career Program.

Purpose: To provide career planning, developmental experiences, and job assignments that will enhance motivation and job performance. The program utilizes and develops a person's strengths and corrects weaknesses, as possible. Some weaknesses, such as poor decision-making ability, cannot be corrected in a short time; other weaknesses, such as poor oral communication skills, may be corrected more easily and quickly.

Duration: Operates throughout a person's career.

Description: Consists of many of the components of the high-potential development program, but at a slower pace, without singling people out and making them part of a special program and assigning them to special bosses. The standard career program embodies a management philosophy that treats all employees as valuable corporate resources and is concerned with maximizing all employees' productivity. These tasks require conducting accurate and thorough performance evaluations, setting goals, providing challenging job assignments, giving feedback, ensuring accuracy and realism of expectations, and providing for periodic evaluation and redirection of career plans. These are basic elements of good supervision. Unlike the high-potential program, which has specific career plans for each participant, the standard career program places the responsibility for career planning on the individual. Supervisors discuss career opportunities with their subordinates. In addition, a voluntary, self-administered career planning program is available to assist the individual in assessing strengths and weaknesses, establishing a training program, and identifying opportunities in the company.

Participants: Employees at all levels in the company throughout their careers.

Control: Training is provided for supervisors. The personnel department offers career planning materials and monitors employees' career progress.

The personnel department may also offer a one- or two-day career planning program (or different programs for special groups, such as women or minorities).

Applicability: As a management philosophy, the program is presented in a company brochure and distributed widely. It is supported by supervisory training and by evaluating supervisors on those elements of good supervision associated with subordinates' career development.

Advantages: The program provides all employees with information about career opportunities and ties supervisory practices with career development. It treats career development broadly by including not only opportunities for promotion but also job challenge, opportunities for achievement, enhancement of strengths, and maximum utilization of skills and abilities.

Disadvantages: Supervisors differ in their abilities to provide feedback, create challenging assignments, and delegate responsibility. The program becomes meaningless if the elements of good supervision are not implemented.

Costs: The program provides a unified focus for continuous training and development activities. Therefore, costs may not be appreciably greater than if there were no program.

Recommendation: Build the program over time. Have a master plan of career development modules (for example, supervisory training courses, self-administered career planning) and slowly develop and implement the modules until they constitute a coherent career development and training system.

7

* * * * *

Adapting Programs to the Organization's Philosophy and Needs

Chapter Five contrasted two companies that differed in their support for manager development, and Chapter Six described comprehensive development programs. This chapter offers questions that can help to determine a company's philosophy of manager development and evaluate programs the company offers its managers.

Companies differ in the career management systems they offer to their employees. Consider the extreme condition of a company that is low on the situational characteristics associated with career motivation. It provides few opportunities for achievement, low group cohesiveness, little encouragement for goal setting, and, generally, few rewards and opportunities. This company is likely to treat its employees as resources to meet current business needs rather than treating them as corporate assets that need to be developed to meet future needs. The company is not likely to move its people between departments, and it probably discourages development-oriented transfers within departments. No distinction is likely to be made between employees with high potential and others; the assumption is that as vacancies arise, the best people are selected for promotion. Little attention is given to preparing young managers for higher-level positions. Policies like these are liable to lead to complacency; they present few problems in the face of organizational change, because they specify standard procedures. Employees are unlikely to be highly involved in their work, however. They will not be advancement-oriented, and they will not have a strong sense of career identity. They are also unlikely to be committed to the company's goals, except with respect to their own job security. They will probably be dependent on bosses for emotional support, and they probably will not have high self-respect in their work.

Now consider the opposite extreme: an organization high on the situational characteristics associated with career motivation. This company is likely to believe in hiring the most able and highly motivated employees, treating them as corporate resources for the future, training them as generalists, moving them between departments every twelve to eighteen months, distinguishing high-potential employees from those who will become specialists in particular areas, and rapidly promoting the most able who demonstrate high potential for advancement. Companies with such policies find it difficult to maintain them in times of organizational change and economic constraints, when the work force must be consolidated and there are few promotional opportunities. These employee-development policies require a commitment at the highest levels of the company if they are to be maintained over the long run.

Over time, a match is likely to develop between the organization's philosophy of career development and its employees' career motivation. Certain types of employees are attracted to and selected by certain organizations. For example, an organization high in situational dimensions reflecting opportunities for achievement and innovation is likely to search for and attract people who are high in career resilience. Organizations low in such opportunities may not care about personality characteristics associated with career resilience and will not be impressed by candidates with high career resilience.

Organizational conditions may affect the employees' attitudes and motivations. Little positive reinforcement for a job well done, and few opportunities for achievement, engender low career resilience. Low support for career development engenders low career insight. Few opportunities and rewards, and little encouragement for work involvement, discourage the development of career identity. This is not to say that a company's climate cannot improve, however. Organizational development efforts enhance work climate and achievement opportunities, thereby increasing employees' career resilience. These effects, in turn, may lead to support for career development, which will increase employees' career insight. Furthermore, offering opportunities and rewards, encouraging involvement through job challenge, and emphasizing the importance of employees' roles in the organization may increase employees' career identity, as well as reinforcing their career resilience.

What to Ask to Determine a Company's Philosophy of Manager Development

A company's programs, policies, and procedures for career development depend on the answers to eight basic questions, as presented below.

To What Extent Are Employees Treated as Corporate Assets? The more employees are treated as corporate assets, rather than just as resources to meet current business needs, the more development-oriented job moves are likely to be made. Job and organizational analyses can be used to coordinate such moves so that a number of people can benefit simultaneously. Job matches can be made, not just on the basis of skill requirements but also on the basis of a person's career motivation level. Bosses should be trained to provide environments that enhance career motivation, and individuals whose career motivation is low should be assigned to bosses who are best at generating career motivation.

Does the Company Want to Develop Generalists, or Specialists Within Departments? Job and organizational analyses can help answer this question. If a common set of skills is applicable to jobs in different departments, and if unique skills can be acquired fairly easily, then a generalist philosophy makes sense, especially if having knowledge of many elements of the business is beneficial. Nevertheless, a department may view job moves as disruptive, preferring instead to develop its own people within the department. Such a development philosophy would take advantage of the variability of skill requirements between jobs within the department, moving people into different positions and adding job responsibilities to increase their knowledge of the area. Movement between departments may be more desirable for people in midcareer who have already acquired expertise in particular areas and have advanced to sufficiently high levels (for example, middle management) to make knowledge of the "big picture" desirable.

Who Has Control over Promotion and Transfer Decisions? Such decisions may be made by a central personnel official, a committee, a department head, or the supervisor whose department has the vacancy (London, 1978; London and Stumpf, 1984). The more such decisions are decentralized—under the control or influence of the immediate supervisor—the more subordinates are likely to perceive a relationship between behavior and work outcomes. Decentralization assumes that supervisors are trained to make fair and reasonably accurate decisions, but such decentralization also makes it more difficult to transfer and promote managers while still keeping in mind their needs and the needs of the corporation. In contrast, centralized decisions—under the control of the personnel department—make it difficult to take into account simultaneously the needs of the department losing the person as well as those of the department gaining the person. Personnel committees may offer workable solutions. One company has standing committees at each level of management. These committees annually evaluate the progress of managers one level below in the departments represented by each committee member. The committee members are also responsible for filling vacancies in their own departments. Often, personnel transfers are made for the development of individual employees. Knowledgeable about the employees and the departments, the committees are concerned with both manager development and meeting the daily needs of the business.

To What Extent Does the Company Depend on Promotion from Within to Fill Vacancies? In many companies, promotion from within is traditional. It rewards competent, loyal employees with promotion and ensures that higher-level positions are filled with individuals who are knowledgeable about the organization's activities. In some cases, however, it may be desirable to select people from outside the organization, to bring in new blood and/or to develop an area in which the company is not experienced. Whether vacancies are filled internally affects the question of what career opportunities are likely to be available, as well as the competition for them.

To What Extent are Bosses Responsible for Assisting Subordinates in Career Planning? A boss may serve as counselor or coach to a subordinate. Many supervisory behaviors pertain to the subordinate's career development. These include providing information about career options, clarifying the basis for promotion and transfer decisions, clarifying the basis for performance appraisal, giving frequent feedback on job performance, providing information about company changes and their effects on subordinates, recognizing difficulties subordinates have in adapting to change, and encouraging subordinates to establish and periodically revise career plans. Companies that expect subordinates to engage in career planning should reward bosses for developing their subordinates and should give bosses discretion over important career outcomes. Bosses often recognize that helping subordinates with career issues is an important part of the job, but one they neglect because it is not recognized at higher levels. Career development could be made part of a boss's responsibility in the same way that compliance with affirmative action objectives is often incorporated into the evaluation of a boss's performance.

Another frequent complaint from bosses is that they do not control outcomes that are important to their subordinates.

Perhaps the most important outcome is salary. Merit pay increases are often trivial or nonexistent. Many bosses, particularly those at lower organizational levels, also have little say in promotion and transfer decisions. Bosses can make recommendations to higher levels but, because of their limited control, cannot use promotion as a reward. Nevertheless, these bosses should help their subordinates understand not only how their behaviors and accomplishments contribute to promotion but also what part the immediate supervisor plays in the process. The boss should also demonstrate the value of promotion for obtaining desired outcomes—more challenging assignments, higher pay, greater likelihood for recognition, and so on. Often, employees at lower organizational levels do not recognize the benefits that go along with promotion; hence, they are not advancement-oriented.

Should There Be a Comprehensive Manager-Development Program Encompassing Many Career Development Components, or Should Efforts Be Limited to Separate Programs Operated on an As-Needed Basis? The multidimensional nature of career motivation, as well as the job and organizational characteristics that affect it, suggest that career development programs should not operate in isolation from one another; comprehensive, integrated programs are necessary. Such programs might include orientation training, goal setting, special job assignments, meetings with top executives to discuss career opportunities, and so on. Separate comprehensive programs, however, should be offered to those who have different needs or who contribute in different ways to the company. For instance, a diagnosis of future human resource needs may predict substantial middle- and top-management vacancies, while job and organizational analyses may reveal that a fast-track advancement program is necessary to prepare high-potential young managers for middle-management positions and positions above. This circumstance leads to the next question.

Is It Beneficial to Identify High-Potential Employees and Put Them on a Fast-Track Advancement Program, Separate from Those with Average Potential Who Are on a Standard Career Track? There are many potential problems with dual career tracks. One is that they create an impression that those in the high-potential program are crown princes and princesses, while the others have received the kiss of death. Another problem is that they create friction between the high-potential young managers and their bosses and subordinates, who are often older and feel threatened by the fast-tracker. The early-career development programs already recommended aim to avoid these problems by providing motivational components for all young managers within a dual career system (that is, a fast-track program together with a meaningful standard career track). Some companies keep their list of high-potential managers secret. This avoids clashes between the annointed few and the others. It also avoids raising the expectations of those in the program. However, it eventually becomes apparent who is in the program and who is not by the frequency of job changes and the type of assignments a person receives. Telling people they are on a fast-track program clarifies what the company expects of these managers and allows the company to hold special group meetings and other programs for those on the fast track.

To What Extent Should the Organization Designate Specific Career Paths? Some organizations foster career development by designating career paths and providing career opportunities for following the chosen paths. These career paths may specify the sequence of jobs an individual should have in moving up the organizational hierarchy; there may be several different paths within a department. Career paths may also cross departments, but they usually remain within the boundaries of a specific area of the business. For instance, there could be a career path to prepare engineers for management responsibilities within engineering.

The company may require that young managers complete career planning forms, which ask them to formulate their goals and design their own career paths. The form may ask for specific assignments the individual wants to have in the future, or it may ask the individual to specify desired job families. The latter approach provides more flexibility than the approach of identifying specific jobs (these may not even be open when the individual is ready for them). Career planning mechanisms

usually provide an opportunity for revising the career plans at
least once a year.

Comparing the Manager-Development Philosophies
of ECHO, Inc., and DYNAMO Corp.

In considering the differences between ECHO and DYNA-
MO, we learned that ECHO treated its young managers as meeting the current needs of the business, while DYNAMO treated its
young managers as corporate assets for the future: They did
contribute to current business needs, but they also were being
prepared for middle-management positions. Both companies adhered to a philosophy of promotion from within. DYNAMO estimated needs for middle managers and top-level managers five to
ten years in advance and recognized the need to hire and prepare young managers if sufficient talent were to be available to
meet those future needs.

Another element of a company's philosophy involves the
question of whether to train generalists or specialists. DYNAMO
trained managers to be experts in elements of management that
were applicable to jobs in many different departments. This approach was particularly important at middle- and top-management levels, because these managers were frequently rotated
between departments; a middle manager in engineering might be
moved into personnel, or a middle manager from real estate
might be moved into construction. Technical expertise was less
important at this level than the ability to manage the work and
the people.

ECHO, in contrast, was becoming more segmented, as departments assumed their own identities: There had been several
company reorganizations, and different departments were operating under different restrictions brought about by changes in
the industry. A similar reorganization also took place at DYNA-
MO, but the company maintained its generalist philosophy. At
the same time, it recognized that young managers not in the development program had to be hired and trained as specialists in
certain departments (for example, computer programming).
These individuals were brought in because they had specific ex-

pertise, and it was intended that most if not all of their total careers with the company would be spent in these particular areas of expertise. Consequently, DYNAMO was attempting to maintain a dual philosophy of manager development with different career ladders. Specialists were able to advance to middle management within a single department. Those trained as generalists moved between as well as within departments as they rose to middle management. (It was anticipated that those trained as generalists would have better opportunities to rise above middle management than those trained as specialists.)

Another element of company philosophy and organizational design is the extent to which management staffing decisions are centralized. One finding from the boss interviews was that second- and third-level ECHO and DYNAMO managers did not have good understanding of how promotion and transfer decisions were made in their companies. The bosses provided input about candidates to higher-level managers but were usually not involved in the decision-making processes. Promotion and transfer decisions were decentralized, in that they were made by middle- and top-level managers in each department, which often made it difficult to coordinate moves between departments. Because DYNAMO had a history of moving people between departments, however, there was considerable coordination between higher-level managers, who often sought people from other departments to fill their vacancies. ECHO appeared to have less coordination between departments, and so it was more difficult for a young manager to move between departments. Several study participants from ECHO even complained about the difficulty in moving between units within a department.

Despite the flexibility of job movement at DYNAMO, several young managers in the company complained that there was not enough central control over job assignments. They wished that the development program coordinator had more input into this process—perhaps because they felt that they would have greater influence over their job assignments that way. While the young managers from DYNAMO did not hesitate to make their career goals known to their bosses and to higher-level managers, this disclosure was not always effective, at least from the young managers' point of view. As the survey results already cited have shown, many young managers felt that factors beyond merit contributed to promotions.

Another element of corporate policy is the question of whether development of skills and broadening of experience are viable reasons for changing jobs. This question recalls the extent to which young managers are viewed as corporate assets versus resources to meet current business needs. Generally, DYNAMO tried to move someone when the person could benefit from the move but did not make a transfer when it might have been detrimental to the needs of the business; corporate as well as individual needs had to coincide in staffing decisions. ECHO, in contrast, did not seem to pay attention to the development potential of a job reassignment. A person was moved if the immediate needs of the business called for it, but it was not considered legitimate to transfer a young manager solely for the benefit of his or her career.

Neither ECHO nor DYNAMO offered its young managers specific career paths. ECHO did not foster career development, and the idea of planning for future career moves seemed pointless to many of our study participants from ECHO, since there were not many opportunities for movement, either at the same level or to higher levels. In contrast, career planning was an important part of the manager-development program at DYNAMO. Each individual was encouraged to think about career alternatives and discuss these with bosses and higher-level managers. Each year, the young managers revised what job or jobs they wanted next and designated general career paths (for example, in marketing and finance or in engineering and systems implementation). One manager wished he could mention the jobs he did not want; he thought listing only a few desired jobs limited his options, because he might like and benefit from many positions, but there were a few positions he was certain he did not want.

Some of the study participants from DYNAMO complained that their desired career paths were not considered when staffing decisions were made. As one participant put it, if he had to wait until the position he wanted next was available, he might be waiting forever. Nevertheless, the career planning effort was useful to the participants and to the company in considering what experiences would be needed to promote movement in specific directions while still allowing for twists of fate.

How the Company Affects the Manager

So far we have reviewed the cases of five people, whose experiences demonstrate the interaction between individual characteristics and the situation. Here are their companies.

From DYNAMO, we have met Lydia Brown, who would not tolerate a company that did not meet her high expectations; Marilyn Bentley, who needed a level of positive reinforcement that the company could not provide; and Wayne Converse, who found that the boss and the type of assignment made all the difference to his success. From ECHO, we have met Jim Boyd, who was disappointed by the lack of responsibilities in his assignments and by the low work commitment he perceived in his co-workers; and Carol Baylor, who found that she could control her career and gain self-confidence working within the system. Now we also meet Ray Markham of ECHO and Deborah Harley of DYNAMO. Ray's experience shows how frustrating the lack of support for career development can be. Deborah's experience shows how a company that applies the career motivation guidelines we have outlined can develop managers and produce success stories.

Sticking With It: The Case of Ray Markham. Company and departmental policies, as well as the supervisor's philosophy of manager development, determine the level of support for career development, the encouragement of involvement in a subordinate's career, and the availability of career opportunities and rewards. These factors, in turn, may influence the individual's career insight and career identity. The effects of these conditions may depend on the individual's career resilience. Those with high career resilience are likely to develop career insight and identity much more quickly than those with low career re-

silience, who require considerably more support for career development and more encouragement of involvement.

Ray Markham, an Ivy League graduate who had been
with the company for about five years when I met him, was
evaluated by the assessment staff as high in career resilience. His
high career insight and identity emerged over time as he learned
more about the politics and social climate in his department. He
had had a series of assignments at first level in the installation
and maintenance department during his first two years with
ECHO. He had been rated outstanding and was scheduled to participate in the company's one-year development program for
high-potential first-level managers. (The personnel department
operated the program for about two years before abandoning it
in the face of little support.) Before he was placed in the program, however, his boss's boss (at third level) was transferred,
and the person who replaced him insisted that Ray again prove
himself before being allowed to enter the program. Ray thought
this demand was unfair, to say the least. He also felt that his career could benefit by a move to a new department. Such a move
would give him broader experience and perhaps lead to more
rapid advancement. In addition, he felt that his future in his
current department was not bright, and that he would be better
off in the long run if he could transfer to another department
early in his career.

Ray believed that the finance department would be a
good place for him. This department was looking for someone
with his background, and he got in contact with the boss who
had the vacancy. He was interviewed for the job and received an
offer, but his third-level boss would not release him. The third-
level manager was severely disappointed in Ray's lack of loyalty.
He argued that, after all, the installation and maintenance department had trained him, and the department deserved something in return. Ray insisted that his training was not wasted
and that he certainly would use it to benefit the company, but
in another department. This argument did not go over well, and
the third-level manager's irritation was registered on Ray's next
performance appraisal. This incident delayed his entering the
high-potential development program for a year.

Ray confronted another career barrier about a year after

completing the program. While finishing the program meant that he was ready for promotion to second level, it certainly did not guarantee promotion. When a second-level job became available, Ray was temporarily assigned to the position as an acting second-level manager. Unfortunately, the job function was eliminated several months later, and Ray was sent back to his former first-level position, even though he had already vowed to himself that he would never return. Several months later, the assistant vice-president promised Ray that he would have the next promotion in the department, but it did not materialize for six more months.

Ray's major complaint about ECHO was lack of support for career development and few opportunities for advancement. Ray felt that he should have advanced more quickly, given his qualifications and his performance ratings. His new boss agreed. Ray learned that demonstrating loyalty and patience would pay off more quickly in his department than pursuing his career interests aggressively. While his social perceptiveness increased, his job involvement—and, to some extent, his need for advancement—seemed to have declined as a result of the department's reactions to his career initiatives. At various points during his four and a half years with the company, he had sent his résumé to other companies. He said that he would have left ECHO if he had not been concerned about his job security and if the job market had been better.

Deborah Harley: The Case of a Rising Star. Many of the people in our sample of managers were probably typical of the average college graduate today. They had B averages, they were involved in some extracurricular activities, and they sought jobs in business. While they had fairly low desire for career advancement upon entering their companies, they worked hard and did well. Deborah Harley was such a person. She had had a sequence of tough jobs, which required demonstrating strong supervisory skills and gave her an opportunity to shine by solving problems and increasing performance indices in a line department. Her excellent performance at DYNAMO led to her promotion to second level; in the process, she gained the respect and friendship of several middle- and top-level managers.

At the time of assessment, Deborah Harley was twenty-four years old. She was a friendly and almost bubbly person who could warm up to a vice-president at first meeting just as easily as she could to someone on her own level. She seemed as if she could be a real pal, joking around and making fun, but she was also very definite about not letting people take advantage of her. She could show a rough work crew who was boss; in fact, she had been able to tame a racially tense work group. Her forte seemed to be straightening out disorganized departments.

Deborah had been with the company for three years at the time of assessment. After graduating with majors in math and economics from a large state school, she was hired by DYNAMO as a computer programmer in the data-processing department. She soon had an opportunity to enter the firm's manager-development program, and she was transferred to the engineering department. She worked on a project involving the design of facilities for a new type of electronics equipment. She reported to a third-level manager whom she described as a dynamic individual. Others in the department were older and, in Deborah's opinion, not very bright. While she enjoyed her work, she asked for another job with supervisory experience.

After only nine months in the engineering department, she was transferred to the customer service department as supervisor of a group of service representatives. She found that the department was down to earth, but that the people were not much more intelligent than those in engineering. The job was a challenge for two reasons. First, all nine of her subordinates were black women who had been with the company for many years. The racial tension wore off after a few weeks, when her subordinates realized that Deborah was not as young as she looked (they thought she was nineteen at first) and that she meant business and knew what she was doing. Second, Deborah's boss was trying to upgrade the department's performance on response time to service requests; his goal was to decrease response time by 30 percent. Deborah achieved that goal in her work group within three months, whereas neither of the other two first-line managers in the department met the goal.

After six months in this position, Deborah was transferred to a special project, working directly with the fourth-level manager. This project entailed designing guidelines for a new procedure to handle service requests. Working on the project gave her exposure to the fifth-level manager (an assistant vice-president), as well as to other top officials of the company. While the project took a month longer than the boss originally had anticipated, the outcome was successful, and Deborah was placed in charge of monitoring the program.

The assessment staff evaluated Deborah as moderate in career identity. Her need for advancement was somewhat low, although her need for recognition, desire for leadership, and financial motivation were fairly high. She demonstrated a commitment to her work, identification with the company, and a need for job security. Work was very important in her life, although she was also concerned about spending time with her fiancé and their friends.

Deborah's career insight was high. She clearly wanted to advance to a middle-level management position. She also had a good idea of how she would balance her career with her home life. She intended to be married in about a year and then wait to have children until she was promoted to third level. She felt that if she had a child before that time, her career motivation would be questioned and her opportunities for promotion might be hampered. She seemed to understand her strengths and weaknesses and had realistic expectations for her career.

Deborah's career resilience was high, in that her self-esteem, adaptability, initiative, and concern about doing high-quality work were all high. She was high in risk taking and low on fear of failure. While she was evaluated as high in competitiveness, she was also high in need for supervisor approval and in reliance on others.

The clinical psychologist's report on her projective tests indicated that her responses appeared to be sincere, matter-of-fact expressions of her thoughts and feelings, showing no indications of either unusual introspection or defensiveness. For the most part, she appeared to be a practical, realistic person who was more comfortable dealing with concrete, everyday events than with tasks that required imagination or independent thinking (despite her attempts at and aspirations for the latter). She seemed to be satisfied with herself, felt that she compared well with others, and believed that she had impressed others favorably. Her responses indicated that while she initially found giving orders difficult, she now found this task easy and natural, yet she seemed to remain uneasy about (and probably was inconsistent in) assertiveness. Her confidence in her ability to fulfill a supervisory role, the psychologist felt, was likely to fluctuate a great deal. Similarly, her reaction to decision-making situations was apt to be direct and decisive at some times, cautious and dependent at other times. She appeared to be accepting, respectful, and deferent toward supervisors, and she was comfortable in a subordinate role. Her projective responses indicated that she relied heavily on company policies and regulations, appreciating them as a source of information and guidance to her in making decisions.

When we interviewed Deborah seven months after assessment, she was married and very happy. She and her husband had purchased a home and a car, and they were working hard to make ends meet. She had had another assignment change since we had talked to her. She was now in a staff assignment, formulating procedures for a consolidation of offices. She found this job exciting and a great responsibility, since her recommendations would have a major effect on the lives of the employees involved.

A year later, Deborah had been promoted to second level and was doing very well. Her boss had nothing but praise for her. She had been assigned to head a consolidation effort in her department, and it was a huge success. She designed procedures for explaining the consolidation to the employees, determined a way to use employees' input in reassigning them, and brought the consolidation off in less time than expected. She was then assigned to manage the largest office in the department. Her boss felt that she could achieve third level in about three more years. He sat down with her and mapped out what jobs she should have to prepare for the promotion. He felt that she was in an excellent position, since she compared favorably to the few people who would be in competition with her.

Deborah is someone who is able to make the most of the

right opportunities. Unlike Marilyn Bentley, Deborah did not have a stellar academic background. Unlike Lydia Brown, Deborah did not have grand expectations. Deborah was a good worker who believed in putting all her energy into the job. She was well liked by her subordinates and by her bosses. Both Deborah and Lydia began their careers with a healthy pattern of career motivation. They were high in career resilience and insight. Deborah's moderate career identity was increasing with each successful experience and with the encouragement of her supervisors.

Deborah's current boss felt that if she had any weakness, it was her lack of technical knowledge. He recommended that she read and know all there was to know about the latest developments in the field. Such studying would help her to use this information and could lead her to discover a breakthrough: This behavior is what the company needs and what will advance her career the most. He also felt that it was necessary for Deborah to understand the factors that affect the earnings of the total company; she needed to know the "big picture," as he put it. He also felt that Deborah needed more flair. She was a hard worker and a problem solver, but to reach third level and attain higher levels, the boss believed, she would have to demonstrate greater sophistication and overall knowledge.

Conclusion

Implicit in this chapter is the belief that a certain philosophy of manager development is better than another. Young managers should be treated as long-term corporate assets; the process for making staffing decisions should allow for movement between departments; developing skills is a viable reason for transferring young managers; and career planning mechanisms should be instituted and their use should be reinforced. Each of these elements of corporate philosophy is a continuum; in other words, they are not a matter of "all or none." Moreover, a company may have a dual approach to any one of these elements, as in the example of DYNAMO's trying to develop both generalists and specialists. What is important, however, is that attention be given to the development of young managers early in their careers, and that bosses be reinforced for their contribution to their subordinates' career development.

The next chapter looks in more depth at a variety of strategies for manager development and considers their likely impact on career resilience, insight, and identity.

8

❋ ❋ ❋ ❋ ❋

Selecting Human Resource Strategies and Techniques for Manager Development

Chapter Six described different motivational strategies, from those aimed at directly affecting managers' behavior to those aimed at indirectly affecting managers' behavior through leadership style and the company's policies and procedures. This chapter reviews these techniques in more detail and then offers an estimate of the extent to which each probably contributes to career resilience, career insight, and career identity, as well as an estimate of the overall costs and benefits of each program. The techniques are grouped according to whether they focus on the individual, the situation, or company policies and programs.

A good way to read this chapter is to review the topics covered, read about the techniques and programs of most interest, and then use the chapter as a reference when the need for a description or an opinion about a particular technique arises. Special attention should be given to the last two sections, which consider the value of the programs and offer some recommendations.

Focus on the Individual

Recruitment

Some companies do better than other companies in attracting able and highly motivated managers. Recruiters in different companies vary in their aggressiveness. One company may do a better job of scouting and wooing candidates than another. Moreover, companies differ in what they offer college graduates in salary, job challenge, development programs, and promotion opportunities.

Selection

Common selection techniques measure abilities and skills associated with managerial success. For example, tests measure verbal and math abilities; interviews examine background and interpersonal orientation (for example, leadership experiences). Some companies use assessment centers for selection. This process uses behavioral exercises, interviews, personality tests, and other techniques to measure decision making, organizing and planning, leadership, and other basic managerial skills. With this process, however, less attention is usually given to measuring needs, interests, and the personality characteristics associated with career motivation. Many organizations use personality profiles in their selection of managerial personnel, but the variables used are generally based on educated guesses, and the methods are not validated. Methods need to be designed and validated to examine these variables as possible predictors in the selection process.

Realistic Job Previews

Realistic job previews increase the retention and satisfaction of employees. My career motivation study indicated, however, that companies may attract college graduates into management with promises of programs that do not materialize or rates of advancement that are unrealistic. For instance, the college graduate may be led to believe that because a company is large, there will be ample opportunity to move between departments, depending on the young manager's interests. Yet such movement may be very difficult and, in fact, discouraged. Another example is that a manager-development program may be on the drawing board and will be used to attract college graduates, but the program never gets off the ground, does not operate as intended, or affects very few newly hired managers. A program that promises job movement and rapid advancement may be used to entice the college graduate, but organizational and economic changes may make it difficult to continue operating the program in the way it was intended to operate. The result is that employees' expectations cannot be met, a disappointment that contributes to dissatisfaction and possibly to increased turnover. A fear among recruiters is that presenting a realistic picture may dissuade high-potential college graduates from accepting employment with the company. Methods of conveying realistic job conditions and career opportunities need to be investigated, along with their effects on the quality of young managers recruited and on their long-term attitudes, turnover, and productivity. The best solution, however, would be to promise and deliver attractive jobs and development programs so that job previews can be both realistic and positive.

Orientation and Awareness Training

Orientation training focuses on job responsibilities of managers at all levels. This orientation training includes a description of how promotion and transfer decisions are made, what types of skills are required, and how many opportunities are available for advancement, so that young managers can set realistic goals and have a good idea of what behaviors are necessary to attain those goals. Orientation training goes a long way toward enhancing career insight and career identity.

Another element of orientation training involves learning about the whole company. Bosses of young managers frequently complain that their subordinates have a very narrow view of their job responsibilities and that they do not understand how they fit into the whole corporate operation. Understanding based on orientation contributes to an appreciation of the significance of one's position and enhances cooperation with other departments.

Methods for orientation training are not limited to courses. They also include meeting with top executives and the opportunity to observe them on the job. Training techniques are discussed in more detail in Chapter Ten.

Motivation Assessment

The Career Motivation Assessment Center. The career motivation study used a two-day assessment center, which focused on individual characteristics associated with career motivation (see Chapter Three). In-depth interviews, behavioral exercises, personality and projective tests, and several questionnaires and essays were used in the assessment. Later, the material on each participant was reviewed, and ratings were made on the dimensions of career motivation, which fall into the three domains of career resilience, career insight, and career identity. Selected results were then fed back to the participants. The intention of the feedback in our research program was to understand whether the participants viewed themselves in the way we saw them. The feedback was meant to be a positive experience, and suggestions for actions the participants might take were discussed only when this question was raised by the participants. Such an assessment, however, could be used as part of a career counseling process. Young managers who feel that they could benefit from such an assessment could be screened by counselors. If the counselors felt that the assessment data would be valuable, the employee could be sent through the center. The results would be fed back to the employee but would not be available to the employee's department and would not be used to make decisions about the employee.

The career motivation assessment center would provide input for career planning, but its intention is broader. Focusing on personality variables such as belief in oneself, need for achievement, risk-taking tendency, and independence (elements of career resilience), the assessment center provides the individual and the counselor with in-depth information, which can help not only in matching individuals to jobs but also in providing suggestions for improving interpersonal relationships, taking initiative, seeking more rewarding assignments, and so on.

The assessment process also provides information on career insight, which includes not only the nature of one's career goals but also one's sensitivity to the social and political environment on the job, as well as the accuracy of one's self-perception. Information about career identity is helpful in understanding one's needs in comparison to others in the company and in relation to organizational conditions and opportunities. The career motivation assessment center should be most valuable for individuals who feel they lack career direction, self-confidence, and/or a sense of independence.

Self-Assessment Workbooks and Workshops. Some companies, such as General Electric, offer self-assessment techniques for career planning. Self-assessment generally consists of a sequence of self-paced, self-administered workbooks that focus on the employee's skills and help the employee identify viable career opportunities for job transfer and promotion. One element in the sequence often requires the employee to meet with his or her boss to discuss strengths and weaknesses and match them to job opportunities. Workshops have also been designed to help groups of employees work through the sequence of career planning activities.

The self-assessment workbooks and workshops usually focus on career planning. They assume that the individual will be changing jobs and possibly moving up in the organizational hierarchy; there is obviously no point in such career planning if movement is constrained by organizational circumstances or policies.

Another aspect of these activities is that the burden for career development is placed on the employee, and this effect is appropriate: It should be the employee's responsibility to develop and implement his or her own career plans. The organization and the bosses provide supporting material and encouragement, but the prime responsibility rests with the individual. A potential problem, though, is that an employee with initiative may begin a career planning sequence with all good intentions but never finish it, because of resistance from bosses, failure to locate needed information, or failure to realize that, ultimately, decisions affecting one's career are made by others. Clearly,

attention must be given to communicating how staffing decisions are made and how the employee can influence these decisions. The career planning program that requires employees to
express their career interests will be worthless if those interests
are not taken into account in personnel decisions. In general,
career development programs are valuable only to the extent to
which they are in line with organizational realities. (See Chapter Ten for a discussion of computer-based self-assessment techniques.)

Motivation Awareness Training. Instead of a major assessment process, many individuals may benefit from being made
aware of what characteristics constitute career motivation and
where the average young manager in the company stands on
these variables. Individuals can then think about this information in relation to themselves. This training could be geared to
individuals with average self-awareness and average ability to be
objective about themselves. Most people could probably benefit from such awareness training, but the extent of the benefits
and their impact is likely to be less than could be obtained
through individual assessment and feedback. (See Chapter Six
for a description of a personal motivation awareness program
for new managers.)

Career Counseling. Career motivation assessment and
feedback is probably most valuable when used in conjunction
with counseling. This combination can add considerably to the
cost of the process, and it is certainly not necessary for everyone. A career counselor is of questionable value if there is no
initial assessment, against which the validity of the counselor's
perceptions can be checked. The role of the counselor is to help
employees develop action strategies for enhancing their strengths
and minimizing the impact of their weaknesses.

Focus on the Situation

Supervisor Training

Supervisors should be trained both on the nature of career motivation and on the situational factors that contribute to
career resilience, career insight, and career identity. The train-

ing should suggest different strategies for supervising those who are high in career motivation and those who are low. For instance, while the individual who is high in self-confidence, risk taking, and independence (components of career resilience) is likely to benefit from a challenging assignment which he or she can work on alone, the individual who is low in self-confidence, risk taking, and independence is probably going to need more structure and more interpersonal concern.

An outline for a one-day workshop on motivation strategies for increasing productivity is presented in Exhibit 3. The

Exhibit 3. Outline for a One-Day Workshop on Motivation Strategies for Increasing Productivity.

Common Management Strategies and Problems (30 mins.)
Participants are asked to state their approaches to management and their most serious management problems. From these statements a list is made of traditional management techniques and issues. This list serves as a basis for discussion and comparison during the seminar.

Understanding Motivation: The Essence of Good Management (15 mins.)
This is an introduction to the role of motivation in directing employees' behavior and increasing their effort. A distinction is made between what employees bring to the job (their abilities and their desire to work hard) and what supervisors can do to enhance motivation.

Career Motivation: Employees' Career Insight, Career Identity, and Resilience (15 mins.)
Essential elements of career motivation are described.

Case Study (30 mins.)
The background, job history, and current position of a young first-level manager are presented. The case is used as a basis for understanding motivation and relevant management strategies.

Management Strategies for Increasing Motivation (30 mins.)
Ways of directing, controlling, and organizing work to enhance employees' career insight, identity, and resilience are discussed. This discussion gives participants a practical set of guidelines, such as those presented in Chapter Six, for more effective management.

(continued on next page)

Exhibit 3. Outline for a One-Day Workshop on Motivation Strategies,
for Increasing Productivity, Cont'd.

Focus: Job Design, Leadership Style, Goal Setting, Performance Appraisal, Feedback, and Reinforcement (60 mins.)
For each of these crucial areas, motivation strategies are recommended, practical examples are given, and evidence for their effectiveness is provided.

Discussion of Applying the Motivation Strategies to Management Problems (30 mins.)
Returning to the issues raised by the participants at the start of the seminar, we ask the participants to describe how they would apply the motivation strategies.

Developing a Management System (30 mins.)
The participants are guided in how to use the principles discussed in the seminar to revise their approaches to management. They leave with a new set of strategies they can apply on the job.

---

goals of the workshop are to acquaint managers with career motivation concepts; increase managers' awareness of differences in motivation among subordinates; and suggest strategies for enhancing career resilience, insight, and identity.

Job Redesign

The career motivation guidelines focus on several elements of job redesign. These include the amount of autonomy in the job; the extent to which the employee is held accountable for his or her work; the employee's control over work methods and goals; and opportunities for achievement, creativity, using a variety of skills, and developing new skills. Bosses should learn to vary job characteristics to meet subordinates' needs. Some individuals can take a strong dose of a certain element of job redesign; others must build up to it.

A factor that should be considered in job redesign is the environment, including the physical setting, the quality of interpersonal relations, and the compensation system. These factors must be favorable if job redesign efforts aimed at increasing job challenge and opportunities for achievement are to be successful.

Leadership Style

The manager-development guidelines in Chapter Six touch on many elements of leadership style. They suggest that bosses should learn about goal setting, performance appraisal, feedback, acting as counselors or coaches, and reinforcement. These elements are discussed below.

Goal Setting. The manager-development guidelines state that employees' career insight can be increased through support for their career development. This support involves encouraging goals and formulating action plans to achieve them. As previously noted, the boss should clarify the basis of performance appraisals and of promotion and transfer decisions. In the process, the boss should also try to foster realistic expectations. Subordinates should be helped to set realistic goals and to understand what to expect when they attain them. Work and career goals are important, but they should not be achieved at the expense of other important or necessary behaviors not included in the goals. Goals should be specific, moderately difficult, prioritized, and easily measured. They should be set and evaluated at regular intervals (for example, quarterly). The goals should also specify the manner in which they will be accomplished. They should be put in writing and established jointly between bosses and subordinates.

Performance Appraisal. The manager-development guidelines suggest that several points should be emphasized in training bosses to conduct performance appraisals. Performance consists of the behaviors and outcomes of doing the job. Behaviors do not always reflect job outcomes, since the outcomes may not be totally under the individual's control. The format for performance appraisal is less important than what is done with the information. Bosses should avoid rating a person the same way on all elements of performance unless such a rating is justified; that is, the boss should distinguish between different facets of performance that may not be related. A person may be good in one area, but not in another.

A distinction should be made between performance and potential. Potential for advancement refers to demonstration of the skills needed at a higher level. Performance does not always reflect potential for advancement: An individual with good performance may not necessarily be able to perform well at a higher level; alternately, an individual whose performance is not up to par may be confronting unusual problems beyond his or her control and still could have potential for advancement.

Potential to rise to a certain level should be evaluated only by a person at that level or above. Therefore, a second-level manager can evaluate a first-level manager's potential to advance to second level, but not to advance to third level. The assessment center has been very useful in evaluating potential for advancement two levels above the present level. A boss two levels above is unlikely to have enough awareness of the individual's behavior to judge his or her potential, but assessors two levels above can evaluate behavior in the assessment center in relation to the managerial skills that are required at the higher level.

Psychologists often recommend a problem-solving approach to performance appraisal, meaning that emphasis should be placed on correctly identifying the cause of any deviation from what was expected, rather than on blaming the individuals concerned. Judgments about the causes of performance deficiency, or even of performance improvement, should await input from the employees themselves. Supervisors who have good day-to-day relationships with their subordinates are likely to have much more success with performance appraisals than supervisors do who are distant from their subordinates.

Feedback. Bosses must establish their credibility as sources of feedback, on the basis of their own expertise and/or creating a climate of interpersonal trust. In general, people rely on sources close to them for feedback. When paired with goal setting, performance feedback increases the probability that individuals will meet or exceed their goals. Effective feedback is specific, timely, behavior-oriented, clear, frequent, and presented in relation to the performance of others.

Performance goals and performance feedback should be tailored to fit the person. For high performers with potential for growth, feedback should be frequent enough to provide corrective action but not frequent enough to be controlling and detract from initiative. For adequate performers who have settled into their jobs and probably would prefer to advance no higher in the company, very little feedback may be needed; after all, the average performer has displayed reliable and steady behavior in the past, knows the task, and knows what is needed. Low performers should be removed from the work group if their performance does not improve. They should be monitored closely and given very specific feedback, and the connection between feedback and such negative sanctions as termination should be made explicit.

Boss as Counselor or Coach. As noted above, the boss is in a position to evaluate subordinates' job performance and their potential to rise at least one level in the corporate hierarchy. The boss should be aware of what career opportunities are available within the organization and should provide assignments to expand subordinates' capabilities in line with these opportunities. The boss should also provide subordinates with feedback and make suggestions for improving performance and/ or career opportunities. These suggestions must be offered in a nonthreatening way. The boss should understand any nonwork aspects of subordinates' lives that affect career issues. Bosses may be most effective as counselors when subordinates have undergone substantial self-assessment and have set goals jointly with bosses. As mentioned by supervisors interviewed in the career motivation study, counseling should not be limited to a formal, once-a-year event but should be done continuously on an informal basis.

Another important function of the boss is to demonstrate the value of promotion for desired outcomes, explaining, for example, that promotion leads to more challenging assignments with higher pay and greater likelihood of recognition. Such demonstrations should help enhance young managers' advancement motivation. (The boss's role in developing managers is the subject of Chapter Nine.)

Reinforcement. Positive reinforcement is an important element in an individual's career resilience. Reinforcement intended to increase desired behaviors should be frequent and, at first, given at regular intervals. Once desired behaviors are established, they should be reinforced intermittently. Proper use of reinforcement can also decrease undesired behaviors—for example, by withholding positive outcomes (an action termed negative reinforcement) and by using punishment, if necessary. In general, it is wise to minimize any consequences of failure that result from risk taking. In all cases of negative reinforcement, the subordinate should know the reason for the action.

Summary

Supervisor training should focus on the elements of good management. These may be summarized in the following six points (really another way of stating the manager-development guidelines from Chapter Six).

- Enhance job challenge for those who can handle it.
- Structure work, as necessary. Build a cohesive work group and demonstrate concern for employees. Increase employee participation in decision making.
- With the participation of subordinates, set specific career and work goals.
- Base performance appraisals on the achievement of key responsibilities and on other crucial job behaviors.
- Provide frequent feedback.
- Reinforce desired behaviors through positive reinforcement and eliminate undesired behaviors through negative reinforcement.

Company Policies and Programs

Rewarding Bosses for Developing Young Managers

The bosses interviewed in our research often complained that they were not reinforced for paying attention to their subordinates' career development. Many of them held that this was an important part of their jobs, which they neglected because it was not recognized by higher-level managers. Bosses should be expected to encourage subordinates' career development, and they should also be rewarded for doing so.

*Giving the Boss Discretion Over Important
Career Outcomes*

Another frequent complaint from bosses in our research was that they did not control outcomes important to their subordinates. Perhaps the most important outcome to them was salary. Merit pay increases or bonuses were often trivial or standardized; in a few cases, high-performing young managers were told that they did outstanding jobs, and they were rated outstanding by their bosses, but their ratings were changed so that outstanding ratings could be given to employees of longer tenure so that the latter could maintain their salary levels.

The young first-level managers in the study and their immediate supervisors recognized that immediate supervisors had little say in promotion and transfer decisions. The boss could provide input to higher-level managers but had no power to use promotion as a reward. Both first- and second-level managers tended to be unclear in explaining how promotion and transfer decisions were made. The manager-development guidelines suggest that clarifying these processes is important in helping young first-level managers understand not only how their own behaviors and accomplishments contribute to promotion but also what part immediate supervisors play in the promotion process.

Supervisors should learn how they can influence subordinates' motivation. Relevant factors under supervisors' control include the elements of job design, work assignments, goal setting, and feedback. Social reinforcements (for example, public praise) can also be very important. Our research participants from ECHO often complained that their skills were not fully utilized; they felt that a college degree was not necessary to do their jobs, and they believed that their bosses would not try to transfer them to more meaningful positions because bosses were afraid of losing good workers who would be needed if job demands increased. Since there is often considerable variability in how a job can be done, bosses have discretion in how they structure assignments and delegate authority. Such discretion can be used to enhance young managers' career motivation.

Career Paths

Some companies have detailed career paths that suggest logical moves between jobs. The more specific these career paths are, in some cases, the less functional they tend to be, because a specific job designated on a career path may not be available when an individual is ready for it. A better approach is to develop career paths based on job families. Such a path specifies only the type of job that a person should have next.

Another strategy is to develop a unique career path for each individual, usually with substantial input from the person involved. This strategy, sometimes called a career matrix, asks the individual to specify what jobs he or she would like next. There are several problems with this strategy, however. One is that the information is not used when higher-level managers make promotion and transfer decisions. Another is that individuals are unrealistic about the jobs they list. For instance, someone in the engineering department who has a strong desire to be in public relations may specify one or more public relations jobs on the matrix, without regard to the fact that he or she does not have the experience to be moved into the public relations department. A career matrix should be established jointly between the boss and the employee, on the basis of information about career opportunities and job requirements. The career matrix and a suggested career path can clarify career goals, as well as paths to those goals, and thereby enhance career insight.

Succession Planning

Succession planning involves defining the requirements of future positions and determining the availability of candidates and their readiness to move into various jobs. Replacement charts are occasionally used to record possible successors for key positions. Succession planning is usually done by supervisors, with little input from subordinates. Ideally, succession planning and career planning should be united, so that individuals understand the relationships between their career objectives and the organization's goals. Realistically, however, the organization often determines an employee's destiny. Succession planning, like career paths, may have the disadvantage of boxing people into particular jobs or sequences of jobs and can also decrease the extent to which a wider body of managers has equal opportunity for obtaining particular vacancies.

Despite these advantages, organizational continuity requires replacing employees with individuals who have similar qualifications. A less specific procedure than formulating replacement charts is to compile promotion lists, frequently during annual meetings held by department managers or human resource development committees. Each individual's advancement potential is discussed, and those who are rated ready for promotion are ranked on a promotion list. Each department may keep its own list of first-level managers who are eligible for promotion to second level. The lists are usually secret. While promotion lists have many of the same disadvantages as replacement charts, they provide more flexibility, in that specific individuals are not designated as possible replacements for specific positions. Thus, it is possible to draw from a pool of prescreened candidates in making staffing decisions.

Job-Matching Systems

Aligning individuals' abilities and interests with job requirements is the ultimate goal of most staffing decisions. The idea behind job matching is that an inventory of human resource talent is compared, person by person, with the requirements of available jobs. Individuals in the talent pool are generally those with high potential or those who have been rated ready for promotion or transfer. Searching the talent pool increases equal employment opportunity by ensuring that all potentially qualified candidates are considered. Many companies utilize computerized information systems to make job matches. An essential component of such matching systems is a job function code, which applies to a broad cross-section of positions and individual qualifications. That is, an individual's skills and abilities are described along the same dimensions used to describe jobs. Therefore, the dimensions must be applicable to a variety of job functions.

The disadvantage of job-matching systems is that often

they are not used as intended. In many cases, vacancies are filled by individuals known to the decision makers. Nevertheless, I have encountered several cases of effective use. The computerized job matching system enabled managers with vacancies in their units to search the company's personnel files for individuals who were ready to move into the vacancies. This information was supplemented by information on the candidates' performance and career preferences.

Job Posting

Publicly posting position vacancies encourages employees to apply for openings and prepare themselves for future openings. Obtaining a proper match between positions and employees then depends on bosses searching for candidates and on managers seeking new positions. Job posting should be accompanied by policies intended to ensure fair treatment of employees. I have encountered cases of managers who did not apply for openings in other departments because they feared that their supervisors would be vindictive. In at least two cases, employees applied for jobs in other departments and received job offers, but their current bosses refused to release them.

A job-posting system and self-nominations permit employees to seek broader experiences in developing their own skills. Being turned down for a position can have positive aspects if the rejection leads to the recognition of skill deficiencies. The company may require feedback to be given to individuals who are rejected, although in most cases feedback is not given. Overall, job posting can increase employees' understanding of company procedures and facilitate communication up and down the organizational hierarchy.

Managers filling vacancies often do not give candidates much consideration if they nominate themselves, however. Companies that use job posting for management vacancies often ask employees who are interested in vacancies to get their bosses to nominate them. This procedure makes sense, since the bosses are in a good position to evaluate individuals' skills, but the bosses must be willing to lose these employees. A more objective approach would be to allow self-nominations for those who have been evaluated in an assessment center. The manager who must fill the vacancy would then have reliable and valid information about the candidate's abilities.

A Formalized Sponsor or Mentor Program

This program involves assigning new employees, during their first year in the company, to experienced managers. The mentor need not be the new employee's immediate supervisor. The mentor meets with the new employee every few weeks, helps him or her learn the ropes, provides advice, and so on. Such relationships often continue on an informal basis for many years, and may evolve into bona fide mentor–protégé relationships.

The term *mentor* is a buzz word used by many participants in the career motivation study. They believed that having a mentor was important to advancement, if not absolutely necessary. Several of them felt they already had mentors. The bosses generally had different impressions about mentors. They felt that the concept entailed a close relationship between a young manager and an executive at fifth level or above, and they doubted that first-level managers could develop such relationships. Nevertheless, there were several participants in the study who were promoted to second level partly because of the influence of fifth-level managers. In these cases, it was clear that the fifth level was following the career of these young managers and did something to enhance their career progress, but this process did not entail close personal relationships. A better term might be *sponsorship*.

Bosses, while they may not be sponsors or mentors, can still be important role models for young managers. An effective boss can demonstrate desirable behaviors, and an ineffective boss can demonstrate undesirable behaviors. Unfortunately, young managers are not always able to distinguish between effective and ineffective bosses. This situation suggests that young managers' first assignments should be to bosses who are good performers and are likely to be effective role models.

Appraisal of Potential

Assessment Centers. Assessment centers are used to evaluate managerial potential and have been used in several ways.

One use is for early identification of high-potential managers. Young managers judged by their bosses to have high potential are sent to the assessment center during their first year or two with the company. Those who do well may be placed in a high-potential development program or may be given special opportunities leading to rapid advancement. The difficulty some companies have with this approach is that young managers generally do not do as well in the assessment center as the more experienced first- and second-level managers. This finding suggests that careful attention should be paid to who attends the assessment center.

Another early-career use of assessment centers is for development. A company that hires highly qualified and motivated young managers into a high-potential development program may hold that the young managers' potential for advancement has already been evaluated and that the assessment center is unnecessary for this purpose. It is useful, however, for highlighting people's strengths and weaknesses, and this information suggests the career experiences that will be most helpful in preparing people for middle management.

Supervisor Ratings. A potential-appraisal system trains bosses to collect data on critical incidents and rate subordinates on dimensions important to performing well at the next level. Ratings are generally made every three years or so. Employees can request that their supervisors wait a year before rating them, in hopes of having more opportunities to demonstrate potential during the year. When properly used and combined with feedback, ratings can be a valuable tool in helping young managers understand the behaviors that contribute to demonstrating potential for advancement.

Careers Center

Several companies have experimented with careers centers. The major element of such centers is a booklet describing job opportunities in the company (for example, notices of position vacancies) and information about the company's career development programs and policies. The information is generally in looseleaf binders, so that it can be updated periodically. The

center may contain a library of books about career development, as well as workbooks for self-assessment. A career counselor (possibly an outside consultant hired on an as-needed
basis) may be available to evaluate and discuss employees' abilities and interests and help formulate career plans. Employees
who want more in-depth analysis may be referred to career
guidance agencies outside the company.

Communicating Promotion and Transfer Policies

A company should have written statements and guidelines for how positions are to be filled (how candidates are
sought, whether a single supervisor makes the decision to fill a
vacancy or whether a committee makes it, and so on). Such policies should aid decision makers and promote fair treatment of
employees. Informing employees about how promotion and
transfer decisions are made should help them understand how
performance and experience contribute to these decisions.

Job Rotation

Young managers may be moved to new jobs periodically
as a way of exposing them to different elements of the business.
This approach assumes that generalists are better managers than
specialists. One method of job rotation is to provide a young
manager experience in different jobs within a single department. The assumption here is that it is important to develop expertise within a single department (which may have many varied
jobs) before moving into other departments. Movement between departments can be delayed until the individual reaches
middle management. The length of time on each job assignment
may vary from several months to a year or more. The person
should not simply observe but should actually work on the job
and be expected to make a contribution to the unit. The sponsoring unit (the person's original department) should agree to
take the individual back, unless the individual agrees with another unit to assume sponsorship. The individual's salary should
be paid by the unit in which he or she is working, especially if
the assignment is for more than four or five months.

Developing a Company Philosophy
of Early-Career Management Development

The programs, policies, and procedures for the development of young managers depend on the answers to the basic
questions discussed in Chapter Seven. These concern companies' policies with respect to treating employees as corporate
assets, developing generalists versus specialists (within departments and in the company at large), delegating control over promotion and transfer decisions, depending on promotion from
within to fill vacancies, expecting bosses to be responsible for
assisting subordinates in career planning, having a comprehensive manager-development program that encompasses many career development components versus separate programs operated on an as-needed basis, identifying high-potential employees
and putting them on a separate, fast-track advancement program, and designating specific career paths. (See Chapter Seven
for a detailed discussion of these basic questions.)

Answers will suggest the type of development programs
required for young managers. At one extreme, a company may
believe in hiring the most able and highly motivated young managers, treating them as corporate assets for the future, training
them as generalists, moving them between departments every
twelve to eighteen months, distinguishing them as high-potential managers different both from managers in specialist positions and from those who are up from the ranks, and rapidly
promoting those who continue to demonstrate high potential.
Such policies, as explained in Chapter Seven, are difficult to
maintain in times of organizational change and economic constraints. Such development policies require commitment at the
highest levels of a company if they are to be maintained over
the long run.

At the other extreme is the company that treats young
managers as resources for meeting current business needs, does
not move people between departments, and discourages development-oriented transfers within departments. The assumption
of this company is that the best people will be promoted when
vacancies arise; little attention is given to preparing young man-

agers for higher-level positions. Such policies are likely to lead to complacency; they are scarcely affected by organizational change. With this scenario, bosses probably have to learn to deal with young managers who are not highly involved in their work, not advancement- or achievement-oriented, do not have a strong sense of career identity, are not committed to the company's goals (except as their own job security may be affected), depend on others for emotional support, and do not have high self-concepts with respect to work.

A company that has a high-potential development program may also want to have a standard career program for managers who are competent performers but do not have the potential or motivation for rapid advancement. The standard career track gives them opportunities for promotion and transfer, but not at a rapid pace. The components of such a program were reviewed in Chapter Six.

If a company offers two such programs, which program should a person be in? This question suggests the need for a preliminary program to screen young managers. In some cases, it may be possible to identify high-potential managers when they are hired and put them directly into the high-potential program. In many cases, however, it may not be possible to make that determination right away. Also, the first year with the company is a time for becoming acclimated to the company's policies and procedures and for learning the work. Appendix A of Chapter Six outlined a program for developing new managers. The career development activities reviewed above could be integrated into the comprehensive programs discussed in Chapter Six or could exist alongside them as support services.

Anticipated Effects of Manager-Development Programs on Career Motivation, and Estimates of the Costs and Benefits of These Programs

Table 5 lists the programs discussed above and suggests the career motivation domains likely to be affected by each program. The table also indicates an estimate of the overall costs and benefits of each program. These judgments of costs and

Table 5. Anticipated Effects of Early-Career Development Programs on Career Motivation, and Estimated Costs and Benefits.

| | Career Motivation Domains | | | Estimated | |
Programs	Career Identity	Career Insight	Career Resilience	Cost[a]	Benefit[a]
Focus on the Individual					
Recruitment		X	X	L	H
Selection		X	X	L–M	H
Realistic Job Previews		X		L	H
Orientation and Awareness Training		X		M	M
Motivation Assessment					
Career Motivation Assessment Center		X	X	H	H
Self-Assessment Workbooks and Workshops		X	X	L–M	L–M
Motivation Awareness Training		X		M	M
Career Counseling		X		H	L–M
Focus on the Situation					
Supervisor Training	X	X		M	M–H
Job Redesign	X		X	L–M	M–H
Leadership Style	X	X	X	M	M–H
Goal Setting		X		L	H
Performance Appraisal		X	X	L	L–H
Feedback		X	X	L	M–H
Boss as Counselor or Coach	X	X		L–M	L–M
Reinforcement		X	X	L	H

Focus on Company Policies and Programs

Rewarding Bosses for Developing Young Managers	X	X	X	L	H
Giving the Boss Discretion over Important Career Outcomes	X	X	X	L	H
Career Paths	X	X		L	L–M
Succession Planning	X	X		L	M
Job-Matching Systems	X	X		H	L
Job Posting	X	X		L	L–M
A Formalized Sponsor or Mentor Program	X			L	L–M
Appraisal of Potential					
Assessment Centers	X	X	X	H	H
Supervisor Ratings	X	X	X	L	L–M
Careers Center	X	X		L	L
Communicating Promotion and Transfer Policies	X	X		L	M
Job Rotation	X		X	H	H
Developing a Company Philosophy of Early-Career Management Development	X			L	H

Components of a Comprehensive Program

Assignment to a Boss Who Is a Good Role Model and Concerned with a Young Manager's Development	X		X	L	H
Skip-Level Reporting	X	X		L	M–H
Meeting with Fellow Young Managers	X	X		L	M
Meeting with Top Executives about Career Issues and Sitting in on Higher-Level Meetings	X			L	L–M
Opportunities for Exposure to Top Executives (for example, Giving Presentations)	X	X	X	L–M	M–H
Evaluation after First Year (High Risk/High Reward)	X	X	X	M–H	M–H
Special Assignments that Grow in Responsibility over Time	X	X	X	L	H
Company Coordinator	X			M	M

[a]L = Low; M = Moderate; H = High

benefits are not just financial but also psychological. Moreover, the costs and benefits refer to those incurred by both the individual and the organization.

Another point to remember is that the costs and benefits (as well as effects on motivation) are likely to vary for a given program, depending on how it is conceptualized and implemented. For example, a job redesign effort to increase job challenge may entail a very simple, inexpensive change that makes the job much more meaningful. Again, it may require substantial changes in work methods and procedures for employees on several different jobs. Redesigning one person's job to make it more challenging may make another person's job less meaningful; a cost may be incurred that will not be immediately evident.

Another consideration is that the programs listed in Table 5 are not independent. For instance, feedback is an important part of performance appraisal and assessment. Moreover, the programs do not operate in isolation. For example, effective job redesign to increase challenge requires a conducive environment —for example, a supportive boss. As another example, the effects of leadership training depend on the leader. Similarly, the elements of good management (goal setting, performance appraisal, feedback, reinforcement) depend on how they are implemented by the boss. This idea is incorporated into the manager-development guidelines as well as into the discussion of leadership style, above, which lists various suggestions for supervisors who want to enhance career motivation.

Some programs in Table 5 are likely to affect more than one domain of career motivation. For instance, assignment to a boss who is a good role model and concerned with a young manager's development could have a pervasive effect on career motivation because the boss influences the subordinate in many ways. The boss determines the nature of the subordinate's work (for example, the amount of challenge and responsibility), the information that the subordinate has about career opportunities in the company, and the type and extent of reinforcement that the subordinate receives. Many of the programs have impacts on career insight because they provide information about the individual and/or help the individual understand the political and social environment. Table 5 emphasizes the importance of the boss's role and of the company's policies in affecting that role. Bosses can be more effective if they have discretion over important career outcomes and if they are rewarded for developing young managers.

Table 5 assumes that a program is implemented under fairly optimal conditions. The table indicates that many programs are likely to have low costs and high benefits. Such programs include aggressive recruiting; selecting candidates on the basis of career motivation as well as ability; realistic job previews; job redesign; goal setting; performance appraisal; feedback; proper use of reinforcement; establishing and communicating company policies regarding performance appraisal, promotion, and development; assigning young managers to effective role models; and giving young managers special assignments. Several programs have high estimated costs and high benefits. These include assessment centers for evaluating managerial abilities and potential for advancement, the career motivation assessment center, job rotation, and high-risk/high-reward programs for high-potential managers. While the costs of operating these programs may be very high and the logistics difficult, they are likely to have substantial long-term benefits that far outweigh their costs. The programs may affect the entire climate of the organization, the quality of work life experienced by the employees, and the long-term strength of the organization.

A number of programs are expected to have low costs as well as low benefits. These include offering career paths, job posting, training bosses as counselors, formal mentor or sponsor programs, a careers center, supervisory ratings of potential, and meetings with top executives.

Table 5 also shows one program that should probably be avoided because of its high cost and low benefit: the job-matching system. As mentioned earlier, experience has shown that such programs often do not operate as intended. Another program with potentially high cost and low to moderate benefit is career counseling. Counseling is probably beneficial for a few individuals, but it probably works best in conjunction with such programs as a career motivation assessment center, an assessment center to evaluate managerial potential, job rotation, and efforts to communicate promotion and transfer policies.

The above judgments need to be tested. Look over Table 5, and consider what would be required for a particular program or technique to affect a domain of career motivation.

Conclusions and Recommendations

Human resources programs that deal with career development are often implemented solely because there is some feeling that they are needed; little attention is given to their costs relative to their benefits. Furthermore, there are no sound criteria for evaluating their benefits. This chapter has considered the costs and benefits of almost forty programs or approaches to early-career manager development. It has also considered the impacts of these programs on career identity, career insight, and career resilience, the three major elements of career motivation. The programs with the presumed lowest costs and highest benefits do not focus on such career planning and development efforts as career paths, succession planning, job matching, and mentoring; rather, they are based on sound management principles—realistic job previews, enthusiastic recruitment, valid selection methods, job challenge, goal setting, thorough and accurate performance appraisals, feedback, and proper reinforcement. Bosses should be rewarded for developing young managers and should have discretion over such important outcomes as decisions about which subordinates are promotable. They should also have input into who is actually promoted. The company should develop a clear philosophy of early-career development, communicate this philosophy, and maintain it consistently. Certain programs that are particularly desirable for high-potential managers include special assignments that grow in responsibility over time; assignment to bosses who are good role models and are concerned with young managers' development; and periodic meetings with fellow young managers to compare career goals and progress.

Accurate assessment of advancement potential is a cornerstone of successful career development. Before determining potential for advancement, however, it makes sense to determine potential for development. That is, the young manager must learn about his or her strengths and weaknesses and develop an appropriate sense of self-esteem and independence before establishing a career direction. Therefore, some type of career motivation assessment, which may be partly self-administered with computerized scoring and feedback, should be developed. Periodic evaluation and feedback are important for developing a sense of insight, competence, and realistic desire for advancement. Changing jobs within or between departments is also desirable for understanding the corporate environment, improving one's skills and abilities, and developing involvement with the work and loyalty to the company.

Chapter Six recommended three early-career manager development programs: the first year in management; a standard development program; and a high-potential development program. The latter two programs establish two early-career tracks, but they would be part of a comprehensive corporate human resources development program that continues at higher levels of management and includes one set of programs and policies for the assessment, development, and promotion of middle-level managers and another set of programs for top managers and executives. A person's movement through these programs is triggered by different events in his or her career. For example, promotion to the first level initiates the individual's participation in the first-year-in-management program. High performance and potential ratings from one's supervisor may result in being sent to an assessment center for additional evaluation of advancement potential. For those on a standard career development program, the annual supervisory appraisal is also a time for evaluating eligibility for the high-potential program. The appendixes in Chapter Six review the features of these three programs, including their goals, developmental components, and operation.

This chapter has emphasized the importance of the supervisor in affecting subordinates' career motivation. The next chapter gives some examples from our study of ECHO and DYNAMO. The examples from these two companies allow us to consider the role of the boss in two different settings with different philosophies of manager development.

9

✳ ✳ ✳ ✳ ✳

The Boss's Role
in Developing Managers

The boss can make a big difference in the opportunities available to the employee and in the employee's outlook on career opportunities. The boss plays a major role in structuring the situational conditions that generate career resilience, career insight, and career identity. Many of the situational factors described in the preceding chapters are under the boss's control. Subordinates' career resilience may be influenced by how much control the boss gives them over their work goals and work methods, the amount of input they have in making decisions affecting their own careers, the extent to which the boss encourages them to take risks, the competitive atmosphere in the department, and the general relationship between supervisor and subordinates. Career insight is tied to the accuracy and clarity of feedback subordinates receive from the boss, the extent to which the boss encourages subordinates to set career goals, and the extent to which subordinates are informed about different career paths open to them. Career identity is affected by how the boss structures subordinates' jobs, recognizes subordinates' good performance, provides opportunities for advancement, and gives able subordinates opportunities to demonstrate their leadership skills.

This chapter examines how several bosses perceived their roles in manager development. The cases include bosses who were concerned about their subordinates' development as managers, as well as bosses who were much less concerned about it. One case demonstrates that the presence of a well-structured manager-development program, such as the one at DYNAMO, does not necessarily mean that the boss will be an enlightened proponent of manager development. Similarly, the absence of such a program, as at ECHO, does not necessarily mean that the boss ignores subordinates' career development; on the contrary, there were cases of ECHO bosses who cared about their subordinates' development and, in fact, fought departmental policies so as to further subordinates' career progress.

There was a major difference between bosses in the two companies, however. At DYNAMO, college graduates hired into management were treated as corporate resources to be developed for the future. At ECHO, which did not have a manager-development program, most bosses viewed recent college graduates in the same way they viewed their other subordinates: All managers were viewed simply as meeting the current needs of the business, and there was little concern for their development to meet future business needs.

Bucking the System at ECHO

John Gilligan, a second-level manager in the construction department, had some definite ideas about manager development. After twenty-one years with the company, he was given his first opportunity to supervise. He had requested a transfer to his present position to try to implement his ideas for manager development. He had given development much thought, and he had some opinions about how it should occur and what the role of a boss should be. Since taking this job, two and a half months earlier, he had tried to put his philosophy of development into effect. His approach was that work should be fun. He believed that his job was not to produce, but to help his subordinates produce, and he thought their work should be challenging, interesting, and important. Everyone had some routine work to do, but he felt it should not be a major part of the individual's assignment. While he believed in enriching subordinates' jobs, he was a hardliner when it came to meeting performance objectives. This attitude was necessary in a department that measured performance on several quantifiable indices. Nevertheless, he soon had several run-ins with his boss and with others about what his proper role should be and how his subordinates should behave.

John thought that he managed people differently from the other second-level managers in the department. He realized that he could not treat all his subordinates equally because they had different levels of competence. He believed in giving the work to the workers. He believed in positive feedback and also in being as candid as possible. John's strategy was to run his "show" with as much enjoyment and fulfillment as possible. He felt this was especially important because there were few opportunities for promotion in the company. "If you can't make the most of your present job, then you are in trouble," he said.

John was in a department that showed little concern for the development of its people. Many managers in his group would have loved to have different jobs, but the department was reluctant to transfer them for fear that the workload would increase and that there would not be enough trained people. It was hard to transfer to another department, and movement within the department was also difficult. The current work of the department was considered more important than moving people from job to job for their development. Bosses felt that such training would be costly and would cut down on productivity.

John Gilligan disagreed. He had initiated several job moves for himself in the department and wanted to help his subordinates move as well, but since movement was difficult, he felt that his subordinates could increase their skills and responsibilities in their present jobs. John's boss was concerned only with meeting performance objectives; and, of course, John also realized that performance was crucial. But John was willing to go out on a limb for his subordinates. He delegated work and increased subordinates' responsibilities. Higher management seemed to feel that any change from the status quo was a threat. John saw his actions as risky, but at this stage of his career he felt that he did not have much to lose. He knew that additional promotions for him were unlikely and that he must make the most of remaining at his current level.

John's attitude stemmed at least in part from a need to do something meaningful and from a feeling that he must initiate his own job challenge because it would not come from his supervisors. He also felt an obligation to the people who worked for him. He reasoned that they felt the same as he did about their jobs: If he was bored with his job, they were also likely to be bored; if he felt that his talents were not properly utilized, then they probably felt the same way. John wanted to turn the situation around, even if it meant bucking the system in his department.

A few days before John was interviewed, a subordinate told him that the morale in the group had improved considerably since he had taken over. This comment made him feel good. He had shown that he was willing to share his knowledge and get involved in his subordinates' problems, but at the same time he gave them the freedom to run their own jobs. One of John's subordinates told us this was the first time in over a year that she had felt she was important and that she was accomplishing something for herself and the company. Spurred by John's encouragement, she began to formulate a strategy for obtaining a transfer.

John helped his subordinates recognize what had dawned on him many years earlier: Career planning and development mean nothing if the department is not responsive. He carefully structured his own opportunities and realized that his career progress would be limited to making his present job more exciting. He tried to bring the same job excitement to his subordinates by encouraging their individual contributions and personal growth and by showing his concern for them. He hoped that after he had demonstrated to his supervisors that his group was doing good work under his leadership, he would have more power to restructure their jobs, to give more responsibility to those who could handle it, and to help the most able and motivated managers advance.

Manager Development in the Marketing Department

The goal of ECHO's marketing department for developing its people was to train marketing professionals. The department wanted its people to develop their selling skills and hoped that they would stay in sales for most of if not their entire careers. A sales job at ECHO required considerable technical and managerial expertise in addition to the communication skills and aggressiveness needed for effective selling. Some areas of sales dealt with specialized products and services, which were often custom-designed.

Dorothy Miles was a second-level manager in ECHO's marketing department, with six people reporting to her. Her subordinates worked closely with customers to assess their needs and design services. They began working with clients by doing a needs assessment. This step was followed by presenting the results, providing a cost-benefit analysis for services recommended, and implementing the services if the sale was made. Dorothy felt that her department was in the limelight. Her subordinates' jobs were as much glamour positions as anything in the company could be. The job required a range of skills and personality characteristics. The first-level position, called corporate account executive, required patience and judgment. The account executive had to know how much time to spend with the client and understand the client's needs as well as those of the company. The department was developing a reputation for providing a valuable service and for not trying to sell equipment clients did not need.

Dorothy's approach to the development of her subordinates was to concentrate on increasing their skills and identifying their potential. Since marketing was a growing area of the company, there were likely to be many opportunities for transfer and promotion for those who did well. When Dorothy had first been assigned to the position, about a year before, she had begun by identifying areas important to the job. She developed an evaluation system based on a list of job requirements. She observed her subordinates on the job, recorded the frequency with which they met different requirements, and graded each individual on each requirement in comparison to the rest of the group. She held frequent coaching sessions with her subordinates to discuss their performance and suggest ways to improve. If a subordinate needed attention, she believed it was important to do something immediately. It was also important, she felt, to provide a quantitative description of the person's behavior. She encouraged her boss and their bosses to go out with her subordinates on client contacts. She wanted her supervisors to know the people in her group, the problems they faced, and their abilities to solve problems. She recognized that, to broaden their skills, some of her subordinates might want to change jobs in the future. Since the department was fairly new and most of her subordinates were new to this type of work, however, her primary emphasis was on building the skills relevant to their jobs rather than on preparing them for other jobs in the marketing department or in other departments.

Dorothy's attention to her subordinates' development dealt primarily with evaluation and feedback, which were crucial, given the early stage of development of her department and her people. She recognized that, later, other elements might be more important, such as preparing people for transfer and promotion. Dorothy's management style, in terms of the domains we have been discussing, was aimed at supporting career resilience through both positive reinforcement and opportunities for autonomy, achievement, and creativity. She frequently sent her people to training courses and brought in experts to give them pointers. She encouraged her people to take risks and provided constructive feedback.

Stick-to-the-Rules Management

One boss in ECHO's accounting department believed in sticking to the rules, no matter what. Bob Richards felt that he should be on call twenty-four hours a day and that his job was vital to the business, even if his contribution was indirect. He felt that young managers were paid handsomely and that the company deserved their loyalty. In his opinion, the work they did was not worth the money they were paid. Bob even believed that his subordinates worked best when they were united on an issue—against him. He realized that they were not pleased with his leadership, but he talked about having an open-door policy and open lines of communication. Chances are, though, that his behavior was inconsistent. Bob admitted that his subordinates were his greatest source of stress. He was frustrated when they did not communicate with him. He realized that several of them disliked their jobs and wanted transfers; but, since he had been in the same position for the last six years, he believed that job movement was unimportant. His focus was on getting the job done; he had no interest in manager development. His authoritarian leadership style and his tendency to give little feedback, whether positive or negative, created considerable stress among his subordinates.

The Impact of Departmental Policy

As mentioned in Chapter Five, ECHO tried to develop specialists, rather than generalists who could move from department to department. The reason for this policy was that the departments were run almost in isolation from one another. Creating specialists seemed to lock people into assignments. Each department had so much invested in its people that it could not afford to release them, or so top management believed.

Joe Morris, a boss in the engineering department, complained that he had been on his present assignment for eight years. Joe had developed and managed his job in such a way that no one else could take it over. The department did occasionally transfer people, but such change occurred almost overnight; there was no planning to prepare people for it. Joe believed that high-caliber people should be moved through the business, with career paths mapped out in advance. Although this procedure had not been followed in his department, the department had hired an outside consultant to conduct meetings with managers about their career development and work problems. Unfortunately, there was no mechanism to bring about the changes recommended in these group discussions, partly because there was no one in the department who had responsibility for the career development of people within it.

Joe had had no input to his job assignments during his career, and his subordinates were likely to have just as little influence over their careers. He saw nothing he could do to improve the situation for them. He could recommend people for changes in assignments, but he knew that in most cases such recommendations would fall on deaf ears. Since the department had made an effort to keep its size down, people were not replaced when they retired. As a result, the span of control (the number of people reporting to one boss) had increased for many supervisors.

While Joe would have liked to spend more time with his subordinates on their career development, he had a tough time meeting his objectives. He regretted that the career development of his subordinates was not something for which he was evaluated and rewarded. He claimed that if subordinate development had been part of his performance appraisal, he would have spent more time working with his people. He knew that it would be difficult to move subordinates into jobs more in line with their career interests. He realized that he could change the nature of their work and give them more responsibility and opportunities to make decisions. Unlike John Gilligan, however, he did nothing about this realization.

Another boss in the engineering department, Frank Geer, complained that he was being transferred the next day to another job at a remote location. His current boss advised him that he would continue to be responsible for his present job until they found a replacement, while his new boss advised him that he would be responsible for his new position immediately. While he tried to reason with his new supervisor, his arguments were to no avail. Frank's strategy was simply to leave his present position and move to the new one immediately.

Frank described the experience of a young manager who had come into his unit. First he made sure that the manager attended the necessary training courses, then he put the manager into a position with the same responsibilities as other managers who had been on the job for many years. The more the young manager accomplished, the more Frank expected of him, but he could not promise the young manager that his good performance and potential would be rewarded by advancement. According to Frank, the environment in the department was not so much stressful as it was dulling. Young managers were well paid, and the job market was such that there were few opportunities outside the company, and so they were stuck.

Managing Subordinates
in a Manager-Development Program

Chapter Five described DYNAMO's manager-development program. An important element of the program was that it trained generalists. The young first-level managers were moved from department to department every twelve to eighteen months to learn different elements of the business. For their first assignments, they reported to third-level managers. The boss's job was to evaluate the potential of the recruit for moving to higher levels of the company. After the first year, the boss made the decision of whether the subordinate should stay with the company or be terminated. Retention implied that the subordinate had potential to advance to at least third level.

For the second and third job assignments, young managers reported to second-level managers. The first assignment was a special position, in that the subordinate was given different projects and often had considerable visibility to higher-level managers, but the next positions were more mundane. Responsibility increased, however. The young managers were often placed in jobs supervising eight to ten nonmanagement people, who had worked for the company twenty to thirty years. The young managers knew that once they had proved themselves, there would be opportunities to move on.

One participant in the study, who was very successful in many job assignments and had been promoted to second level after four years, was Deborah Harley. (Her case was described in Chapter Seven.) Her current boss, Carl Schwartz, was a third-level manager in his mid-thirties and a former participant in the manager-development program. He described the program as giving young managers crucial assignments to prepare them for higher levels. They were moved from job to job so that they would learn the business. This movement was difficult, however, in the current stagnant economy. With little growth, the trainees became frustrated and lost their desire to advance. Carl felt that second- and third-level managers did not take enough risks for their trainees. He wished that the bosses could be evaluated on how much attention they gave to developing their people. (The same point was made by a boss in ECHO, as noted above.)

Carl evaluated Deborah's performance as excellent, and he mentioned that he had gone out on a limb to secure her promotion. As one of his goals, he had decided that he would promote at least two trainees during the year, and Deborah was a beneficiary. Carl had set this goal for himself because he believed that if a young manager had high potential and the program promised rapid advancement, then advancement opportunities should be created. Carl believed that some trainees felt that the company was in business for the sole purpose of their development. While he wanted to discourage this attitude, his attitude was that the manager-development program contributed to the continued vitality and viability of the company.

Carl believed that it was important for trainees to have jobs on the operations side of the business. Many of the trainees preferred low-risk staff jobs or rotations to corporate headquarters. Deborah's job experiences had been primarily in the field, and so she was a "diamond in the rough." Carl encouraged his trainees to discover when it would be time for them to change jobs and the types of jobs that would be good for them. He felt that such encouragement was the mark of a good manager. Trainees influenced their own careers through their bosses. A boss could be very helpful in recommending a trainee, but securing a promotion required a higher-level manager.

Carl stated that he had changed his management style within the last few months because performance in his department had improved and his subordinates did not require so much close supervision now. He tried to show that he could be replaced, because he hoped to move on himself. He felt that his unit was the toughest in the company; they had a number of problems, and the work was highly visible. He mentioned that Deborah accepted the pressure without question and seemed to be the best performer in the group.

As another example, Bev Martin was a young second-level boss at DYNAMO. She gave the impression that self-doubt never entered her mind. She stated that she was very concerned with her subordinates' career development. She viewed herself as a mentor to her high-potential subordinates. She cared about their futures and was willing to discuss their careers with them. She was aware of her subordinates' goals and their family situations. She tried to introduce them to people who could be important to their careers and tried to let others see their work. She gave them as wide a background as possible by giving them special assignments that required a variety of skills. Bev believed that a first-level manager's job assignment is not as important as the boss's style of management. One of the advantages of the manager-development program was that it gave young managers a sequence of job assignments and, in the process, exposed them to different bosses who had different styles of management. The young managers could observe these different styles and develop styles of their own.

Bev believed in the value of social rewards, such as praising people in front of others and helping them develop reputations as excellent performers. Some management trainees got reputations as people bosses wanted to have working for them. She stated that she expected as much work from a subordinate as a subordinate could give her. She thought that people often misused their time, working overtime just to impress others. Bev thought that this was undesirable and that someone had to break the mold.

Bev believed that most young DYNAMO managers found their jobs meaningful. An advantage of being able to move from job to job was that even if management trainees had positions they disliked, they could put up with them for a year or so, knowing that other jobs were in the offing. The management trainees had recourse to higher levels if they were dissatisfied with job assignments. First-level managers thought nothing of going over their bosses to talk with third-level or even higher managers. Many management trainees knew corporate officers quite well. Many managers who were not in the development program resented the trainees; there was a halo that went along with being a participant. Top management recognized that the trainees were the future leaders of the business and valued the program highly.

In general, Bev felt that there was pride in being part of the manager-development program. The participants attended meetings, and they often knew what was happening in the company before other people did. Their performance was closely followed, and there was a thick job folder about each trainee. Bev mentioned that she was not a trainee, since she had been hired as an accountant, considered to be a specialized position. Nevertheless, she had changed departments several times and was now considered a general manager. She used her own experiences as evidence that being a member of the development program was not required for movement and advancement in the company, but she emphasized that young managers who were part of the program had many more career opportunities open to them than managers who were not participants.

Will the Boss Be Supportive?

Mal Wilcox, a third-level boss at DYNAMO, seemed tough-minded and callous. He appeared to be exactly as one subordinate had labeled him: insensitive. A former patricipant in the manager-development program, Mal stated that he motivated his subordinates by giving them responsibility for particular assignments. He noted that because of many changes in the company, the work was becoming unstructured, and it was necessary for the management trainee to impose a structure. He was much more concerned that his subordinates get their work done than that they be exposed to higher-level managers. Mal noted that many management trainees in the past had been promoted to higher organizational levels, even though they had not deserved promotion. Moreover, he felt that many average performers had been kept in the program but should have been dismissed.

Mal felt that opportunities were not handouts to trainees; rather, opportunities were insights that trainees got by doing their jobs. For instance, if a trainee discovered a way to save the company money, the trainee got a "brownie point." Mal felt that some trainees did not dig into their jobs enough to acquire the basic understanding needed to do their jobs. This was a problem, because the development program attempted to move people into new assignments every twelve to eighteen months.

Mal viewed himself as a resource for his subordinates. He tried to give them positive and negative feedback. He looked for assignments that he hoped would lead to improvement in their behavior. He described how he had asked one subordinate to give a presentation before a vice-president. Mal provided no coaching beforehand, and the young manager did a poor job. After the presentation, Mal criticized her style. The subordinate felt that this was an important learning experience, but that Mal could have helped her in a more constructive way by coaching her before the presentation.

Teresa Cole was another second-level boss at DYNAMO. She described her management views as avant-garde, although a certain resentment seemed to inform her views. Nevertheless, her perspective revealed some real problems with the manager-development program.

Teresa stated that the management trainees at DYNAMO were supposed to have exceptional skills, but that, in her mind, they did not. Teresa admitted, however, that she was not an easy boss to work for. She had a negative opinion of the manager-development program. Buzz words like *visibility* and *mentoring*, she felt, were used by the trainees meaninglessly. The management trainees did not understand the risks of exposure; they believed that if they gave presentations to vice-presidents, the vice-presidents would automatically recognize their skills and put them on a fast track upward. The trainees put more emphasis on politics and exposure than on learning and working. There was no understanding of team effort; the trainees felt that whatever they did must be good. They wanted to be

protected and get the credit. They emphasized their own careers, not their potential contributions to the company. They
did not recognize the real centers of information and power.
The trainees expected everything to come their way, without
their having to gain a broad overview of the business. They
adopted the attitude that customers and business needs got in
the way of their careers. The norm of dedication to service was
waning; many young managers seemed to avoid field experience. If the trainees were truly outstanding, Teresa believed,
then no job would seem like a threat to them.

Teresa felt that some other bosses treated trainees as
though their development mattered more than getting the work
done. Unlike Teresa, these bosses tended to be former trainees
themselves. Teresa believed that young managers were often
promoted only because it was supposed to be time for them to
be promoted. She told of being promised that she would be
promoted, but the promotion never materialized. She also said
that it was almost impossible to fire poorly performing managers who were part of the development program. She described
an Ivy League college graduate who, in her opinion, had demonstrated total lack of concern for the business, yet she had
been unable to fire him. Top-level managers in the company
moved him to a new and better position, and she was left where
she was.

Teresa believed that young managers who were not
trainees were more interested in developing their current work
because they would be staying in it longer. Trainees knew that
they would be transferred, and this knowledge generated mini-
mal interest in developing expertise. There were actually few
promotional opportunities in the company at the time, but
bosses of trainees still encouraged them to seek promotion because they did not want the trainees to lose motivation. Teresa
mentioned that in trying to fill a vacancy a few months before,
she had interviewed a number of first-level people to interest
them in transferring to her group. She was angry that many of
them had asked about access to the third-level manager, totally
disregarding her authority in the unit. In her department, third-
level managers had no time for trainees, she stated. Teresa

wished that trainees would exhibit more initiative and creativity in doing their work. Most of their energy seemed to be taken up in discussing and worrying about their career prospects. She felt that the trainees did not take risks because they did not want to do anything that was bad politically. As a result, they tended to be passive managers.

Conclusions and Recommendations
for Assessing Development Support

While ECHO did not have a manager-development program, some bosses in that company were very concerned about their subordinates' career development. At DYNAMO, which had a strong program, some bosses were alienated by the program and felt it was counterproductive. In general, these bosses were the exceptions. ECHO bosses tended to be unconcerned about their subordinates' careers and were more concerned about whether they were getting their work done. At DYNAMO, it was important for subordinates to do good work, but emphasis was also placed on developing their potential for advancement. As stated before, the distinction seemed to be between treating young managers as persons simply meeting current business needs (ECHO's philosophy) versus treating young managers as corporate resources being prepared for middle management, in addition to meeting current business needs (DYNAMO's philosophy).

One assumption behind the manager-development program at DYNAMO was that advancement opportunities exist, but a downturn in the economy and other changes in the business had decreased the number of opportunities available. Therefore, the expectations of the young managers for rapid advancement were not being met. This circumstance generated some hostility toward the company. At ECHO, where such expectations were low to begin with, the young managers were more apathetic about the lack of advancement prospects. Nevertheless, at both companies the young managers wanted interesting, challenging assignments. The reaction was different at each company, however. At DYNAMO, when assignments became dull and young managers felt they were not learning anything, they would go to their bosses or higher to complain. At ECHO, feelings of underutilization were prevalent, but young managers felt they had few opportunities to change the situation. Most ECHO bosses simply did not think about how to make subordinates' jobs more challenging and rewarding, while such thinking was part of career development at DYNAMO; it was especially important to the young manager's first year in the company, when the boss was supposed to give the young manager several important job assignments.

ECHO bosses who wanted to were able to create positive work environments. This effort made it more reasonable for subordinates to think about career development within the limits of the organization. Some bosses at DYNAMO created negative environments for management trainees. The intention of the development program was to provide support for career development and encourage involvement through challenging assignments and opportunities for job movement. While this philosophy was difficult to maintain as opportunities declined, the company felt it was crucial to support the program if there was to be sufficient talent for the future at middle and higher levels of management. The bosses learned how to enhance their subordinates' development under these conditions, although some bosses felt there was too much emphasis on development.

Now consider some of the following questions about your company and the bosses you know (or about your own behavior as a boss). (These questions parallel the manager-development guidelines in Chapter Six.)

To what extent do bosses, or to what extent do I . . .

- give subordinates positive reinforcement for good work?
- provide opportunities for achievement?
- encourage innovation?
- de-emphasize negative consequences of failure?
- enhance group cohesiveness?
- show concern about subordinates' personal welfare?
- encourage goal setting for job and career?
- provide information about career opportunities?

- give performance feedback to subordinates?
- create challenging jobs?
- encourage participation in professional activities?
- provide opportunities for promotion?
- give subordinates a chance to try out leadership roles?

To what extent does the company . . .

- give supervisors discretion in rewarding subordinates' good performance (for example, with merit pay increases)?
- allow redesigning of jobs?
- encourage innovation (for example, by welcoming changes for improved efficiency)?
- accept occasional failures?
- reward cooperative behavior and use project task forces requiring collaborative effort?
- show concern for the individual (for example, in benefits, time off for personal reasons)?
- provide mechanisms for goal setting?
- disseminate information about career opportunities?
- generate measures of performance and feed them back to employees?
- increase levels of responsibility?
- provide financial support for involvement in professional activities?
- create promotional opportunities and transfers to more meaningful, responsible assignments?
- expect managers to act as leaders, to describe what needs to be done, and to do it?

Now, consider the congruence between the boss and the company. The boss's philosophy of manager development and the company's policies and procedures are all important to manager development. Ideally, they work in tandem to enhance career motivation. When the company does not support career development, however, bosses can do a great deal to create more favorable work climates, as John Gilligan tried to do at ECHO. Nevertheless, bosses cannot compensate entirely, since many important resources and rewards, such as promotion and transfer opportunities, are not under their control. Several of the examples from DYNAMO also indicate that bosses are not always supportive of the company's policies and programs.

The company's stance toward manager development is a matter of business need, historical circumstances, economic conditions, and the leadership styles and attitudes of top executives. Factors such as these may be grouped under the label *organizational culture*. The culture is not easily changed, but bosses' attitudes can be controlled through selection, socialization, training, role models, and so on. The next chapter considers training courses as a resource for developing managerial and leadership skills and, in the process, enhancing career motivation.

10

❋ ❋ ❋ ❋ ❋

Training Programs
for Developing Management
Skills and Leadership

Broadly speaking, career development may be viewed as a sequence of job assignments, training courses, and other activities aimed at achieving career goals. Training refers to acquiring the skills needed to do our jobs and move into new jobs at the same level or at higher levels of the organization. Training minimizes and, in some cases, overcomes our weaknesses. In addition, training enhances our strengths. It rarely reverses weaknesses, and it rarely builds new strengths. Therefore, training requires understanding ourselves and seeking experiences that enhance our abilities, meet our needs, and help us to accomplish our goals. Thus, training is as much the responsibility of the individual as it is the responsibility of the organization. We must determine what experiences we need and want, and then we must get the most out of these experiences.

Many organizations offer courses, tuition aid, and special programs (for example, workshops and guest lectures at department meetings) to keep managers up to date with current ideas and trends in how to manage better. Supervisors are expected to coach new subordinates and guide the careers of more experienced subordinates. In this sense, the organization and the boss provide the resources and create the environment for learning and growth. The individual's responsibility is to take advantage of these resources.

This chapter covers two types of management training: (1) skill and knowledge training, and (2) leadership training. Skill and knowledge training enables the manager to supervise others. Supervision includes directing and coordinating work. It involves knowing how, when, and to what extent it is necessary to structure subordinates' work, design meaningful jobs for them, involve them in goal setting, give them responsibility, and give them feedback on their performance. It also requires developing a supportive work climate. Leadership training involves learning about creating and communicating a vision of the future, coaching subordinates, facilitating their work, and building networks and coalitions of people in other departments. It also involves learning how to deal with ambiguity and adapt to change.

Managers vary in the degree to which they are enablers (applying managerial skills and knowledge) and leaders. To the extent that the work environment is complex and changing and requires initiative and independent action, the manager must be a leader to be successful. Consequently, managers do not have to be at the top of the organizational ladder to be leaders. To a certain degree, every manager is a leader. Enabling and leading are both important roles. The question we must ask ourselves is "To what degree do we need to become better enablers and leaders?"

Skill and Knowledge Training

Types of Skills. Just as managing is not one profession or one role, there is not a single set of managerial skills that are important under all conditions. Traditionally, management is thought of as organizing, directing, planning, and controlling the work of subordinates. Administering, monitoring, communicating, evaluating, decision making, problem solving, resolving conflict, and other functions also come to mind. These functions suggest a host of skills.

Developability. Some skills are more easily developed than others. By the time we begin our careers, certain individual characteristics have been established (London and Stumpf, 1982). These include intelligence, decision making, and perhaps the ability to work with others. For instance, recent research (Streufert, cited in Goleman, 1984) into the mental processes that are crucial to the world of work suggest that most successful corporate leaders think in a style notable for its complexity. It does not depend on measured intelligence but is an approach to decision making called *cognitive complexity.* It is the ability to plan strategically without being locked into one course of events, the capacity to acquire ample information for decision making without being overwhelmed, and the ability to grasp relationships between rapidly changing events. It is "the mental capacity, the temperament, and the inclination to confront complexities even in small problems" (Goleman, 1984). People without this capacity are common; according to Goleman, "They see problems in isolation from each other, and often rigidly hold to a single overriding goal." Cognitive complexity is particularly important to the highest levels of management.

A study of more than two thousand managers identified such important managerial competencies as being able to spot hidden patterns in an array of facts and having a sense of spontaneity in self-expression (Boyatzis, 1982). Such skills are not simply learned on the job; they are "intertwined with a network of cognitive, emotional and motivational tendencies" (Boyatzis, cited in Goleman, 1984).

While it may be possible to increase a manager's cognitive complexity, the cost to the corporation and the time involved may make training on such a characteristic unfeasible. Companies usually rely on selection to be sure that the people entering the organization already have such skills and capacities. Nevertheless, developmental job assignments and courses may be valuable to those who are already fairly strong on these characteristics, so that they can enhance their abilities and prepare for higher-level positions. Some skills, such as communications ability, can be changed more easily, and an effective training program may lead to considerable improvement.

Chapter Six outlined eight guidelines for bosses to follow in fostering subordinates' career motivation. These are a guide to the skills managers should have. A set of courses following the guidelines would focus on giving positive reinforcement; providing more opportunities for achievement; providing opportunities for risk taking, by rewarding innovation and reducing fear of failure; fostering positive interpersonal relationships and developing a positive group climate; supporting career development, by encouraging goal setting; giving subordinates feedback on job performance; designing meaningful, responsible jobs; and fostering subordinates' advancement prospects, by giving them leadership opportunities, recognition, assignments visible to top management, and financial rewards.

Skill Diagnosis. A diagnosis of the skills that need to be improved should precede training. Unfortunately, this process is often informal and sometimes haphazard. For example, I am often sent course brochures and advertisements for workshops. If one looks interesting, I may enroll. Occasionally, my boss recommends a workshop, perhaps because he feels I need work in the area or because he has attended it and felt it was worthwhile. Sometimes skill diagnosis is more systematic. A career counselor may give me some tests and then tell me what skills need improvement. I may attend an assessment center run by my company. This is a two- or three-day experience, during which I take tests and participate in group discussions, business games, and decision-making simulations. The assessment staff observes my performance and rates me on a set of dimensions reflecting my managerial ability—decision making, organizing, planning, oral communication, written communication, and so on. My boss and I receive feedback on my performance and discuss the implications of the results for my future advancement prospects, as well as what I can do to make the most of my skills and minimize my weaknesses.

The advantage of the assessment center is that it provides

information on how well I do on a variety of standardized tasks. Also, there are several observers, and so there is input from different sources. The assessment center exercises are designed to be realistic, and studies show that assessment center results reflect on-the-job performance and predict success better than most other techniques (such as supervisory ratings) (Thornton and Byham, 1982). Nevertheless, since we cannot all attend assessment centers, we should take advantage of information about our performance available from our peers, bosses, and subordinates.

IBM's Computerized Skill Diagnostic. IBM has developed a computer program that asks the respondent questions about fifty competencies, such as planning, risk taking, and demonstrating sensitivity. Managers fill out this questionnaire for themselves and their subordinates, and their bosses fill it out for them, using a rating scale of 1 to 4 for each of the competencies. The analysis averages the responses, and the report lists the competencies seen as most needed for development. The manager then uses this information to select management courses offered by the company.

IBM requires all managers to have forty hours of classroom instruction a year. Some of this time involves learning about new company policies and procedures. A manager can take an outside course or workshop (for example, a program offered by a university) to satisfy the requirement. Every four years, the manager is required to return to the corporate headquarters training center for a week of classes, guest lectures, and discussions on management topics.

A Self-Diagnostic Test. Reread the checklist at the end of Chapter 9. Use it to assess whether you have the skills to implement the guidelines for manager development discussed in that chapter. Ask your boss, a co-worker, and/or several subordinates also to fill out the checklist, describing you. Discuss their responses with them. Also consider what actions you could take in areas where you need improvement.

Training Methods. There are numerous training methods. These include information presentation (lectures, films, reading material), group discussions, self-paced learning, cases, and simulations (for example, business games). The desire to design more effective training methods has led to the development of a sophisticated training technology. Audio cassettes, videotapes, films, workbooks, and computer programs are examples of techniques used alone or in combination with others. The goal in all cases is to present the material clearly and in a manner that will maintain interest.

Some training experts warn about giving more attention to the method used than to the content covered (Gagne, 1962). One method that seems to be very effective is behavior modeling, discussed below; it is also considered by London and Stumpf, 1982.

Behavior Modeling. The early works of such psychologists as Watson, Thorndike, Skinner, and others in behavior modification have contributed substantially to the training field. The essential notion of behavior modification is that individuals repeat behaviors that lead to desirable consequences (that is, reinforcements). While some training programs rely solely on behavior modification, others combine behavior modification with additional procedures.

Behavior modeling applies certain behavior modification principles to training. Assume that a class is being trained in a management skill, such as giving feedback. A videotape is used to demonstrate how the supervisor should give feedback to a subordinate. Managers in the class then role-play the situation while being observed by the instructor. The instructor rewards appropriate behavior with verbal praise and corrects inappropriate behavior. The trainees' supervisors are also trained to reward appropriate behavior, so that classroom learning transfers to the job setting.

The principles involved in behavior modeling are as follows:

- *Modeling:* Trainees are taught learning points and are provided with examples via videotape.
- *Role playing:* Trainees play the role of supervisors, and subordinates engage in an interaction similar to the one on the videotape.

- *Reinforcement:* The instructor uses social reinforcement (for example, praise) to encourage trainees to apply the demonstrated behavior.
- *Transfer of training:* Supervisors are trained to reinforce the subordinates when they exhibit the behavior taught in the training program (Goldstein and Sorcher, 1974).

Behavior modeling uses behavior modification by demonstrating to the trainee the nature of the situation (the stimulus) and the desired behavior (the response). Trainees are reinforced with praise (the consequence of their behavior) when they demonstrate the desired behavior during the practice session on the job. This procedure requires (1) clearly specifying the behaviors that are to be trained, (2) observing behaviors and measuring their occurrence, (3) rewarding the desired behavior, and (4) observing appropriate changes in behavior (Miller, 1978). Behavior modeling has been shown to be effective in training such elements of supervision as goal setting, giving feedback, giving positive reinforcement, dealing with performance problems, and handling racial issues.

Hartford National Bank's Behavior Modeling Program. Being a bank branch manager requires proficiency in a number of varied skills. The branch manager sells the bank's products and services, analyzes financial statements, makes credit decisions, negotiates loans, enforces audit and security procedures, and complies with many policies and procedures. These are technical skills acquired in training courses and through experience in lower-level positions in a bank. A key ingredient to effective performance for all branch managers is dealing with people: the irate depositor, the eager trainee, the harassed teller, the tough-minded division manager. An assessment of branch managers' strengths at Hartford National Bank and the areas where they needed development found that the greatest need was in basic interpersonal skills (Wise and Zern, 1982).

The officers of the bank agreed that a behavior-modeling program would best suit the needs of the branch managers. The human resources staff began developing the program by first identifying eleven skills that needed development. These were maintaining desired performance, dealing with employees who were having performance problems, giving performance feedback, conducting performance appraisals, conducting salary reviews, establishing goals, assigning work effectively, achieving objectives through teamwork, coaching effective sales performance, reducing resistance to change, and enhancing upward communication. A behavior modeling module was developed for each of the eleven skills. Each module had five major components:

- a brief reading assignment, which introduced the module and emphasized the importance of the skill.
- a list of action steps—a "roadmap"—that outlined the components of the skill and indicated how the principles were put into operation.
- a custom-made, videotaped behavior model showing one good example of a manager following the action steps in a simulated but realistic situation.
- videotaped skill practice, during which management trainees practiced the skill and received feedback on the extent to which they followed the action steps and the general principles in an experience-based role rehearsal.
- a skill-use plan, which required trainees to plan the means by which they would transfer the newly acquired skill to their jobs.

After putting seventy-five randomly selected managers through the program, the bank compared them to managers who had not yet received the training. The results showed that the program had significantly reduced turnover and increased performance. Subordinates felt that the managers who had received the training were more willing after training than before training to explain decisions and to solicit and listen to ideas.

Types of Management Training Programs

The relevance of a training program depends on the person's career stage and organizational level. For example, orientation programs are offered to people when they enter the organization or when they change roles (for example, advancing a level or moving into a new department). The new-manager orientation training outlined in Chapter Six is an example. Orientation training is used at all levels to indoctrinate newcomers. For example, newcomers are frequently given an orientation to the organization, covering its objectives and the benefits it offers as well as formal rules employees are expected to follow. Orientation sessions may also be held for newly promoted individuals to help them get acquainted with their new peers, introduce them to top executives, and explain procedures and behaviors expected of them. In addition to the content of orientation programs, the fact that they are offered suggests to the new employees the importance of their roles (London and Stumpf, 1982).

Another type of training is a workshop designed for top managers, to acquaint them with broad policy issues facing the business. For example, AT&T periodically runs a corporate policy seminar for its top managers. Approximately sixty fifth- and sixth-level managers participate during each one-week session. The aim is to increase top managers' understanding of critical outside forces. Issues covered are political, social, and economic. Human resources and technological advances are emphasized. Outside experts and AT&T professionals make presentations and moderate group discussions. New seminars are designed when the need arises, depending on issues facing the company. For instance, AT&T recently designed a new program to help top managers understand and deal with the increasingly competitive environment now being faced by the company since the breakup of the Bell System.

Some of the AT&T entities have instituted policy seminars for middle-level managers. These seminars allow dialogue on the critical issues facing particular operating units. For instance, after divestiture one region of AT&T Communications held a transition seminar for all its managers. The goal of the week-long sessions was to understand changes facing the business and what would be expected of the company's managers. The need to be more innovative and cost-conscious was emphasized.

Technical Management Training. In addition to the need

for training in interpersonal skills that require modifying attitudes and behaviors, there is a growing need for more technical training in the solid productivity skills that can affect an organization's profits. A strong proponent of this approach is William S. Mitchell, director of human resources at the Metropolitan Life Insurance Company (Lean, 1984). He recommends concentrating less attention on training in such supportive functions as interpersonal skills and communications and focusing more on skill building in such areas as work-level forecasting, work scheduling, resource scheduling and allocation, resource quality improvement, work simplification, organization structuring, productivity control, and cost analysis and control.

Another technical management strategy is competency-based training. This process identifies those characteristics of managers that will be compatible with the company's values and then works to develop them in all managers, first by identifying highly competent managers and analyzing their skills. A comparison to others who are judged less competent reveals competency gaps, which for current employees should be corrected by training whenever possible and for newcomers by changing selection criteria.

Outside Seminars. The Institute for Management Studies (IMS) is a nonprofit organization that sponsors day-long mini-courses given by top management scholars. IMS offers monthly sessions at many locations around the country. Member companies can send people for a fee of about $90 per attendee. The announcement for each program indicates who should be interested in the seminar (what level of managers from which functions). For example, one seminar may be designed for senior executives in marketing, planning, and human resources, while another seminar may be designed for middle managers from the finance, legal, and administrative areas. Sessions focus on leadership development; planning and organizing; or executing, controlling, and evaluating work. Recent topics have been leadership and the exceptional executive, the importance and value of linking corporate cultures and strategies, and strategic management.

University Programs. Many business schools offer extension courses on their campuses or at other convenient locations

(London and Stumpf, 1982). Examples include two-day semi-nars on improving white-collar productivity, and setting and im-plementing management goals, presented by the Wharton School of the University of Pennsylvania. The Harvard Business School offers two- and three-week courses in managing corporate con-trol and planning, marketing management, and a program for senior managers in government.

New York University offers a week-long management ef-fectiveness program for high-potential middle managers. This program is designed to assist managers in diagnosing their inter-personal, judgmental, and analytical skills as they relate to execu-tive-level positions; update technical skills in finance, marketing, and organizational behavior; and facilitate career management.

Pennsylvania State University designed a two-week hu-man resources management program for senior corporate direc-tors of human resources and for other line and staff executives responsible for human resource functions. The program covers managerial career planning and development, managing organi-zational change, quality of work life, trends in union–manage-ment relations, strategies for behavior management, and the expanded role of the human resource professional.

Looking Glass, Inc.: A Simulation for Assessment and Development. Designed by the Center for Creative Leadership in Greensboro, North Carolina, Looking Glass, Inc. is a business simulation (McCall and Lombardo, 1978). It includes roles for twenty top-level managerial positions across four hierarchical levels, three divisions, and three functional areas. Consequent-ly, there is considerable variation in the role requirements for each position. A trained staff observes the participants during the six-hour simulation and provides group and individual feed-back on more than a dozen managerial skills. Another simula-tion, based on the Looking Glass format, has been designed by Stumpf at New York University for use by financial services managers (Stumpf, 1984).

Comprehensive Company Programs

Many large companies have training departments that of-fer management courses. Some companies (such as IBM, as described above) require attendance at certain training programs or require a certain number of hours of training per year.

Some companies offer sequences of training courses: One course or workshop builds on what was learned in previous training experiences. I believe that an organization should have a comprehensive, integrated manager-development program that includes not only bosses who follow the manager-development guidelines but also company policies and procedures that provide the necessary resources. Training programs should contribute to the overall manager-development policies in these organizations. The following examples describe comprehensive management-training programs offered by several organizations.

Union Carbide Corporation. Union Carbide offers several series of development programs tailored to specific classes of employees. These series include programs for supervisors, programs for managers, and programs for executives. Participation in each series is voluntary, but attendance is based on a job-related need and requires departmental sponsorship. Program goals are to help individuals who are already doing effective work to do even better in preparing individuals for future career growth within the company. All programs are designed to complement other forms of skill development, such as on-the-job training and attendance at university or other external programs.

Union Carbide's Corporate Management Development Unit offers a needs analysis guide for each series of programs. Potential participants are instructed to discuss with their bosses the areas that need development. They are also asked to review their career plans, reflect on their strengths and weaknesses, and seek feedback from peers that might clarify the areas needing work. Once the areas to be improved are identified, individuals are directed to the needs analysis guide to select the specific programs designed to meet their needs. The programs include finance and accounting, time management, and productive conflict management. A special program on managerial skills analysis is also available to help individuals diagnose their managerial strengths and weaknesses (Wall, Awal, and Stumpf, 1981; Colarelli, Stumpf, and Wall, 1981).

Xerox Corporation. Xerox (London and Stumpf, 1982) has established minimum, mandatory training requirements for managers. Its programs start with individuals who have not yet held management jobs and extend to those in senior management positions. The management preparatory course, lasting one week, covers fundamentals of management and provides participants with an opportunity to think about whether they want management positions. A one-week course for newly appointed managers covers company values, important personnel policies and procedures, and general managerial skills. A two-week middle-management course deals with managing people. It covers interpersonal skills, observation methods, and feedback techniques and concludes with a one-and-a-half-day planning process. A course lasting two weeks, for upper-middle managers, and a one-week course for executives cover business strategy and planning and are run by business school professors.

Sentry Insurance. Sentry has recently developed an extensive, formalized manager-development program (Lee, 1984). The six-part program includes more than twenty courses, which take a Sentry employee from the first level of supervision to the top of the corporate ladder. The program begins with an assessment center for employees who are interested in management careers. The assessment center provides feedback on strengths and weaknesses and gives a flavor of what management is like. Employees can nominate themselves for assessment if they have at least one year with the company, are performing satisfactorily, have some knowledge of the basics of management, and have the endorsements of their bosses. First-time superiors take a self-paced course on the nuts and bolts of Sentry's management process, as well as a traditional classroom program on selection, interviewing, hiring, performance appraisal, equal employment opportunity guidelines, and affirmative action. After that, courses are offered on such topics as stress management, decision making, problem solving, delegation, and motivation. Executive-development courses focus on mentoring and on an executive profile, which compares individuals' own assessments of their management skills with those of their co-workers. Selected top managers attend three-month executive-development programs at Harvard and Stanford.

Corning Glass Works. Corning's manager-training begins by teaching the newcomer "how we do things around here: what our products are, how managers are evaluated, how we set our objectives, how people get promoted" (Lean, 1984). David Groff, who is in charge of management education for Corning, believes that manager development should be continual and should represent the corporate position. Corning offers about eighty regularly scheduled manager-development programs at numerous times throughout the year, and between twenty and forty other programs are scheduled less often. Most are in such "hard" managerial skills as marketing, pricing, engineering, statistics, and accounting.

Anheuser-Busch. Anheuser-Busch is trying to implement stronger ties between manager development and productivity improvement and has strengthened evaluation efforts by tying them more closely to productivity (Lean, 1984). For instance, Anheuser-Busch is investigating how much the seminars on motivation, for example, influence absenteeism. The company also uses more skill-specific development, as opposed to generic management training. The courses in such basic management skills as coaching, leadership, stress management, and writing skills emphasize company-specific applications, using real-work simulations and role playing.

Choosing a Management Training Program

Both the number and the variety of management training programs suggest that there is no one best way to develop managers. Companies use what has worked for them in the past and what they feel will work for them in the future (London and Stumpf, 1982). Starting out with highly capable, motivated managers is an important step in developing a high-quality management team. Thus, manager selection and development should be integrated efforts. Moreover, organizations should rely on many forms of instruction (simulations, video feedback, cases, role playing, group discussions, and so on) rather than on only one type. Management programs should be based on specific needs, and organizations should eliminate programs once those needs are met (Morgan, Hall, and Martier, 1979).

Evaluating Training Programs

The extent to which evaluation is important will depend on the benefits expected from the training program and the cost of the program (London and Stumpf, 1982). If a major investment in training is expected to increase productivity or sales, then it is important to measure the impact of the training program on these outcomes. If training is inexpensive and intended only to improve morale, then evaluation may be less important. In most cases, however, training is costly, and substantial benefits are anticipated; yet rigorous training evaluation is rare (Goldstein, 1980). Some reasons for this deficiency are that evaluation adds to the training cost, is time-consuming, and may mean a delay in obtaining the full benefits of the program. Some of those who design and implement training programs also claim that they know the value of the programs and so do not have to conduct evaluation studies. Sometimes individuals who advocate programs, without providing empirical support for the programs' benefits, do not want to risk discovering negative results.

Overcoming this resistance to training evaluation is essential. Training should be viewed as an investment, not as an expense. Thus, organizations need to know the return on training investments, just as they do on other investments. Training evaluation need not be expensive, time-consuming, or complex; fairly simple, practical research designs can provide sufficient data for meaningful evaluations.

Steps in the evaluation process include determining what criteria should be measured and what research design should be adopted. Rigor is typically sacrificed, to some extent, because of limited resources. The goal in designing most evaluation research projects is to identify methods that provide the most accurate and meaningful information by means of the least resources. (See Wexley and Latham, 1981, and Goldstein, 1980, for in-depth treatments of training and evaluation.)

Leadership Development Training

At the outset of this chapter, a distinction was made between management and leadership, and it was argued that all managers, at least those with supervisory responsibilities, are leaders, to varying degrees. That is, the leadership role is not reserved solely for top managers, although it is likely to be a more important part of their jobs than it is for those at lower levels of the organizational hierarchy. Since all managers may be leaders, however, let us describe what is meant by leadership and how it can be developed.

Peters and Waterman (1982) describe effective leaders as visionaries, coalition builders, facilitators, cheerleaders, and coaches. Bennis (1984a, 1985) recently completed a study of ninety chief executive officers. He found that leaders are effective because they create attention and pay attention; they provide a strong, constant model (a role model people can shoot for—and at); they permit and encourage risk taking; they enjoy developing others and are in control of their own envy; their self-esteem is not totally dependent on the job, since they have hobbies and other interests outside of work; they have professional values; they stand up for their beliefs and encourage others to do so; they have an esthetic sense; they balance their ambition, values, and professional expertise; and they have a sense of purpose and add spirit to the organization.

Margolis (1984) believes that managers at her company, Bristol-Myers, need seven core attributes to be effective leaders: (1) the capacity to act—to take initiative and make changes, (2) emotional security (the capacity to feel), (3) the ability to manage upward, (4) the ability to pay attention to the non-routine, (5) the know-how to manage group processes (knowing when to elicit participation from subordinates in decision making), (6) interpersonal ability, and (7) adaptability.

According to Margolis, managers at Bristol-Myers need to be organization builders, developing and evaluating people and sustaining commitment in a competitive environment. The company tries to foster these characteristics in managers by holding them accountable early in their careers, giving them challenging and responsible jobs, moving them into different areas of the business so that they will have a broad outlook and understanding of external forces, and giving them regular feedback on their performance. (This manager-development strategy is similar to the one followed by DYNAMO and outlined in Chapter Five.)

Another description of leadership that has implications for leadership training was compiled by O'Connor (1984). She views leadership as having three components: (1) understanding (having a realistic perspective on and awareness of what is happening in the work environment); (2) envisioning (recognizing and developing subordinates' skills, seeing the whole corporate picture, forecasting the future, and interpreting situations to revise forecasts as changes occur); and (3) acting (being action-oriented, exhibiting risk taking, being flexible, experimenting).

Schein (1984) offers a similar argument. He says, first of all, that since management is a proactive set of occupations (see Chapter One), we must teach people to be responsive early in their careers. This training should not be on the basis of simulated responsibility in business games, but should be derived from real responsibility on the job. This formulation corresponds to my notion of developing career resilience, the domain of motivation that concerns our belief in ourselves, need for achievement, and willingness to take risks, as well as knowing when to be independent and when to be cooperative. Organizations and managers enable employees to become leaders by positive reinforcement, providing opportunities for achievement and risk taking, and promoting supportive work climates.

Schein goes on to say that managers need to be clear about their talents, motives, and aspirations. This self-reflection should take place in relation to their work in the present and future, not in relation to their careers. Schein feels (and I agree) that managers spend too much of their time on career planning. This idea corresponds to my concept of career insight—the domain that concerns having clear, realistic, and flexible goals and an understanding of our strengths and weaknesses, and having an understanding of the social and political environment of the organization. Enabling conditions for career insight are support for career development and feedback on performance.

Schein also believes that we need to do more to train leaders as visionaries and entrepreneurs. Organizations need to be attractive enough so that visionaries will select them as employers. Thus, organizations need a climate that will support managers' visions of the future and allow them to act on their visions and make them come true. This belief corresponds to my concept of career identity—the domain that concerns being involved in our jobs, professions, and organizations and having needs for advancement, recognition, leadership, and money. Organizations and managers foster these characteristics by designing challenging jobs and providing opportunities and rewards.

Bennis (1984b) says that being a leader is like "learning how to play the violin in public." Leaders need outside observers who can help them understand their own behaviors; Bennis feels that we give insufficient attention to the role of personality and self-understanding in leadership. Quoting Karl Marx's statement that "man's consciousness of self is the highest divinity," Bennis recommends that leaders learn how to manage themselves. Bennis calls this "the creative deployment of their characters," and he calls for a "restoration of self" in leadership theory. This, he argues, is "healthy narcissism" (1984a). But what types of training courses promote leader development?

Previous chapters have described manager-development programs that encourage career resilience, career insight, and career identity. These programs center on organizational policies and procedures and supervisor behaviors. In the next section of this chapter, we outline training courses, workshops, and other activities that also may contribute to the development of these domains of career motivation. As we have seen, these domains are tied to Schein's conceptualization of leadership as being proactive and responsible (career resilience), learning about ourselves (career insight), and having a vision of the future (career identity). Thus, the activities we are about to consider can be called *leadership training.*

Promoting Career Resilience: Examples of Proactive Training

- *Junior boards:* High-potential young managers are appointed for from several months to a year to sit on a junior board. The purpose of the board is to discuss major issues facing the company and advise the board of directors or top officers on these issues.

- *Chairing a committee or task force:* Asking a junior executive to chair a major committee or task force on an important problem facing the organization.
- *Responsible job assignments:* Giving young managers significant supervisory responsibility in line positions (a policy followed by DYNAMO's manager-development program).
- *Giving presentations to top executives.*
- *Attending high-potential assessment centers measuring skills needed at higher levels.* This is usually a two- to three-day experience, during which the manager's potential to perform at a higher level is assessed.

Developing Career Insight:
Examples of Training for Self-Understanding

- *T-groups:* The National Training Laboratories Institute for Applied Behavioral Science offers human relations laboratories called T (for training) groups. T-groups use small, unstructured groups to help trainees develop insights about themselves and others. While T-groups tend to be stressful, they lead to valuable self-insight.
- *Motivation or personal awareness workshops:* Such a workshop has been discussed as part of a new-manager orientation program. Participants observe videotapes of managers describing their experiences and bosses describing their styles of management. The participants discuss how the questions addressed in the tapes apply to them. Then they set action goals in the areas where they want to improve.
- *Career motivation assessment and feedback:* The motivation assessment center, or a shortened version of it, could be used to assess individuals on relevant personality characteristics, needs, and interests. The participants could then get feedback on their results, as well as some help in interpreting and applying the results to their career directions.
- *Postassessment development:* After a career motivation assessment or a skills-based assessment center to evaluate potential for advancement, exercises may be used to help participants understand the assessment results. Workbooks, business simulations, diaries, and other methods (see below)

may help participants enhance career insight, improve leadership skills, and establish more meaningful career identities.

- *Development journal:* Managers may keep a record of their job experiences and important related events to help them reflect on these experiences and understand their linkages better. Managers can then see whether their careers are moving in the directions they intend.
- *Diaries and personal journals:* Sometimes writing out thoughts and feelings can put a new perspective on them, particularly when we go back after some time to read them again and think about changes that have occurred since they were written.
- *Self-assessment:* Many books are available which have self-analysis inventories and guides (see, for example, Bolles, 1980; Kotter, Faux, and McArthur, 1978). Companies such as General Electric and Bell of Pennsylvania have experimented with offering managers a series of workbooks on skills self-asssessment, guides for supervisor–subordinate discussions, and aids in seeking career opportunities within the company. Another workbook helps managers compare a profile of their skills to the skills required at higher levels of management. The American College Testing Program offers a microcomputer software package called "Discover: A Computer Based Development Program for Organizations" (1984) and designed to help employees manage career changes. Five modules help employees (1) analyze their present career satisfaction and understand the career changes they may face, (2) assess themselves on interest, skills, and values, (3) gather information about career opportunities, (4) help identify decision-making styles and improve decision-making skills related to career moves, and (5) identify realistic goals and establish action plans to increase the likelihood of success.
- *Outward-bound:* Outward-bound programs take work groups to remote campsites for experience with wilderness survival or for participation in physical, group exercises. The programs are intended to help individuals understand their relationships with others as well as develop greater trust and cohesiveness in the work group (Long, 1984; Van Zwieten,

1984). Proponents of this approach argue that it heightens one's self-awareness, sense of control, and receptiveness to the work environment. The Japanese use a similar method for middle managers, which includes lessons on humility (Phalon, 1984). Managers first recite their weaknesses publicly; they finish the program when they have successfully completed modules intended to overcome their weaknesses.

- *Support groups:* Managers get together to share their experiences and provide each other with help. This approach works well when the managers are from different departments or organizations and are not in competition with each other for career opportunities. One such group, the Chief Executive Roundtable sponsored by the New York–based American Woman's Economic Development Corporation, is a group of ten women business owners who meet monthly to help each other with business problems (Jacobs, 1984).

- *"Consultraining":* Hornstein and MacKenzie (1984) write that management education can be a way of achieving organization development. They offer two one-week courses, occurring about one year apart, for upper-middle management. Called "consultraining," the aim of the courses is to help managers develop the competencies they need to perform effectively in changing situations. Discussion and exercises in the courses focus on diagnosing interpersonal relationships; roles; values; and feedback. The first week results in an action plan for increasing personal and unit effectiveness. Participants during the first week are from diverse work sites, while those in the second week are from the same work site. The second week focuses on a team effort to solve a real organization problem. The training improves managerial skills through feedback, increases the use of cross-organizational task forces to solve problems, and increases the acceptance of organization-development consultants.

- *Role-orientation training.* The goal of this type of training is to increase managers' awareness of the role of a manager and the value of success in the managerial role. McClelland (1965) uses such an approach to train would-be entrepreneurs in the value of achievement and power. Miner (1984) has a role-

orientation program aimed at increasing advancement motivation. Miner has found such programs effective because
they focus on changeable interests and attitudes that are
linked to behavior.

Developing Career Identity:
Ways to Encourage Visioning the Future

- *Computer conferencing:* Managers participate in computer
  hookups with fellow managers in the same or other organizations around the country to address issues concerning general, prespecified topic areas. Many networks of this type
  address the issue of productivity improvement. The goal is to
  develop a fresh and broad perspective by dialogue over long
  periods of time. The advantage is that participants can work
  on the network at their own convenience. They can express
  their views to many people and obtain the views of their co-
  participants without having to attend meetings or contact
  each participant individually.
- *Frequent discourse:* Many organizations are encouraging
  managers to talk in open forums about major issues facing
  their businesses. Rather than following the dictum "ready,
  fire, aim," the thought here is to give careful consideration
  to issues and uncover new ways of dealing with them before
  acting. Examples of relevant questions for discussion are
  "How can costs be cut? What moral issues are involved in
  how we do business? What values guide our business activities?"
- *Humanities programs:* In the 1950s and the 1960s, it was
  popular for organizations to send high-potential managers to
  year-long university programs in the humanities. The idea
  was that this "broadening" would make better general managers. The trend in the 1970s was away from these courses
  of study and toward technical and business programs related
  more directly to corporate needs. The trend today is toward
  a better-balanced approach. Schein (1984) recommends that
  business schools require courses in history, philosophy, and
  ethics. He also suggests that fluency in at least one foreign

language be required for a business graduate degree. The rationale is that as businesses become more international in scope, we must understand foreign cultures to be successful abroad.

- *Sabbaticals:* Some companies, such as Xerox, Polaroid, and IBM, offer executives time off with pay to participate in community action projects, research, special scientific endeavors, and government or professional activities not directly related to their functions in the organization. Such programs benefit the community as well as the company's reputation. They tend to provide the participant with new experiences and a sense of self-renewal.

Conclusion

This chapter has examined management skills and knowledge training and leadership training. Some skills, such as cognitive complexity, are not easily developed once a person has started his or her career. The manager-development guidelines in Chapter Six suggest skills for training, including how to give positive reinforcement and provide more opportunities for achievement. Skill diagnosis should precede training. The IBM diagnostic is an example of a computerized approach for collecting and combining input from the boss, subordinates, and the manager. Behavior modeling was described as an example of an effective training technique. Types of manager training run the gamut from focusing on technical skills (such as planning work schedules and improving productivity) to examining corporate culture and changing interpersonal skills. Large companies often have comprehensive sequences of manager-training courses.

We have seen a parallel between Schein's (1984) conceptualization of leadership and the three domains of career motivation: Leadership is proactive and responsible (career resilience), learning about ourselves and the environment (career insight), and visioning the future (career identity). Training for leaders focuses on one or more of these leadership attributes.

All managers may be leaders, to a certain degree. This observation applies to managers at all levels of an organization, and it also applies to managers at all career stages. The next chapter examines the career motivation of midcareer middle managers, with special emphasis on the meaning of development for plateaued managers—those who are unlikely to advance to higher organizational levels.

11

❋ ❋ ❋ ❋ ❋

Motivating and Developing Midcareer and Plateaued Managers

Many of today's managers in the middle of their careers are also in the middle of the management hierarchy. They grow older, but their jobs remain the same. Their careers are plateaued. These people are guardians of the organization's culture and tradition, but they are also often barriers to change. The contribution of middle managers to corporate productivity is diminishing, partly because of their middle position in the corporate hierarchy and partly because their jobs are frequently stagnant and meaningless. As Kets de Vries (1978) observes, "Careers can be a major source of stability, but also a source of frustration. Career plateaus are the natural consequence of the organizational funnel, particularly in periods of limited growth. The inevitable consequence is that most managers will come to some form of a halt in their careers" (p. 50).

So far, this book has addressed the development needs of managers early in their careers, because early development is

207

crucial to what happens later in the manager's career. But what about those who have reached middle management, perhaps fairly early in their professional lives, and find themselves asking, "Is this all there is?" This chapter examines the role of middle managers and the consequences of being plateaued. The pressures on middle managers are considered in relation to demographic and economic trends. Characteristics of plateaued managers are compared to high flyers, and men are compared to women in midcareer. The development needs of middle managers are reviewed, and development programs, including some nontraditional alternatives, are suggested. Finally, reasons for, and the nature of, midcareer crisis are examined, along with successful and unsuccessful coping strategies. Kets de Vries (1978) explains the value of considering all these aspects of midcareer problems and needs: "These matters, important for both individual and organization, will enable us to traverse the quicksand that can be midcareer and make it a station on our route to personal growth and generativity, instead of the beginning point of a lifelong decline into boredom, frustration, and stagnation" (p. 62).

Pressures on Middle Managers

Warren (1984) distinguishes between pressures on middle managers from the environment external to the organization and from the environment internal to the organization.

The External Environment. Economically, we have moved from a period of growth to one of "stagflation." With the influx of foreign manufacturers and the deregulation of some major industries within the United States, competition for goods and services has become fierce. Technology is progressing dramatically. Microprocessors and the latest devices in telecommunications have helped us be more competitive, but we are doing it by cutting costs rather than by increasing our productivity. Demographically, women, minorities, and baby-boomers have flooded the labor market.

The Internal Environment. More than ever before, managers face pressures from top management to cut costs and get more out of fewer people. Managers also face more competition from peers for the best jobs. Today's corporations have higher standards; they cannot settle for mediocrity in an environment where the price of failure is bankruptcy. In addition, today's jobs are less structured than ever before. The job security of the manager is rapidly decreasing as technology advances. The days of the generalist manager may be waning, as companies realize the need to have specialists at all levels of management. (This was the reason for the increased segmentation of departments at ECHO, as discussed in previous chapters; recall, too, the difficulties DYNAMO had maintaining a development program, and the negative reactions of the high-potential managers in the program as advancement opportunities declined.)

Fear of failure is higher, as new technologies become obsolete before they can be introduced into the workplace. For example, many managers feel the need to have personal computers because everyone seems to be using them, but managers worry about what to do with them; they want to be shown how they can use and benefit from the new technology, rather than exploring the possibilities for themselves and inventing their own creative applications.

Stein (1984) argues that middle managers are caught up in organizational traditions that do not make sense today. Most people spend time circumventing organizational constraints, but think of how their time could be spent if the constraints did not exist! For example, in one large corporation the officers decided it was time to make personnel systems more responsive to the needs of the business. One area they identified as needing more responsiveness was job evaluation—the process of establishing new jobs, writing job descriptions, and identifying proper rates of compensation. Writing detailed job descriptions and getting them approved by the evaluation committees were complex chores. Considerable resistance was created between the committees, which took their time to do the work, and managers, who needed to fill the positions immediately because the work had to get done. A task force changed the system by making managers accountable for evaluating the jobs under their control and by having a monitoring process to spot-check new jobs to be sure that the level of compensation was worth what the work required. Theoretically, the new procedure should have given managers more discretion and responsibility and cut the costs of having full-time personnel on evaluation committees, but the organization decided to keep the job evaluation experts as consultants to managers who might need their help. Also, some top managers did not see why their middle managers should be responsible for job evaluation, and they decided to let the job evaluation consultants make the decisions, as they had in the past.

The organization described above tried to give middle managers more responsibility, but many organizational changes take responsibility away from managers. Such changes include the heightened industrial democratization of the workplace; the emphasis on participative management and on increasing spans of control; and third-party rights efforts (for example, the equal employment opportunity–affirmative action programs in many organizations) (Stein, 1984). Matrix organization structures have led to more conflict and strains, as managers have become unsure of the appropriate reporting relationships and responsibilities. Increasing spans of control and participative management, in contrast, have required learning the skills related to managing interactions between subordinates, rather than simply directing the work of subordinates.

Schlesinger and Oshry (1984) describe the role of middle managers in contrast to roles at other levels in the organization:

> Each level has its role in the organization— top managers are shapers, workers are producers, and middle managers are integrators—and each layer also has problems that hinder its work. [One problem with the role of integrator is] rooted in the organization's promotion track and reward system, which values functional expertise and technical competence over collaboration and promotes differentiation, often at the expense of needed integration. So, isolated from top management and the work force and differentiated from peers by departmental and functional orientations, middle managers have few channels for sharing and sup-

port. [Moreover,] the job of the average middle manager is not much better, in terms of its inherent motivating potential, than the job of the average U.S. worker [p. 10].

Schlesinger and Oshry (1984, p. 12) argue that middle managers' problems stem from inadequate organizational structures and inadequate support from top management, rather than from middle managers' inherent lack of skills, character, or intelligence: "Blame, however, seems to befall the people holding the jobs rather than the job itself, and the message of inadequacy is getting through to middle managers, who are beginning to believe it themselves." Schlesinger and Oshry's solution is for middle managers to unite as a power bloc and begin to coordinate and integrate their own activities in the organization.

The most pervasive change increasing pressure on middle managers has been the rapid pace of change itself (Stein, 1984). Managers are not able to resist change as they did in the past; change happens too quickly these days. There is no time to resist change or even to react to it. In the past, it was possible to ride the crest of change and become obsolete slowly during one's career. That is impossible today. The need for an increasingly educated work force means that middle managers now have to avoid obsolescence. Ambiguity and lack of structure are the norm, not the exception. Stein also believes that the mean time between surprises in business is rapidly decreasing, as is the mean time to make decisions. Constrained by chains of command, and by the felt need for analysis and control at all levels of management, managers find it difficult to make decisions. The result is decreased responsiveness and fear of failure.

Middle Managers' Discontent

The eroding contribution of middle managers is evident in a recent survey conducted by *Industry Week* ("Not Eyeball to Eyeball . . . ," 1984). This study found that about 42 percent of the middle managers surveyed expected to leave their current jobs within five years, 36 percent were more likely to seek jobs now than they were two years ago, 46 percent of middle managers believed that their colleagues also wanted to change jobs, and only managers fifty-five years and older appeared content to stay at their jobs. Few middle managers in the survey (only 13 percent) were concerned about their pay; 22 percent believed that advancement opportunities were good, while 41 percent said that advancement opportunities were poor.

Unfortunately, top managers were out of synch with the middle managers' discontent. Middle managers were more unhappy than their bosses realized: 59 percent of the CEOs in the *Industry Week* survey expected that 15 to 48 percent of their management cadre would still be there in five years; 39 percent thought they would lose fewer managers than they had in the previous two years. CEOs viewed lack of career opportunities as the greatest source of middle managers' dissatisfaction, but only 17 percent of the CEOs planned to increase opportunities as an incentive for middle managers to stay.

Performance of Plateaued and Nonplateaued
Middle Managers

Job performance depends on the needs and desires of employees, and these needs and desires vary with career stage, life situation, and career prospects. One study (Carnazza and others, 1981) surveyed 384 middle managers (99 percent male) in a northeastern industrial firm. The study compared those who were plateaued with those whose prospects for promotion, as seen by their bosses and themselves, were still good. Managers with low likelihood of promotion performed better when they and their bosses agreed on clear performance objectives, when the managers received feedback on specific tasks and overall performance, and when the managers knew the basis on which performance was evaluated. Many organizations spend their resources on managers with high likelihood of promotion and on problem performers, but ignore the effectively performing managers who have low likelihood of promotion. This study found that plateaued managers performed more effectively to the extent that they had "challenging, satisfying, and clearly defined jobs; jobs that the managers [felt were] important to the company; and jobs that [gave] the managers a chance to show what they [could] do" (p. 23).

Middle managers with high likelihood of promotion performed better when their contributions and efforts were recognized and appreciated by their co-workers and supervisors. In addition, those who perceived that they had the requisite skills and abilities for promotion, who were willing to relocate, and who did not see age as a hindrance to moving received higher performance ratings. The study also revealed that these results occurred whether the classification of being plateaued or having promotion opportunities was made by the boss or by the incumbent.

Interestingly, there was only 50 percent agreement between bosses and subordinates on the "plateaued" classification. The finding of similar results for each grouping indicates that the acceptance of plateauing may occur on both conscious and unconscious levels: A person may openly deny being plateaued but may also accept it, because of subtle cues sent out by the organization. Nevertheless, for managers to have aspirations for promotion, regardless of how the organization has classified them, suggests that the managers have not given up, or perhaps that to reject the possibility of future promotion, which in our culture is a pervasive indicator of success, is too threatening.

To summarize, Carnazza and others (1981) suggest that assessment of the chances for future career advancement in midlife help managers understand the factors that affect performance. Those without advancement potential perform better when they have clear performance goals and feedback on how well they have achieved those goals. Those with advancement potential perform better when they receive recognition—not just from bosses, but from co-workers as well.

Other studies have examined attributes of midcareer managers. One study (DuBois, 1981) conducted in-depth interviews with ninety people approximately fifteen years after they had graduated from Columbia University. These were privileged individuals; many of them had "made it." Unlike the sample from the study cited above, this group consisted of thirty males, thirty working women, and thirty housewives. DuBois summarized her results as follows (the results from the housewives are also included here because they help us to understand the impact of one's role in midlife):

> Men seem to center their lives primarily around their careers, and men who are happy in their careers are happy in most other areas of life. Men enjoy older children more, and invest more in parenting as their children age. Children's aging happily coincides with men's career plateaus, so that they are most interested in their children at the same time that they are less concerned with advancement in their careers. The two processes seem to complement each other for men.

> The picture for women is not as harmonious. Homemakers seem to structure their lives around their children. Unfortunately, staying at home seems to make it easier for homemakers to avoid confronting their illusions. Many homemakers avoid the issue of what they would do once their children are grown. Some of the homemakers in the study talked about finding jobs, but many were frightened at the prospect of entering the labor force after so many years. Many resolved the situation by focusing more attention on their husbands and by becoming more involved in leisure and artistic pursuits. The women who chose this avenue appeared to get their primary satisfaction in life out of their relationships.

> Working women appear to be a transitional group between men and homemakers. They appear to be conflicted between two major arenas, career and family. They are tied to their roles as parent at the same that they are fulfilled by career involvement. Because of the demands of mothering and feelings of guilt about not staying home to care full-time for their children, going against traditional expectations, working women feel very conflicted and appear unable to reach the kind of integration characteristic of men in midlife. The solution which many working women seem to find is a disengagement from their children. These women, al-

> though they try to incorporate both achievement and relationships in their lives, appear to turn away from relationships and become more narrowly achievement-oriented in midlife [pp. 99-100].

Thus, this study indicates the major differences between men and women in midcareer. For men, work is an important part of life, and their families become more important to them as their careers plateau. Working women feel guilty about their work involvement and have difficulty integrating parenthood and career.

DuBois found that women who enter the work force after raising children expect that because they are just starting their careers, they have considerable advancement potential. Organizations do not see it that way, however, because they view advancement potential in terms of age and the time necessary for having job experiences and the preparation required for higher levels. Consequently, these women are likely to be disappointed when they realize that raising a family means giving up career opportunities, not simply postponing them.

Perhaps the most extensive study of middle managers comes from a longitudinal program of research, which followed managers from the time they entered the company to midcareer. Called the Management Progress Study, the original participating managers were 422 young white males from six telephone companies. One recent report from this research examined the results of eighty college graduates still left in the sample after twenty years (Bray and Howard, 1980). Of these, twenty-two had been promoted to the fourth and fifth levels of management and were counted as definitely successful. Another thirty-nine had reached third level and were counted as moderately successful.

The results showed that high-level managers were more likely to give work the top place in their lives, but they were also apt to expand their lives more than other managers; that is, they tended to achieve in many areas of life. These people were "enlargers," in contrast to "enfolders," who were less successful managers and tended to stabilize and build on existing life structures (Bray, Campbell, and Grant, 1974).

An important finding from this study, however, was that career success and satisfaction with life were not related for this group of managers. Career success and satisfaction contributed in part to life satisfaction, but career success did not necessarily lead to happiness: "The most successful [managers] at work are no more likely to be the most successful in marriage and family life or in recreational pursuits. Nor are they more likely to feel more positive about life . . . or . . . avoid the feelings of crisis that sometimes accompany middle age" (Bray and Howard, 1980, p. 286). The study also found no apparent detrimental effects of career success on life satisfaction. The entire sample comprised males, however. DuBois (1981) reported that successful working women experience conflict with their roles in the home, in contrast to successful working men, who do not experience this conflict and who become more involved with their families when their advancement prospects diminish.

Career Planning and Development in Midcareer

Given these differences between successful and less successful middle managers, what does development mean for those in midcareer? The Management Progress Study found that young managers began their careers with very high expectations of what their lives would be like and how successful their careers would be (Howard and Bray, 1981). For many, reality set in early. Their expectations declined during their first five years with the company. After twenty years, many of those who had plateaued had sound reasons for not wanting additional promotions. Their reasons included not wanting geographical relocations, not liking the politics they felt they would face at higher levels, and not wanting the aggravations of additional responsibility at the next level of management. The directors of the study offer the following advice to organizations: "Don't inveigle the system by dangling promotions in front of those who don't really want them and those the organization shouldn't want at higher levels" (Howard and Bray, 1980, p. 6). They go on to ask, "If promotions are no longer that much of a reward for the typical middle-aged manager, to what ends might midcareers be planned?" They feel that motivation for achievement—which measures the desire to do a difficult job well and achieve on challenging tasks, regardless of advancement—does not diminish over time. This impression suggests the value of enhancing job-challenge and task-accomplishment opportunities for plateaued midcareer managers, regardless of their level in the organization.

One way to do this is by lateral transfers, preferably without relocation to different geographical areas. If this is not possible, an alternative is to enlarge the scope of the present job. Stein (1984) notes that this alternative is likely to be taken as organizations, struggling to cut costs and be more competitive, resize themselves, creating flatter structures and giving managers greater responsibility and more decision-making power. Another way to enrich jobs is to apply principles of job and work-group design. This approach would call for emphasizing such factors as the variety of tasks and skills required; increased autonomy for managers; increased feedback; the significance of the jobs to the organization and to society; and delegation of complete tasks, as opposed to small pieces of a task. One company recently developed a learning guide for its managers to help them redesign their own jobs and those of their subordinates.

Bardwick (1983) suggests a variety of forms for job changes: (1) exchanging people laterally between existing jobs for varying time periods; (2) designing positions so that new jobs require both old and new knowledge and skills; (3) creating temporary work units to solve specific problems, particularly complex problems that require deep study or long-range planning; (4) reappraising those contributions to the organization that are supplementary rather than directly contributory (for example, mentoring and major activities in community or government relations); (5) moving technically expert people into supervisory positions to manage other technical employees; and (6) using some individuals as internal consultants in different parts of the organization (p. 71). In reference to the last suggestion, one company established a new midlevel management position: consultant. The principal requirement for this position is supervisory experience in a field position, which would permit identification with the field manager's problems. The consultant's job is to do whatever is necessary to help clients within the company be more effective. Examples of consulting activities include team building, facilitating group meetings, administering employee attitude surveys and feeding back results, and redesigning work group structures. The consultants go through a development program offered by the company and are encouraged to attend outside courses on organizational development. The company also offers a certification process that requires consultants, after several years of experience and training, to go before a review board, where cases in which they were involved are examined.

The goal of all these efforts is to increase the work involvement of plateaued middle managers. Nevertheless, some people do not want to make the sacrifice of personal time that would be required by a more involving job, especially as the work becomes less important in their lives and as family and hobbies become more important. This unwillingness does not mean lack of interest in a challenging job, however; Howard and Bray (1980) observe: "Career planning may well be a worthwhile effort for middle-aged managers, but mostly for that slim minority that has the ability, motivation, and opportunity to advance to higher rungs of the corporate ladder. . . . To the majority of middle-aged managers, however, corporate realities suggest that career planning is likely to be seen as meaningless, bureaucratic busywork. If the activity could be tied to adding to the challenge for individual control in a job at the same level, it might be much more positively received, providing it didn't call for too big a price to be paid, like . . . moving" (p. 12).

Bardwick (1983) suggests several other possibilities for increasing the plateaued manager's motivation. One is to change the organization's conception of the time frame in which employees are expected to be most productive and creative. A firm might expect five to ten years of competent performance from an employee, particularly when the employee's children are young. This period would be followed by a more lengthy period of much greater work involvement. Bailyn (1980) recommends that organizations create slow-burn paths, rather than fast tracks, to higher corporate levels. Slow-burn movement may mean ten years or more between promotions. This strategy is used in Japanese organizations.

Bardwick also believes that organizations should consider hiring people who are not motivated to advance in the corporation. In fact, there is evidence of self-selection among young people who are advancement-oriented and choose to work for organizations where advancement opportunities are promising (Howard and Bray, 1981). Realistic career previews pay off by not generating expectations for advancement that cannot be met. As Bardwick (1983) states, "It can sometimes be better for an organization to have competent, dependable (plateaued) employees who derive their most important gratifications from interests outside of the job and who have expectations that match current and future realities" (p. 72).

A more traditional way in which organizations try to motivate plateaued employees is to offer symbolic rewards. One company has an "Eagle Award," given to those who, in the judgment of the vice-president, make significant contributions. Retraining is another alternative. In-house education, and tuition benefits for outside courses, give managers a chance to increase their skills and prepare for other jobs within the organization. Bosses should be both trained and rewarded to counsel their subordinates on their development needs and should offer new directions for their work.

Mentoring. The middle manager can make a valuable contribution to the organization by mentoring high-potential young managers. This can be a synergistic relationship (Warren, 1984). The high-potential young manager has enthusiasm, energy, and creativity, while the middle manager has history, a proved track record, and the willingness to produce. Mentoring relationships can rejuvenate older professionals by letting them pass on the wisdom and experience they have learned throughout their professional careers (Hunt and Michael, 1983). Mentors generally are successful people who are knowledgeable, willing to share their expertise, and not threatened by their protégés' potential for equaling or surpassing them. Being mentors gives managers status and esteem in the eyes of their peers and supervisors (Kram, 1980). It is a way to increase one's power base within the organization. Companies can encourage mentoring by giving high-potential young managers special assignments, job rotations, rapid advancement, and programs that increase their exposure to higher-level managers who can serve as mentors.

There are generally four stages of mentoring (Hunt and Michael, 1983). The first is *initiation*. This is a period of six months to one year, during which the protégé realizes what the mentor has to offer. The second stage, *development*, lasting two to five years, gives the protégé opportunities to make decisions. In this stage, the protégé's output is a by-product of the mentor's instruction, encouragement, support, and advice. The third stage is *separation*. This occurs six months to two years after a significant change in the relationship. For example, this change may occur after the protégé has transferred to a new job. If the separation is premature, the relationship may end with both parties feeling anger, frustration, and bitterness. The final stage is *lasting friendship*, as the mentor and the protégé re-establish contact and develop a peerlike relationship. Such a friendship may continue indefinitely.

Enabling. Given the trend toward flatter organizational structures, the manager's role is changing from one of controlling subordinates' work to one of enabling them to produce (Stein, 1984). This role entails managers' having the tools and the discretion to act and to reward subordinates for goal accomplishment. The manager-development guidelines in Chapter Six suggest ways of helping subordinates. These include providing positive reinforcement for jobs well done, and opportunities for achievement and risk taking; creating an environment of interpersonal concern; supporting career development; giving feedback; encouraging job involvement through job challenge; and providing opportunities for promotion and other rewards, to the extent that these are under middle managers' control. Middle managers must have broader visions than they have had in the past. They need to decide what needs to be done and then do it. An applicable phrase is "It's easier to ask for forgiveness than for permission!" In this sense, managers become leaders; they do not wait for direction from higher management, but create the direction themselves.

Another method for helping plateaued middle managers is to teach them about plateauing. "If an employee understands that plateauing originates in the structure of an organization, he or she will feel less angry, less victimized, and less of a failure" (Bardwick, 1983, p. 72). Bardwick believes that career counseling may also help. She emphasizes that counseling, in this case, does not mean the traditional focus on matching the skills or potential of an employee with a present or a future position; rather, the goal is to help managers identify their values, clarify their goals, and generate goals and values that consider their age and the realities of staying at the same organizational level for the rest of their careers with the company. They may need to create new visions or dreams that they can respect and attain, goals that do not include more advancement, money, and power.

To review, we have covered a number of ways to enhance career motivation of midcareer, plateaued managers. These include lateral transfers, resizing, job and work-group design, job changes, job redesign, creating temporary work units or task forces, internal consultantships, changes in organizational expectations about speed of advancement, hiring people who are not motivated to advance, symbolic rewards, retraining, counseling from bosses and professionals, mentoring, discretion for managers to act, and learning about plateauing.

Midlife Crisis

The Management Progress Study found that, at least on the surface, most of the managers had accepted their career plateaus and adjusted to them (Howard and Bray, 1980, p. 5). Some may have felt a sense of failure or may have repressed their anger. Some experienced what is often called a midcareer or midlife crisis, but the majority did not.

One point of view is that everyone experiences one or more personal crises at some points during a career (Levinson and others, 1978). Another point of view is that many people avoid personal crisis: DuBois' (1981) study of midcareer men and women suggested that general midlife issues were not precipitators of crisis; those who had coped with life all along were able to re-evaluate their positions in midlife constructively and accept reality, but those who had had difficulty committing themselves to major life decisions earlier in life experienced feelings of acute distress or crisis upon confronting midlife issues. They did not experience complete breakdown; rather, the outcome of the crisis was personal growth—a reassessment of and coming to terms with their lot in life. This finding is consistent with longitudinal research indicating that severe midlife crises are atypical and that when they occur they generally follow a pattern of poor adjustment throughout life (Vaillant, 1977).

Middle age means coming to terms with our mortality, evaluating our contributions to society, and realizing that our current and future work may not warrant our efforts and enthusiasm. Since people in midcareer do experience crises, to different degrees, it is important to understand this phenomenon and how managers cope with it. We are an achievement-oriented society, and advancement opportunities narrow as managers climb the corporate hierarchy; thus, many people are disappointed and experience a sense of failure (Kets de Vries, 1978).

Precipitating Factors. Kets de Vries has examined not only factors that precipitate midlife crisis but also reactions to it. Precipitating factors include physical events, such as a change in appearance (baldness), menopause, sexual problems, or a breakdown in health. Changes in relationships, such as marital strife, problems with children, or children leaving home ("the empty nest syndrome"), also induce crisis. Career problems that precipitate crisis include being passed over for promotion; awareness of having made the wrong career decision; feeling stuck in the job; termination; and demotion.

Dealing with Midlife Crisis. Kets de Vries identifies four stages of dealing with crisis, depending on whether one faces reality or distorts it and on whether one's reactions are active or passive. These styles are called *constructive, underachieving, defensive,* and *depressive.*

The constructive style is an active, reality-based approach. Managers using this style develop insight by reflecting on their situations, taking stock, and learning. They look for ways to grow, for example, by sharing their resources or by being mentors to young managers. Some managers who confront reality may not find constructive outlets and so settle for less than they had anticipated. Alternatively, they may decide on career change, building on the financial, technical, and managerial resources they already have. (In the language of career motivation, these individuals have healthy career resilience.) The constructive style also requires the insight to perceive oneself and the environment accurately, as well as a strong sense of career identity. For a good example of the constructive style, recall John Gilligan. He was a boss in ECHO's construction department. He was stuck in a department that seemed to care only about getting the work done. John had worked his way up from a nonmanagement position, attending college at night for eight years. Realizing that his future career progress would be limited to creating more excitement in his current-level job, he bucked the system to develop his own job enrichment. He somehow secured a transfer from a technical position, which he had had for many years and which used his engineering skills, to a managerial job that required him to supervise subordinates for the first time. He also applied his own brand of job enrichment to his subordinates' jobs. He worked within the system to change it as much as he could. He had insight into the political and social environment, and he realized that he did not have anything to lose at his career stage.

The underachieving style of dealing with crisis takes a passive approach, but it is reality-based. Managers using this style have low aspirations and are easily satisfied. In fact, *crisis* is too strong a word for what happens to these people; they can do without advancement and without a sense of achievement and have never been the type of person to set the world on fire. Their career identity and resilience are low. They have poor self-concepts, which they have learned to live with. Content with the status quo, the underachieving manager is most likely to become "a rotten tomato on the corporate shelf" (Jennings, 1984). Joe Morris, the boss we have met from ECHO's engineering department, is an example of such a realist who does nothing. He saw the problems, but seemed to lack confidence in his abilities to take the same risks that John Gilligan took. Joe had a tough time meeting his objectives, and so he devoted all his efforts to this task. As a consequence, he ignored the development of the subordinates who helped him meet his objectives. He wished that he could be evaluated on developing people, seeming to believe that only such evaluation would justify spending the time. He did not consider that attention to his subordinates' concerns could improve his own bottom line. Chances are that he regretted not giving the same time to his own development that John Gilligan did. If Joe continues to wait for others to tell him what is important, he is likely to continue being a dissatisfied underachiever.

Defensive managers distort reality in the active mode. These people are prone to stress and panic. A recent study of top executives found that those who failed tended to be insensitive to others and were abrasive and intimidating under stress (McCall and Lombardo, 1983). They either did not bother or were unable to value the needs and contributions of others. Defensive managers deny problems and are quick to blame others. Their behavior may be compulsive. They also may make it clear that, in their eyes, the work of others is never good enough, and so they must do everything themselves. They are likely to deny their own faults and failures. Alcohol may become a convenient escape for them. These individuals have a false sense of resilience, inaccurate insight, and misplaced identity. Of the managers we have met, the one who comes closest to the defensive style is Bob Richards. In one breath, Bob talked about having an open-door policy and open lines of communication with his subordinates; in the next breath, he said that his subordinates worked best when they were united against him. He felt that young managers were overpaid and disloyal.

The depressive style distorts reality in the passive mode. These people blame themselves for their failure and are generally pessimistic. They lack career insight and resilience and probably have never had much chance for success.

Shorris (1981) provides an example of the passive manager who ignores reality. This manager was relocated from state to state as he climbed the corporate ladder. He ignored the needs of his wife, who had given up her career as an artist to marry him. "He was promoted to management from the company's largest plant. . . . She said, 'I am thirty-seven years old and everyone I know is on television.' She drank whiskey with the chairman's wife in the afternoons. Eventually she moved back to her home town and took up painting. He watched television in the evenings" (p. 184).

These four coping styles—constructive, underachieving, defensive, and depressive—demonstrate the interaction of the individual with the environment. The environment goes beyond the work setting. We are the victims of our circumstances, unless we choose to assume responsibility for what happens to us and take action to meet our needs.

Organizations contribute to midlife crisis and affect how managers deal with it. For instance, frequent geographical relocation can destroy a marriage; lack of feedback from the boss may make it difficult for the manager to set realistic goals and evaluate the extent to which they are accomplished; little reinforcement for tasks well done makes it hard to have a positive self-image; lack of opportunity for advancement discourages advancement motivation; lack of job challenge discourages work involvement. The guidelines for manager development in Chapter Six, and the recommendations for midcareer manager development discussed earlier in this chapter, are essential for increased productivity and a higher quality of life for middle managers. The guidelines will not necessarily prevent personal crises for midcareer managers, but they can help managers adjust to changes and disapointments and turn problems into opportunities. The midcareer manager should be alert to signs of personal obsolescence and disappointment and should be able to appraise the future and take appropriate action.

Each of the four coping strategies applies to everyone, to different degrees. Because most of us, even when confronted with difficult situations, are able to function well most of the time, we tend to face reality actively. But consider your answers to these questions:

When do I walk away from a problem?
How often do I procrastinate?

How often do I blame others?
Do I see others as less competent than myself?
What can I do to make my dreams come true?
Am I lazy?
Could I accomplish more than I do?
Do I care? Why?

Think of some other questions to help you understand your coping style. Probe your answers. Finally, ask yourself, "Do I need some help?" If the answers is yes, do something about it; no one else will do it for you. To help you review your career and think about the future, try plotting a career graph.

Most of us have a timetable of career expectations, which evolves and which we track. Tracking is frequently done on the basis of salary, level, or some similar reference as compared to age. (Age is a particularly critical element, because it is the only one beyond our control.) Career graphs prepared in this way allow us to compare past and present results with future expectations—that is, where we want to be at some selected time or age in our lives (Thomas, 1981).

There are many relevant events on a career clock, such as dates of advancement, goal accomplishment, salary increases, and job changes. Looking back over our careers, we can pinpoint when we felt especially satisfied with our work and when we felt especially dissatisfied. By analyzing the reasons why we felt as we did, we can discover and identify ways to plan future career objectives more accurately.

Bryant (1984) has developed a flexible way to help managers analyze and plot their careers. The Personal Career Graph presented in the appendix is an exercise you may enjoy, particularly if you are near or beyond midcareer and have had several significant career events to think about.

Conclusion

Pressures on middle managers, such as the rapid pace of change and a feeling of declining control, create barriers to career development and personal growth, but there are also some positive factors, such as increasing spans of control and more responsibility. Plateaued men become more involved with their families, while working women in midcareer face increased conflict between family pressures and job achievement. Women who return to work after raising families feel that they have many years of high potential ahead of them, but organizations see them as not having time to climb the corporate ladder. Fortunately, there are many ways to enhance the career motivation of midcareer plateaued managers. Serious midlife crises generally are faced only by people who have histories of poor adjustment to major life changes. The constructive coping strategy is a way to assume responsibility for what happens to us and to take action to meet our needs.

Appendix: Creating a Career Graph

by Marshall G. Bryant

The personal Career Graph is a tool that you can use to understand your career better while simultaneously planning future career goals and how to attain them. The graph has been used to identify the need to change jobs, raise questions concerning one's chosen career, emphasize the effect of employee-supervisor differences, and provide personal introspection on job interests.

The graph consists of a vertical and a horizontal arm (see Figure 1). The vertical arm is labeled *Degree of Job Satisfaction* and is bounded by minimum (*Min.*) and maximum (*Max.*) values. These values are determined by the person drawing the curve; they are limited only by the respondent's frame of reference. The horizontal arm is labeled *Time* and is bounded by Beginning and Now. The amount of time covered by the graph is determined by the person drawing the curve. For example, the amount of time selected may be an entire career of many years, the most recent ten years, the period covered since the respondent joined the present employer, or the current job assignment. From our experience of using the graph, it is employed most meaningfully when it covers a period of time long enough to include significant swings or changes in the vertical arm, *Degree of Job Satisfaction.*

In its basic form, the Personal Career Graph is simplistic, and drawing the curve is easy to do. Its meaning and impact come later, in seeing your evaluation of your career displayed graphically. Recollections of past job experiences, and of how job satisfaction was affected by specific work assignments, geographical considerations, working conditions, recognition (or lack of it), supervisory relationships, management policies, and similar influences, all go into the review and analysis of the various changes shown in the curve. It is here, in the context of the changes and their effect on

Figure 1. Personal Career Graph (Example 1).

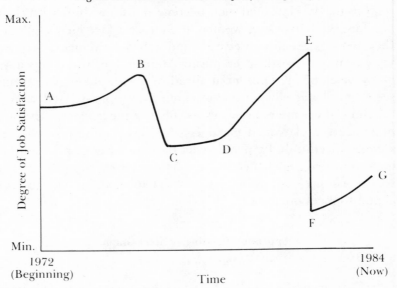

the individual, that the curve takes on its full impact and meaning; it is here that self-analysis and understanding begin.

Figure 1 is an example of a personal career graph. A general analysis of this curve is as follows:

A   Employee joined the company with a high level of enthusiasm and expectation.

B-C   After several projects, good results, and salary increases—all of which raised the level of job satisfaction—the department was reorganized. This reorganization resulted in divided peer groups, a change in supervisors, and work on different projects, which took employee away from the primary area of technical expertise. This latter point was extremely important.

D   Change in supervision and work assignments improved employee's situation.

E   Approval received from employer and from university thesis adviser to pursue work on a project that would meet company objectives as well as employee's personal goal of obtaining advanced degree.

F   Prior to completion of thesis requirements, employee's project was abruptly cancelled, and attainment of degree appeared hopeless. (The events that occurred at this point were rather dramatic, as evidenced by the curve. Without warning, it was announced that, effective immediately, all work on the project would be terminated.)

G   Point where employee began new assignment and where severe depression began to subside.

In Figure 2, we have a familiar bar graph. This individual used the bar shape to indicate an average level of job satisfaction for the entire period of each job assignment. In discussing her career and the rationale for this type of graph, she readily acknowledged that, within each of her assignments, there were times when her level of job satisfaction fluctuated. She saw each assignment as a separate entity.

Figure 2. Personal Career Graph (Example 2).

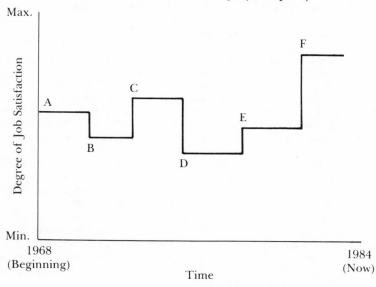

Points *A*, *B*, *C*, *D*, and *E* represent particular job assignments. The differences in the degree of job satisfaction resulted from several geographical relocations (some rated good, others not) and from differences in supervision and type of work (staff versus line operations). Point *F* represents a promotion.

The two most obvious ways to use the graph are in career counseling and in job résumé preparation. This type of graphic review and analysis can be especially helpful in identifying job objectives.

Sometimes we are not aware of the reasons for our high or low levels of job satisfaction, until we begin to analyze the factors that caused us to feel as we did. Relationships with immediate supervisors, higher management, or peers often contribute to our feelings of job satisfaction. Requirements of the job (geographical relocation, overtime, type of work), and the extent to which one is prepared to undertake a particular job, are factors affecting the degree of job satisfaction. Thus, use of the graph and subsequent analysis will go a long way toward answering such questions as the following:

What kind of work do I enjoy?

What kind of work am I prepared to do?

Where do I want to work?

Why do I prefer one kind of work over another?

How do I relate to fellow employees? To supervisors?

Have I spent too much time on a particular job, assignment, or type of work?

Should I now, or soon, broaden my experience?

As a manager, am I becoming a specialist or a generalist?

Am I satisfied with my career? What is lacking?

What should I do to improve my situation?

No graph, regardless of how simple or complex, can answer all these questions, but the Personal Career Graph can help highlight the need for answers to such questions and concerns.

The significance of the Personal Career Graph is not in the ranges of time or values selected for *Degree of Job Satisfaction.* Each person's graph is different. There is no wrong way to draw the curve. Interpretation is left to the individual who drew the curve. Your curve is yours alone.

Points on the curve become significant when the angle or slope of the curve changes sharply or when the direction changes. These are the points where cause and effect are reviewed and analyzed. We should remember that high and low levels of job satisfaction are always in relation to some unspecified standard, determined by each individual.

Perhaps the most important value derived from use of the graph is the direction of the overall curve. If the overall curve is generally in an upward direction, career job satisfaction is positive. If it is not, then a job change is important—if not absolutely necessary. The person is either in the wrong assignment or in the wrong type of work. The problem may be the individual's original career choice.

12

❋ ❋ ❋ ❋ ❋

Conclusion: Applying Manager-Development Strategies and Guidelines

Before discussing possible applications of the major concepts presented in this book, it will be useful to review the ideas discussed so far and to consider some of the connections among them.

Chapter One recommends interactive career planning to create and implement a vision of the future. This requires flexibility and responsiveness to organizational changes that can have an impact on career opportunities.

Chapter Two examines how the organization indoctrinates new managers. We are most susceptible to influence early in our careers when we want to establish ourselves and feel we belong.

An understanding of career motivation serves as a basis for manager development. In my view, career motivation is not one concept. Chapter Three outlines the components of career motivation, grouped into three domains:

- *Career resilience:* keeping our spirits up when the going gets tough by believing in ourselves, needing to achieve, being willing to take risks, and knowing how and when to be co-operative and independent.
- *Career insight:* being realistic about ourselves and accurately relating these perceptions to our goals by establishing goals and having career perceptiveness (understanding the social and political environment).
- *Career identity:* the extent to which we define ourselves by our work through work involvement and desire to advance and obtain what goes along with advancement (recognition, leadership, money).

Chapter Four examines patterns of the career motivation domains, proposing that career resilience sets the stage for the development of career insight and career identity. Self-assessment exercises are offered to help you understand your career motivation and plan action steps for increasing components of career resilience, insight, and identity.

Chapter Five compares the manager-development policies and programs in two companies, ECHO, Inc., and DYNAMO Corp. DYNAMO treated its new managers as corporate resources for the future, while ECHO treated its new managers as means of meeting current business needs, with little regard for their development.

Chapter Six sets forth guidelines for developing new managers' career motivation. These guidelines were operating in DYNAMO and were absent in ECHO. The guidelines are repeated below:

- To support *career resilience*: provide positive reinforcement for a job well done, generate opportunities for achievement, create an environment for risk taking by rewarding innovation and reducing the negative consequences of failure, and show interpersonal concern and encourage group cohesiveness and collaborative working relationships.
- To support *career insight*: encourage goal setting and give career information and performance feedback.

- To support *career identity*: encourage work involvement through job challenge and professional growth, provide opportunities for leadership and advancement, and offer rewards such as recognition and bonuses.

Chapter Seven recommends that, to the extent possible, young managers should be treated as corporate resources. They should be developed as generalists when this fits the organization's needs. Career planning should be instituted and its use reinforced. For example, the process for making staffing decisions should allow for movement between departments in order to facilitate career development, and developing skills should be considered sufficient reason for transferring young managers.

Chapter Eight reviews human resource tools that affect motivation by influencing the individual, the boss's management style, or the company's policies and programs. The most cost-effective programs center on generally recognized principles of good management, including realistic job previews, enthusiastic recruitment, valid selection methods, challenging jobs, goal setting, thorough and accurate performance appraisals, and proper reinforcement.

Chapter Nine provides examples of the boss's role in manager development. The boss plays a major role in giving support to young managers, and the company's policies and programs can facilitate or hinder this process. The questions at the end of the chapter help evaluate the congruence between the company and the boss in following the manager-development guidelines.

Chapter Ten considers manager training methods and ties the career motivation domains to ingredients of leadership. Career resilience implies being proactive and responsible, career insight implies learning about ourselves and the environment, and career identity implies visioning the future. Training methods for enhancing the career motivation domains are also reviewed in this chapter.

Chapter Eleven returns to the theme of the first chapter, interactive planning, which is as important to managers in mid-career as to those just starting their careers. There are many ways for organizations to facilitate the continued development of midcareer managers. Constructive coping is a way for managers to assume responsibility for their own development and to be responsive to organizational changes.

I find the concepts of career motivation and the corresponding manager-development guidelines and exercises to be useful for thinking about my own career and for creating manager-development programs. I do not intend my ideas to be taken as "the one right answer." As you have seen, manager development is not that simple! Rather, this book is intended to provide a theoretical and research base for understanding career motivation. The applications suggested here are designed to integrate and organize principles of good management. My hope is that readers will adapt and apply these concepts to their jobs and organizations to achieve meaningful, on-going manager development. Following are examples of ways the ideas in this book might be applied.

Young Managers

Most of this book addresses the situation of the young manager. The main idea I hope to convey to such managers is the value of being proactive—knowing their strengths and weaknesses, needs and interests; setting goals in relation to career opportunities; taking action to achieve those goals; and being flexible in response to career barriers. The socialization process is a two-way street, meaning that the young manager learns about the organization and becomes part of it but also affects it by creating new projects, establishing new working relationships, and applying new work values. The self-assessment questions and the discussion of patterns of development that appear in Chapters Three and Four are guides for self-understanding. Another potentially valuable lesson from this book is that the organization's policies and programs and the nature of supervision may constrain or facilitate employees' career development. The guidelines for manager development presented in Chapters Six and Seven indicate the type of environment young managers should seek and, in some cases, create by, for example, seeking feedback, opportunities for achievement, job challenge, interpersonal support, recognition, chances to be a leader, and so forth. Finally, there are suggestions for setting career goals and establishing a career direction, which require a foundation of career resilience. The young manager's first task should be to work toward a belief in him- or herself, a desire to achieve, a willingness to take risks, and the knowledge of when and how to act independently and cooperatively. Once the young manager is firmly on the road to career resilience, it makes sense to pursue career opportunities, with an understanding of how to take advantage of them, and to set career goals and try to accomplish them.

Career Women Deciding Whether to Start a Family

Most of the women in the study reported in this book said that they eventually wanted to have children while they continued their careers. Several women planned to wait until they reached middle management before starting a family, feeling that having children prior to being promoted to that level might indicate to management that they were not serious about their careers. They wanted middle-management jobs but cared less about reaching top management, realizing that opportunities to do so were limited and believing that a higher-level management position would require sacrificing time with their families. Other research found that women who had left the work force to start a family and then returned to work when their children were in school believed that advancement opportunities would still be open to them. However, they found that organizations would hire them to fill specific positions but not to prepare them for future advancement (see Chapter Eleven). Career insight fueled by accurate information about career alternatives is especially important to women who value career advancement. Perhaps more than men, women have to be able to analyze the work environment and seek support for career development as they juggle multiple roles, make role transitions, and face career barriers. I hope that an understanding of career resilience, insight, identity, and related factors will help women in this effort.

High-Potential Young Managers

On the one hand, high-potential managers are those who have the least need for development programs because they have the talent and ambition to find or generate the opportunities and environments they want. On the other hand, organizations such as DYNAMO Corp. give high-potential managers considerable attention because they represent an investment in the future. There are problems associated with identifying and being identified with high-potential managers (see Chapters Five, Seven, and Nine). For example, young managers can encounter difficulties both supervising and working for older and more experienced people who may be jealous of their opportunities and salaries. Also, identifying a high-potential group creates expectations for rapid advancement, which cannot always be met because opportunities decline or because the young manager does not succeed. That is why some companies, such as IBM, keep their lists of high-potential managers secret. Whether such a list is secret or not, people eventually recognize who is designated high-potential by the assignments they receive.

The concept of career resilience is especially crucial to the high-potential manager. Others may take it for granted that high-potential managers believe in themselves, want achievement opportunities, are risk takers, and can overcome career barriers. But high-potential managers may not be as resilient as people assume. We found that the training format we designed to orient new managers was also valuable to more experienced high-potential managers (Chapter Six). The high-potential managers needed to understand the elements of career motivation and what they could do to avoid career barriers and create facilitating work conditions. For instance, they needed to understand the subtleties of competitive collaboration—supporting and encouraging others while they try to excel themselves.

Middle Managers

Today's economic conditions require that organizations do more with less. This often means eliminating some middle managers. The result is extreme pressure on plateaued managers who are likely to be in midcareer (see Chapter Eleven). Development for the plateaued middle manager may entail obtaining more responsible, challenging positions at the same management level. It may mean making a midcareer change, or devoting more energy to family and leisure than to career. Organizations and individuals may be able to adapt many of the concepts discussed in this book to deal with such problems. Proactive planning and self-assessment are never-ending processes. Participating in socialization of newcomers can be valuable to middle managers in renewing their commitment to the organization and to their careers. Also, some socialization is necessary any time a person makes a role change, whether to accept a new role or to alter attitudes about a current role (see Chapter Two). Organizations need to adapt their programs and ways of dealing with middle managers to maintain their motivation and utilize them most effectively through appropriate job assignments, training programs, and supervision (see Chapters Eight and Ten).

The Boss

Managers can apply the concepts in this book to their roles as supervisors and leaders (see Chapter Nine). The boss reflects the policies of the organization, but the boss's style of management can create subordinate development independent of, or in interaction with, the organization's programs and policies. I hope that bosses will understand the reasons behind the manager-development guidelines in Chapter Six and will use them.

Personnel Professionals

It is often troublesome that personnel professionals have little influence on their organizations' development policies, such as whether managers are to be trained as generalists or specialists and the extent to which managers are treated as resources for the future or merely as means to meet current business needs. These policies are often set by top managers without professional expertise. This book offers one approach to help human resource specialists recommend policies and generate programs. I recommend that programs be linked in a comprehensive way in order to ensure that their influence on the organization's development policies is pervasive. In this spirit, I outlined programs for new manager orientation, high-potential manager development, and a standard career track (see Chapter Six). In Chapters Eight and Ten training and development programs were outlined and tied to their potential effects on elements of career motivation.

I am in favor of fast-track development programs for high-potential managers and standard career tracks for other managers. Both types of programs begin by socializing the individual into the organization. Both follow the same guidelines for manager development—but the sequence is more rapid for individuals on the fast track, who will have more meaningful, responsible jobs at higher organizational levels.

When promotion opportunities decline, the high-potential program keeps managers competitive with each other by increasing their responsibilities and providing opportunities for merit pay increases. The goal of the standard career track is more difficult to accomplish because it requires developing challenging assignments for more people at lower organizational levels.

Researchers

The research on which this book is based was an intensive investigation of managers early in their careers (Chapters Three and Five). The purpose of the study was to explore the meaning of career motivation. The data provided an understanding of managers' career development at a time when they are especially sensitive to influence. I believe the results show the value of holistic research, collecting and mixing qualitative and quantitative data on both individuals and organizations from multiple sources over time. This book also demonstrates the integration of research, theory, and practice. Certainly, much more research is necessary to (1) examine the meaningfulness of the career motivation dimensions, (2) study development patterns,

(3) test the effects of the guidelines on elements of career motivation, (4) study different organizational philosophies of manager development, (5) examine the role of the boss on subordinates, and (6) apply the career motivation concepts to mid- and late-career stages. We also need more representative and randomly selected samples and better comparison and control groups.

References

※ ※ ※ ※ ※ ※ ※ ※ ※ ※ ※ ※ ※

Ackoff, R. *Creating the Corporate Future.* New York: Wiley, 1981.

Bailyn, L. "The Slow Burn Way to the Top: Some Thoughts on the Early Years of Organization Careers." In C. B. Derr (Ed.), *Work, Family, and the Career: New Frontiers in Theory and Research.* New York: Praeger, 1980.

Bandura, A. "Self-Efficacy: Toward a Unifying Theory of Behavioral Change." *Psychological Review,* 1977, *84* (2), 191–215.

Bardwick, J. M. "Plateauing and Productivity." *Sloan Management Review,* Spring 1983, pp. 67–73.

Bennis, W. "Currents in Leadership Theory and Practice." Paper presented at 44th annual meeting of the Academy of Management, Boston, Mass., August 1984a.

Bennis, W. "Reflections on Bridging Management Thought and Practice." Paper presented at 44th annual meeting of the Academy of Management, Boston, Mass., August 1984b.

Bennis, W. *Taking Charge.* New York: Harper & Row, 1985.

241

Berg, E. N. "Can Troubled Trilogy Fulfill Its Dream?" *The New York Times,* July 8, 1984, pp. 1F, 19F.

Berlew, D. E., and Hall, D. T. "The Socialization of Managers: Effects of Expectations on Performance." *Administrative Science Quarterly,* 1966, *11,* 207–223.

Bolles, R. N. *What Color is Your Parachute?* Berkeley: Ten Speed Press, 1980.

Boyatzis, R. *The Competent Manager.* New York: Wiley-Interscience, 1982.

Bray, D. W., Campbell, R. J., and Grant, D. L. *Formative Years in Business: A Long-Term AT&T Study of Managerial Lives.* New York: Wiley, 1974.

Bray, D. W., and Howard, A. "Career Success and Life Satisfactions of Middle-Aged Managers." In L. A. Bond and J. C. Rosen (Eds.), *Competence and Coping During Adulthood.* Hanover, N.H.: University Press of New England, 1980.

Bryant, M. Personal communication. September 19, 1984.

Buchanan, B., II. "Building Organizational Commitment: The Socialization of Managers in Work Organizations." *Administrative Science Quarterly,* 1974, *19* (4), 533–546.

Campbell, D. P. *If You Don't Know Where You're Going, You'll Probably End Up Somewhere Else.* Allen, Tex.: Argus Communications, 1974.

Campbell, J. P., and Pritchard, R. D. "Motivation Theory in Industrial and Organizational Psychology." In M. D. Dunnette (Ed.), *Handbook of Industrial and Organizational Psychology.* Chicago: Rand McNally, 1976.

Carnazza, J. P., Korman, A. K., Ference, T. P., and Stoner, J. A. F. "Plateaued and Non-Plateaued Managers: Factors in Job Performance." *Journal of Management,* 1981, *7* (2), 7–25.

"Changing a Corporate Culture: Can Johnson & Johnson Go from Band-Aids to High Tech?" *Business Week,* May 14, 1984, pp. 130–138.

Colarelli, S. M., Stumpf, S. A., and Wall, S. J. "Analyzing Managerial Jobs: Quick and Clean." *Eastern Academy of Management Proceedings,* 1981, pp. 80–85.

"Discover: A Computer Based Development System for Organizations." Iowa City: American College Testing Program, 1984.

DuBois, L. "Career and Family in Midlife Men and Women." Unpublished doctoral dissertation, Adelphi University, 1981.

Feldman, D. C. "A Contingency Theory of Socialization." *Administrative Science Quarterly*, 1976a, *21*, 433-452.

Feldman, D. C. "A Practical Program for Employee Socialization." *Organizational Dynamics*, Autumn 1976b, pp. 64-80.

Gagne, R. M. "Military Training and Principles of Learning." *American Psychologist*, 1962, *17*, 83-91.

"GM Shakeup puts 'Official' Stamp on the New Management." *Behavioral Sciences Newsletter*, 1984, *2* (13), 1-2.

Goldstein, A. P., and Sorcher, M. *Changing Supervisory Behavior*. Elmsford, N.Y.: Pergamon Press, 1974.

Goldstein, I. L. "Training in Work Organizations." *Annual Review of Psychology*, 1980, *31*, 229-279.

Goleman, D. "Successful Executives Rely On Own Kind of Intelligence." *The New York Times*, July 31, 1984, pp. C1, C11.

Hackman, J. R., and Oldham, G. R. *Work Redesign*. Reading, Mass.: Addison-Wesley, 1980.

Hauser, D. "Carlton Amdahl's Confession: 'I just couldn't handle it.' " *San Jose Mercury News*, April 24, 1984, pp. 1F, 6F.

Hornstein, H. A., and MacKenzie, F. T. "Consultraining: Merging Management Education with Organization Development." *Training and Development Journal*, January 1984, pp. 52-56.

Howard, A., and Bray, D. W. "Career Motivation in Midlife Managers." Paper presented at the American Psychological Association Annual Convention, Montreal, Canada, September 1980.

Howard, A., and Bray, D. W. "Today's Young Managers: They Can Do It, But Will They?" *The Wharton Magazine*, 1981, *5* (4), 23-28.

Howard, A., and Wilson, J. A. "Leadership in a Declining Work Ethic." *California Management Review*, 1982, *24* (4), 33-46.

Hunt, D. M., and Michael, C. "Mentorship: A Career Training and Development Tool." *Academy of Management Review*, 1983, *8* (3), 475-485.

Jacobs, S. L. "Women Chief Executives Help Each Other with Frank Advice." *The Wall Street Journal,* July 2, 1984, Section 2, p. 21.

Jennings, E. "Leadership and the Exceptional Executive." Paper presented at Institute for Management Studies meeting, Hopewell, N.J., April 1984.

Jones, G. R. "Psychological Orientation and the Process of Organizational Socialization: An Interactionist Perspective." *Academy of Management Review,* 1983, *8* (3), 464–471.

Kets de Vries, M. F. R. "The Midcareer Conundrum." *Organizational Dynamics,* Autumn 1978, pp. 45–62.

Knudsen, K. R. "Management Subcultures: Research and Change." *Journal of Management Development,* 1982, *1* (4), 11–26.

Kotter, J. P., Faux, V. A., and McArthur, C. C. *Self-Assessment and Career Development.* Englewood Cliffs, N.J.: Prentice-Hall, 1978.

Kram, K. E. "Mentoring Processes at Work: Developmental Relationships in Managerial Careers." Unpublished doctoral dissertation, Yale University, 1980.

Lean, E. "What Kind of Management Development Improves Productivity?" *Training and Development Journal,* January 1984, pp. 17–20.

Lee, C. "Sentry Insurance: Training from the Ground Up." *Training,* January 1984, pp. 66–69.

Lehner, U. C. "With His Bid for EDS, GM's Smith Continues to Make Bold Changes." *The Wall Street Journal,* July 2, 1984, pp. 21, 24.

Levinson, D. J., and others. *The Seasons of a Man's Life.* New York: Knopf, 1978.

London, M. "What Every Personnel Director Should Know About Management Promotion Decisions." *Personnel Journal,* 1978, *57,* 550–555.

London, M. "Toward a Theory of Career Motivation." *Academy of Management Review,* 1983, *8* (4), 620–630.

London, M. "Development for New Managers." *The Journal of Management Development,* 1984, *2* (4), 3–14.

London, M., and Bray, D. W. "An Assessment Center to Study

Career Motivation." *The Career Center Bulletin,* 1983, *4* (1), 8–13.

London, M., and Bray, D. W. "Measuring and Developing Young Managers' Career Motivation." *Journal of Management Development,* 1985, *5.*

London, M., and Stumpf, S. A. *Managing Careers.* Reading, Mass.: Addison-Wesley, 1982.

London, M., and Stumpf, S. A. "How Managers Make Promotion Decisions." *Journal of Management Development,* 1984, *3* (1), 56–65.

Long, J. W. "The Wilderness Lab." *Training and Development Journal,* May 1984, pp. 59–69.

McCall, M. W., Jr., and Lombardo, M. M. *Looking Glass, Inc.: An Organizational Simulation.* Technical Report No. 12. Greensboro, N.C.: Center for Creative Leadership, 1978.

McCall, M. W., Jr., and Lombardo, M. M. "What Makes a Top Executive?" *Psychology Today,* February 1983, pp. 26–31.

McClelland, D. C. "Achievement Motivation Can Be Developed." *Harvard Business Review,* 1965, *43* (6), 6–14, 178.

Margolis, J. "Keynote Address: Developing Managers for the Future." Paper presented at 44th annual meeting of the Academy of Management, Boston, Mass., August 1984.

Miller, D. B. "Career Planning and Management in Organizations." *S. A. M. Advanced Management Journal,* 1978, *13,* 33–43.

Miner, J. B. "Using Managerial Role Motivation Training to Overcome Motivational Deficiencies." Paper presented at the Annual Meeting of the American Psychological Association, Toronto, August 1984.

Morgan, M. A., Hall, D. T., and Martier, A. "Career Development Activities in Industry: Where Are We and Where Should We Be?" *Personnel,* 1979, *56,* 13–30.

Nicholson, N. "A Theory of Work Role Transitions." *Administrative Science Quarterly,* 1984, *29,* 172–191.

"Not Eyeball to Eyeball: Managers: More Discontent than Execs Think." *Industry Week,* March 19, 1984, pp. 15–16.

O'Connor, R. Personal communication. September 20, 1984.

Pascale, R. "Fitting New Employees Into the Company Culture." *Fortune,* May 28, 1984, pp. 28–43.

Peters, T. J., and Waterman, R. H., Jr. *In Search of Excellence: Lessons from America's Best-Run Companies.* New York: Harper & Row, 1982.

Phalon, R. "Hell Camp." *Forbes,* 1984, *13* (14), 56–58.

Rowan, R. "How Harvard's Women MBAs are Managing." *Fortune,* 1983, *108* (1), 64.

Salancik, G. R., and Meindl, J. R. "Corporate Attributions as Strategic Illusions of Management Control." *Administrative Science Quarterly,* 1984, *29,* 238–254.

Salancik, G. R., and Pfeffer, J. A. "A Social Information Processing Approach to Job Attitudes and Task Design." *Administrative Science Quarterly,* 1978, *23,* 224–253.

Schein, E. H. "Keynote Address: Developing Managers for the Future." Paper presented at 44th annual meeting of the Academy of Management, Boston, Mass., August 1984.

Schlesinger, L. A., and Oshry, B. "Quality of Work Life and the Manager: Muddle in the Middle." *Organizational Dynamics,* Summer 1984, pp. 5–19.

Sheahan, T. J. "A New Approach to the Three-Year Plan." *Medical Marketing & Media,* 1975, *10* (11), 18–25.

Shorris, E. *The Oppressed Middle: Politics of Middle Management and Scenes from Corporate Life.* Garden City, N.Y.: Anchor Press/Doubleday, 1981.

Stein, B. "Middle Management: An Underused Resource." Papresented at Executive Study Conference, New York City, May 1984.

Stumpf, S. A. Personal communication. November 1984.

Thomas, A. B. "The Career Graph: A Tool for Mid-Career Development." *Personnel Review,* 1981, *10* (3), 18–22.

Thornton, G. C., III, and Byham, W. C. *Assessment Centers and Managerial Performance.* New York: Academic Press, 1982.

Vaillant, G. E. *Adaptation to Life.* Boston: Little, Brown, 1977.

Van Maanen, J. "Breaking-In: Socialization to Work." In R. Dubin (Ed.), *Handbook of Work, Organization, and Society.* Chicago: Rand McNally, 1976.

Van Zwieten, J. "Training on the Rocks." *Training and Development Journal,* January 1984, pp. 27–32.

Wall, S. J., Awal, D., and Stumpf, S. A. "Conflict Management: The Situation, Behaviors, and Outcome Effectiveness." In D. Ray (Ed.), *The Relationship Between Theory, Research, and Practice: An Assessment of Fundamental Problems and Their Possible Resolution.* Mississippi State University: Southern Management Association, 1981.

Wanous, J. P. *Organizational Entry: Recruitment, Selection, and Socialization of Newcomers.* Reading, Mass.: Addison-Wesley, 1980.

Wanous, J. P., Reichers, A. E., and Malik, S. D. "Organizational Socialization and Group Development: Toward an Integrative Perspective." *Academy of Management Review,* 1984, *9* (4), 670–683.

Warren, K. "Plateaued Professionals in Slow Economic Growth." Paper presented at Institute for Management Studies meeting, New York City, April 1984.

Wexley, K. N., and Latham, G. P. *Developing and Training Human Resources in Organizations.* Glenview, Ill.: Scott, Foresman, 1981.

Wise, R. E., and Zern, H. R. "Identifying and Improving Management Skills at Hartford National Bank." *Training/HRD,* November 1982, pp. 56–58.

Index

✳ ✳ ✳ ✳ ✳ ✳ ✳ ✳ ✳ ✳ ✳ ✳ ✳

A

Achievement, need for, and career motivation, 42-43, 47, 77

Ackoff, R., 2-3, 5, 6, 11, 241

Advancement, and career motivation, 46-47, 48, 79

American College Testing Program, self-assessment software from, 202

American Woman's Economic Development Corporation, Chief Executive Roundtable of, 203

Anheuser-Busch: decision files at, 17; training program at, 196

Assessment center: for career motivation, 52-55, 140-141, 158, 162, 163; conducting, 55-56; for potential appraisal, 153-154, 159, 161, 162; for skill diagnosis, 186-187

AT&T: corporate change at, 16, 17; degree of centralization for, 10-11; goal of, 22; and inactive planning, 4-5; policy workshops of, 191

Autonomy, and career motivation, 44, 47-48, 77-78

Awal, D., 194, 247

Awareness training: for career motivation, 142, 158; in orientations, 139-140

B

Bailyn, L., 218, 241

Ballard, H. T., 54

249

Bandura, A., 64, 241
Bardwick, J. M., 217, 218, 219, 221, 241
Bass personality measure, 53
Baylor, Carol: and company philosophy, 129; developmental pattern of, 73-75
Behavior modeling, for skill and knowledge training, 188-190
Bosses: analysis of role of, 165-182; applications for, 237; bucking the system by, 166-169; as counselors or coaches, 147, 158, 161; and development programs, 107-108; discretion for, 149, 159, 162; group sessions with, 92-95, 102; human resource strategies for, 142-148, 158; and managing subordinates, 173-176; policy impact on, 171-173; recommendations on, 179-182; responsibility of, 123-124; rewarding, for manager development, 148, 159, 162; as role models, 159, 160-161, 162; self-assessment for, 180-181; sticking to the rules by, 170-171; as supportive, 176-179; training by, 169-170; training for, 100
Bell Incomplete Sentences Test, 52
Bell of Pennsylvania, and self-assessment, 202
Bell System: breakup of, 4, 191; as decentralized, 10; values of, 22, 28
Bennis, W., 198, 200, 241
Bentley, Marilyn: career motivation of, 60-61; and company philosophy, 129, 135; developmental pattern of, 70, 72; socialization of, 35-38
Berg, E. N., 242

Berlew, D. E., 25, 242
Boeing, productivity through people at, 97-98
Bolles, R. N., 202, 242
Boyatzis, R., 185, 242
Boyd, Jim: career identity of, 69; career motivation of, 61-62; and company philosophy, 129; socialization of, 39-40
Bray, D. W., xiii, 25, 49, 54, 55, 57, 215, 216-217, 218, 219, 221, 242, 243, 244-245
Bristol-Myers: as decentralized, 10; effective leaders at, 198
Brown, Lydia: career motivation of, 59-60; and company philosophy, 129, 135; creating the future by, 7-10; healthy development of, 68
Bryant, M. G., xiii, 226, 227-230, 242
Buchanan, B., II, 20, 24-25, 242
Burke, J., 21
Burr, D., 13
Byham, W. C., 187, 246

C

Calhoun, K. S., 54
Campbell, D. P., 242
Campbell, J. P., 64, 242
Campbell, R. J., 54, 215, 242
Career counseling, for career motivation, 142, 158, 161-162
Career goals, and career motivation, 44-45, 48, 78
Career identity: applications for, 232, 233; boss's role in, 166; career insight related to, 66; and career motivation, 42, 57, 62; career resilience related to, 66-

67; developing and strengthening, 63, 64, 65, 68, 70, 72, 74, 75, 76; and development programs, 105-106, 107-108, 112; and human resource strategies, 141, 158-159, 162; leadership training for, 204-205; and midlife crisis, 223; and organizational philosophy, 121, 129-130, 133, 135; and organizational policies, 101; and self-doubt, 69-70

Career insight: applications for, 232; boss's role in, 165-166; career identity related to, 66; and career motivation, 42, 56-57, 62; career resilience related to, 65-66; developing and strengthening, 63, 64, 65, 68, 70, 72, 74, 75-76; and development programs, 105, 106, 107-108, 112; and human resource strategies, 141, 158-159, 160-161, 162; leadership training for, 201-204; and organizational philosophy, 121, 129-130, 133, 135; and organizational policies, 101; and self-doubt, 69-70

Career motivation: and achievement, need for, 42-43, 47, 77; action plan for developing, 79-80; and advancement, 46-47, 48, 79; assessing, 41-62; assessment center for, 52-55, 140-141, 158, 162, 163; assumptions about, 112; and breaking away from ineffective pattern, 72-73; and career goals, 44-45, 48, 78; case studies of, 58-62; concept of, 41; and dependency and autonomy, 44, 47-48, 77-78; developing and strengthening, 63-80; developmental processes for, 64-

67; and feedback, 45-46, 48, 78; and follow-up interviews, 58; healthy development of, 68; and individual efforts, 73-75; key action steps for, 77-79; managers' views of, 42-47; as multidimensional, 109; and organizational policies and programs, 81-102; patterns for development of, 67-75; redirection of, 68-69; research design for, 49-51; and research feedback to participants, 57-58; research results on, 56-57; and reversing failure, 70-72; self-assessment of, 47-48, 76-80; strategies for, 106-108; and unfamiliarity, 43-44, 47, 77; and work involvement, 46, 48, 79; workshop for, 143-144

Career paths: philosophy on, 125-126, 128-129; strategies for, 150, 159, 161, 162

Career planning: case example of, 7-10; company's view of, 10-16; manager's view of, 3-10; self-assessment of, 7

Career Projectives (Management Apperception Test), 53-54

Career resilience: applications for, 232, 235, 236; boss's role in, 165; career identity related to, 66-67; career insight related to, 65-66; and career motivation, 42, 56, 62; developing and strengthening, 63-64, 65, 68, 70, 72, 73, 74, 75; and development programs, 105, 106, 107-108, 112; and human resource strategies, 140, 143, 147, 158-159, 162; leadership training for, 200-201; and midlife crisis, 223; and organizational philosophy, 121,

129-130, 133, 135; and organizational policies, 101

Careers center, strategies for, 154-155, 159, 161

Carnazza, J. P., 212-213, 242

Center for Creative Leadership, simulation by, 193

Cognitive complexity, and decision making, 185-186

Colarelli, S. M., 194, 242

Cole, Teresa, and supportiveness, 177-179

Columbia University, graduates of, studied, 213-215

Commitment, and socialization, 20, 35

Communication of policies, strategies for, 155, 159, 161, 162

Companies: analysis of policies and programs of, 81-102; attitude surveys of, 90-91; background on, 81-87; career planning viewed by, 10-16; culture of, and bosses, 182; development program comparisons for, 96-97; group sessions for, 91-96; inactive planning by, 12-13; interactive planning by, 13-16; and midlife crisis, 225; and motivation strategies, 108; philosophies and needs of, 119-136; preactive planning by, 13; presidents' letters from, 87-90; productivity through people in, 97-99; reactive planning by, 11-12; socialization fears by, 31; socialization into, 19-40; study results used by, 99-101; training programs by, 193-196; values and norms of, 20-22

Contingency planning. See Interactive planning

Converse, Wayne: and company philosophy, 129; and reversing failure, 70-72

Corning Glass Works, training program at, 196

Counterplanning, concept of, 17-18

Creating the future: case example of, 7-10; and leadership training, 204-205; recommendations for, 5; and socialization, 19-40; strategic planning for, 1-18

Culture, corporate: and bosses, 182; and socialization, 22

D

Delta Air Lines, inward focus of, 31

Dependency, and career motivation, 44, 47-48, 77-78

Development programs, comprehensive: analysis of, 103-118; components of, 159; as comprehensive or limited, 124; effects and costs of, 157-162; goals for, 104; guidelines for, 104-106; high-potential, 110-112, 115-117, 124-125, 156-157, 161, 163; linkages in, 110; motivation strategies in, 106-108; need for, 108-112; for new managers, 110, 113-115, 163; and organizational philosophy and needs, 119-136; standard, 110, 117-118, 163

DuBois, L., 213-215, 216, 221-222, 243

DYNAMO Corp.: attitude survey results for, 90-91; boss's roles at, 166, 173-179; case example at, 131-135; conclusions on, 101-

102, 179-180, 182; development program comparisons for, 96-97; group sessions at, 92-93, 94, 95; impact on, 51; Manager Development Program at, 86-87, 198, 201; managing subordinates at, 173-176; and midcareer managers, 209; participant selection in, 50; philosophy of, 126-129, 232, 236; president's letters from, 88-90; and productivity through people, 98; study results for, 82-84, 85-86; and supportive bosses, 176-179; use of results by, 99-101

E

Early Career Experiences Study, 56
Eastman Kodak, corporate change at, 14-16, 17
ECHO, Inc.: accounting department at, 170-171; attitude survey results for, 90-91; boss discretion at, 149; bosses' roles at, 169-173; bucking the system at, 166-169; case example at, 129-131; conclusions on, 101-102, 179-180, 181; construction department at, 166-169, 223; engineering department at, 171-173, 223-224; group sessions at, 93-95; impact on, 51; marketing department at, 169-170; and midcareer managers, 209; participant selection in, 50; philosophy of, 126-129, 232; policy impact at, 171-173; president's letters from, 88; and productivity through people, 98; sticking to

the rules at, 170-171; study results for, 82-85; training at, 169-170; use of results by, 99-101
Edwards Personal Preference Schedule, 52
Electronic Data Systems (EDS), strong culture of, 31-33, 40
Enabling, by midcareer managers, 220-221
Environments, for midcareer managers, 208-211
Essence, concept of, 10
Expectations Discussion, 54
Expectations Inventory, 52

F

Fact-Finding Exercise, 53
Faux, V. A., 202, 244
Feedback: and career motivation, 45-46, 48, 78; and development programs, 107; strategies for, 146-147, 158, 160, 161, 162
Feldman, D. C., 20, 26-27, 243
Ference, T. P., 242
Fitzgerald, E. H., xiii
Future. See Creating the future
Future Time Line, 54

G

Gagne, R. M., 188, 243
Geer, Frank, policy impact on, 172-173
General Electric, self-assessment techniques at, 141, 202
General Motors (GM): acquisition by, 32, 33; corporate change at, 14, 16, 17
Gilligan, John: bucking the system

by, 166-169, 172, 181; constructive style of, 223, 224

Goal setting, strategies for, 145, 158, 161, 162

Goldstein, A. P., 189, 243

Goldstein, I. L., 197, 243

Goleman, D., 185, 243

Grant, D. L., 54, 215, 242

Groff, D., 196

GTE, as centralized, 10

Guilford Zimmerman Temperament Survey, 53

H

Hackman, J. R., 26, 54, 112, 243

Hall, D. T., 25, 196, 242, 245

Harley, Deborah: and company philosophy, 129, 131-135; and managing subordinates, 173-175

Hartford National Bank, behavior modeling program of, 189-190

Harvard Business School: executive-development program at, 195; summer course at, 67; training programs at, 193

Hauser, D., 243

Herr, B., xiii, 77n, 115n

Hewlett-Packard (HP): productivity through people at, 97-98; values of, 20-21

High-potential development programs, 110-112, 115-117, 124-125, 156-157, 161, 163

HI-TECH, development program comparisons for, 96-97

Hornstein, H. A., 203, 243

Howard, A., 25, 31, 49, 55, 57, 215, 216-217, 218, 219, 221, 242, 243

Human resource strategies: analysis

of, 137-164; applications for, 238; and company policies and programs, 148-155, 159; effects and costs of, 157-162; individual focus of, 138-142, 158; and philosophy, 156-157, 159, 162; recommendations on, 162-164; situational focus of, 142-148, 158

Hunt, D. M., 219, 220, 243

I

IBM: computerized skill diagnostic at, 187, 205; corporate uniform at, 21; high-potential managers at, 236; productivity through people at, 97-98; sabbaticals from, 205; strong culture of, 31; training programs of, 193-194

Ideal Business Day, 54

Inactive planning: by companies, 12-13; by managers, 4-5

Institute for Management Studies (IMS), seminars by, 192

Interactive planning: by companies, 13-16; concept of, 6; by managers, 5-7

J

Jacobs, S. L., 203, 244

Japan: competition from, 15; humility lessons in, 203; slow promotions in, 219

Jennings, E., 223, 244

Jensen, B., xiii

Job Diagnostic Survey, Growth Need Strength Measure from, 54

Job evaluation, and midcareer managers, 209-210

Job-matching system, strategies for, 151-152, 159, 161, 162

Job posting, strategies for, 152-153, 159, 161

Job previews, realistic, strategies for, 138-139, 158, 161, 162

Job redesign, strategies for, 144, 158, 160, 161

Job rotation, strategies for, 155, 159, 161, 162

Johnson & Johnson (J&J): corporate change at, 16, 17, 24; values of, 21

Johnston, M., 32-33

Jones, G. R., 33, 244

Lean, E., 192, 196, 244

Lee, C., 195, 244

Lehner, U. C., 32-33, 244

Leopold, M., xiii, 77n, 115n

Levinson, D. J., 221, 244

Lombardo, M. M., 193, 224, 245

London, D., xiii

London, J., xiii

London, M., 49, 51, 110, 115n, 122, 185, 188, 191, 193, 195, 196, 197, 244-245

London, M., xiii

Long, J. W., 202, 245

Looking Glass, Inc., as simulation, 193

K

Katkofsky, W., xiii

Kets de Vries, M. F. R., 207, 208, 222, 244

Knudsen, K. R., 23, 244

Kodak, corporate change at, 14-16, 17

Korman, A. K., 242

Kotter, J. P., 202, 244

Kram, K. E., 219, 244

L

Latham, G. P., 197, 247

Leadership, effective, 198-199

Leadership development training: analysis of, 197-205; for career identity, 204-205; for career insight, 201-204; for career resilience, 200-201; concept of, 184; factors in, 197-200

Leadership style, strategies for, 145-148, 158, 160

M

McArthur, C. C., 202, 244

McCall, M. W., Jr., 193, 224, 245

McClelland, D. C., 203, 245

McGill, A., 22

McIlhone, M., xiii, 115n

MacKenzie, F. T., 203, 243

Malik, S. D., 28, 247

Management culture, and socialization, 22-23

Management Progress Study, 215-216, 221

Manager development: applications for, 231-239; and assessing career motivation, 41-62; boss's role in, 165-182; company's view of, 2, 10-16; comprehensive programs for, 103-118; concept of, 2; and developing career motivation, 63-80; human resource strategies for, 137-164; idea connections for, 231-234; manager's view of, 2, 3-10; for midcareer and plateaued managers, 207-

230; and organizational philosophy and needs, 119-136; and organizational policies and programs, 81-102; socialization for, 19-40; strategic planning for, 1-18; training programs for, 183-206

Managers: career planning viewed by, 3-10; high-potential, applications for, 236-237; high-potential, programs for, 110-112, 115-117, 124-125, 156-157, 161, 163; inactive planning by, 4-5; individual differences among, 33-40; interactive planning by, 5-7; new, programs for, 110, 113-115, 163; and organizational philosophy, 129-135; preactive planning by, 5; reactive planning by, 3-4; women, 214-215, 235; young, applications for, 234-235

Margolis, J., 10, 198, 245

Markham, Ray, and company philosophy, 129-131

Martier, A., 196, 245

Martin, Bev, managing subordinates by, 175-176

Marx, K., 200

Meindl, J. R., 87, 246

Mentoring: by midcareer managers, 219-220; stages of, 220; strategies for, 153, 159, 161, 162

Metropolitan Life Insurance Company, technical management training at, 192

Michael, C., 219, 220, 243

Midcareer and plateaued managers: analysis of motivating and developing, 207-230; applications for, 236-237; career graph for, 227-230; career planning and devel-

opment for, 216-221; discontent of, 211-212; enabling by, 220-221; external environment for, 208; internal environment for, 208-211; job changes for, 217-218; mentoring by, 219-220; midlife crisis for, 221-226; motivation for, 218-219; performance of, 212-216; pressures on, 208-211; and reasons for plateauing, 216-217; symbolic rewards for, 219

Midlife crisis: company impact on, 225; constructive response to, 222-223; dealing with, 222-226; defensive response to, 224; depressive response to, 224-225; factors precipitating, 222; and inactive planning, 14; for midcareer managers, 221-226; self-assessment for, 225-226; underachieving response to, 223-224

Miles, Dorothy, manager development by, 169-170

Miller, D. B., 189, 245

Miner, J. B., 203-204, 245

Mitchell, W. S., 192

Modeling: behavior, 188-190; by bosses, 159, 160-161, 162

Mone, E., xiii, 115n

Morgan, M. A., 196, 245

Morris, Joe: and policy impact, 171-172; underachieving style of, 223-224

Moses, J. L., 54

Motivation, concept of, 41. *See also* Career motivation

Motivation assessment, strategies for, 140-142, 158

Murphy's Law, for manager development, 5

Murray, H. A., 52

N

National Training Laboratories Institute for Applied Behavioral Science, 201
New York University, training programs at, 193
Nicholson, N., 245
Norms. *See* Values

O

O'Connor, R., 199, 245
Oldham, G. R., 26, 54, 112, 243
Organizations. *See* Companies
Orientation and awareness training, strategies for, 139-140, 158
Oshry, B., 210-211, 246

P

Pascale, R., 21-22, 31, 246
Pennsylvania, University of, Wharton School training programs at, 193
Pennsylvania State University, training programs at, 193
People Express, participative management at, 13-14
Performance appraisal, strategies for, 145-146, 158, 161, 162
Perot, R., 32
Personal Career Graph, creating, 227-230
Personnel professionals, applications for, 237-238
Peters, T. J., 22, 97-99, 198, 246
Pfeffer, J. A., 64, 246
Phalon, R., 203, 246
Philosophy: adapting programs to, 119-136; background on, 119-121; on boss responsibility, 123-124; on career paths, 125-126, 128-129; on centralization of decisions, 122-123, 127-128; comparisons of, 126-129; on comprehensive or separate programs, 124; conclusion on, 135-136; on employees as assets, 121, 126, 128; factors in, 121-126; on generalists or specialists, 122, 126-127; on high-potential program, 124-125; and human resource strategies, 156-157, 159, 162; impact of, 129-135; on promotion from within, 123, 126
Plateaued managers. *See* Midcareer and plateaued managers
Polaroid: sabbaticals from, 205; termination incentives by, 12
Potential, performance distinct from, 145-146
Potential appraisal, strategies for, 153-154, 159
Preactive planning: by companies, 13; by managers, 5
Pritchard, R. D., 64, 242
Procter & Gamble: productivity through people at, 97-98; strong culture of, 31
Productivity through people, 97-99

R

Reactive planning: by companies, 11-12; by managers, 3-4
Recruitment, strategies for, 138, 158, 161, 162
Reichers, A. E., 28, 247
Reid-Ware Three-Factor Internal-External Scale, 53

Reinforcement: for career motivation, 64-65; strategies for, 147-
148, 158, 161, 162
Researchers, applications for, 238-
239
Richards, Bob: defensive style of,
224; sticking to the rules by,
170-171
Rokeach Value Survey, 53
Role readiness, concept of, 24
Rotter Incomplete Sentences Test,
52
Rowan, R., 246

S

Salancik, G. R., 64, 87, 246
Sarnoff personality measure, 52
Schein, E. H., 10, 199, 200, 204-
205, 246
Schlesinger, L. A., 210-211, 246
School and College Ability Test,
52
Schwartz, Carl, managing subordinates by, 173-175
Seig, D., xiii
Selection, strategies for, 138, 158,
161, 162
Self-assessment: for bosses, 180-
181; for career motivation, 47-
48, 76-80; for career planning, 7;
for midlife crisis, 225-226;
sources for, 202; workbooks and
workshops on, for career motivation, 141-142, 158
Sentry Insurance, training program
of, 195
Sheahan, T. J., 17, 246
Shorris, E., 224-225, 246
Skill and knowledge training: analysis of, 184-197; behavior modeling in, 188-190; choosing pro-

gram for, 196; comprehensive
programs for, 193-196; concept
of, 184; and developability of
skills, 185-186; diagnosis for,
186-187; evaluating, 197; factors
in, 184-190; methods for, 187-
190; orientation programs for,
190-191; outside seminars for,
192; policy workshops for, 191;
program types for, 190-193; self-
diagnosis for, 187; simulations
for, 193; technical, 191-192;
types of skills in, 184-185; university programs for, 192-193
Skinner, B. F., 188
Six Cases, 54
Social learning, concept of, 64
Socialization: analysis of, 19-40;
case examples of, 35-40; and
commitment, 20, 35; company
fears about, 31; concept of, 20;
as continuous, 23-24; into corporate values, 20-22; in fifth
year and beyond, 27-28; in first
year, 25-27; indicators of successful, 26-27; and individual
differences, 33-40; and influence
susceptibility, 24-25; as interaction, 34-35; and management
culture, 22-23; methods of, 28-
31; outcomes of, 34; in second
through fourth years, 27; by
strong-culture firm, 31-33
Sorcher, M., 189, 243
Sponsor or mentor program: by
midcareer managers, 219-220;
strategies for, 153, 159, 161,
162
Stanford University, executive development program at, 195
Stein, B., 4, 209, 210, 211, 217,
220, 246
Stoner, J. A. F., 242

Strategic planning: concept of, 2-3; and manager/company interaction, 17-18; for manager development, 1-18; types of, 3-16

Streufert's research, 185

Strong-Campbell Vocational Interest Blank, 53

Stumpf, S. A., 122, 185, 188, 191, 193, 194, 195, 196, 197, 242, 245, 246, 247

Succession planning, strategies for, 150-151, 159, 162

Supervisor ratings, for potential appraisal, 154, 159, 161

Supervisor training: guidelines for, 148; strategies for, 142-144, 158

T

Termination incentives, and inactive planning, 12-13

Thayer, T., xiii, 115n

Thematic Apperception Test, 52

Thomas, A. B., 226, 246

Thorndike, E. L., 188

Thornton, G. C., III, 187, 246

3M, productivity through people at, 97-98

Training programs: analysis of, 183-206; concept of, 183; for leadership development, 197-205; proactive, 200-201; in skill and knowledge, 184-197

U

Unfamiliarity, and career motivation, 43-44, 47, 77

Union Carbide Corporation, development programs of, 194

V

Vaillant, G. E., 222, 246

Values: of companies, 20-22; of productivity through people, 97-99

Van Maanen, J., 28, 34, 246

Van Zwieten, J., 202, 246

Vasko, T., xiii, 115n

Vigil, M., xiii

W

Wall, S. J., 194, 242, 247

Wanous, J. P., 26, 28, 97, 247

Warren, K., 208, 219, 247

Waterman, R. H., Jr., 22, 97-99, 198, 246

Watson, J. B., 188

Westinghouse, and proactive planning, 5

Wexley, K. N., 197, 247

What You Want in Life, 54

Wilcox, Mal, and supportiveness, 176-177

Wilson, J. A., 31, 49, 243

Wise, R. E., 189, 247

Women: applications for, 235; in midcareer, 214-215

Work involvement, and career motivation, 46, 48, 79

X

Xerox Corporation: sabbaticals from, 205; training program of, 195

Z

Zern, H. R., 189, 247